A Time Apart:
Letters of Love and War

Written By
Fred and Norah Egener

Edited by Joan Barfoot

For Mrs. Hillier
with best wishes
Norah Egener

A TIME APART: LETTERS OF LOVE AND WAR

ISBN: 0-921773-34-X

Cover design: Catherine Caple

Printed in Canada

Published by
The Ginger Press, Inc.
848 Second Avenue East
Owen Sound, Ontario
N4K 2H3

FOREWORD
Joan Barfoot

There are many, many accounts of events in the Second World War: of battles and speeches, of tactics and traumas, of victories and causes and tragedies.

There is not so much about love.

At the best and easiest of times, love is a vulnerable commodity. It is by no means flimsy, but it is mysterious, and requires attention and sustenance.

Imagine this: two people, parents, are apart for four dangerous years. They don't know at the moment of separation that that's how long it will be before they see each other again. But for four years they will live on different continents. Their daily jobs, circles of friends, conversations, comforts, deprivations, ambitions, disappointments - all their individual circumstances - will be utterly different. For four years they cannot embrace, or even hear each other's voices.

How does love survive this?

~

In 1941, Norah and Fred Egener were living in Oakville. Fred commuted to Toronto, where he was a solicitor with the provincial department of health. They had a two-year-old son, Waide.

In June of that year, when Fred shipped out with the Canadian army to England, Norah was pregnant with their second child. She was twenty-five years old; Fred was twenty-eight. They had known each other by then for almost a decade. They met one summer as teenagers on holiday in Owen Sound, the hometown of Norah's mother. Norah was born in London, where her father was a businessman. Fred's father was a doctor of music and organist who also wound up in London, although the family generally spent the summer at their Goderich family home.

By 1936, Norah and Fred were both university students. They were in love. It seemed to them a terrible disruption - war - was headed toward the world. Deciding not to delay marriage any longer, they eloped, although they didn't announce their marriage or actually live together for another two years.

Then they had only until June, 1941, when Fred went overseas, to build themselves into a family. And then they had until June, 1945, when Fred finally came home, to somehow sustain themselves as a family.

They did this with letters, hundreds of them. They are written by two intelligent, articulate, often discouraged but determined people intent from the outset on doing their respective jobs - Fred to go to war, Norah to raise their children and build a homefront life.

The care each takes to hold on to their connection is enormous. Letters written over such a distance in space, time and experience, aren't at all like a catch-up conversation at the end of a day. They require detail, description, and careful, truthful exposure of emotion and event.

Within the restrictions of war-time censorship, Fred tries to help Norah see England's fields and cities through his eyes; to feel his impatience and his desire for combat; to smell the dust and mud and taste the olives and oranges of Italy.

He is vivid in his descriptions of loneliness, despair and longing to be home. He has to be far more circumspect about locations, movements and battles, particularly in late 1944 and 1945, when he is involved in serious, desperate actions in Italy and, finally, Holland. Especially in that period there are gaps and omissions in his letters, which can barely hint at his activities.

He does not write to her, for instance, about crawling on his hands and knees, under fire, across a bridge in Italy in 1944 to rescue two wounded fellow soldiers. There is almost never a time, for that matter, when she has more than a vague idea where he is.

For her part, Norah tries to help Fred imagine his growing, changing children, one of whom he has never seen; to describe the household she establishes in Owen Sound with her parents and her sister; to keep him up to date with her circles of friends and acquaintances, the books she is reading, the parties she gives and attends, her interests in politics and other civic activities.

She, too, speaks of loneliness, despair and longing for him to be home. They discuss such issues of the day as events and rumours of the war, rationing, Canada's conscription debate and the threat of Quebec separation. They explore their concepts of duty and loyalty and their gropings toward finding solid frameworks for their lives. They try to give each other courage and hope, but they are also truthful about mistakes, depressions and falterings of purpose.

As a collection, the letters are a testament, not to uncluttered romance, but to endurance and commitment and the best honesty two people can manage.

The correspondence survives because Norah kept Fred's letters and periodically Fred shipped Norah's home to her.

Obviously, selecting from such a massive four-year exchange is as much a matter of deciding what to leave out as it is what to include. The lives and events of some friends and relatives of Norah and Fred have been omitted, as are many details of their children's development and their own busy social lives.

Friends and family members who are referred to include, besides Fred and Norah's respective parents, Norah's sister Eleanor; Fred's aunt Marg; Fred's brother and sister-in-law Don and Kay; Norah's aunt and uncle Pheobe and Ben Legate; Norah's family doctor and his wife, Al and Grace Pollock; and various maids and household help.

Nothing that appears in this collection has been altered, and all deletions are indicated by ellipses.

One last word: reading and editing these letters has been literally a labour of love - an exploration of that elusive and profound emotion that one way or another touches all of us. I am immensely grateful to Norah Egener for opening her heart and history so completely. It is an act of trust not only in me, but in those of you reading this.

INTRODUCTION
Norah Egener

For over forty years, more than four hundred letters that my husband and I exchanged from 1941 to 1945 during the Second World War lay buried and untouched in two large boxes in the attic.

In 1988, several months after my husband's death, I was interviewed by CBC Morningside's Stuart McLean about our Victorian attic. As we looked over the rich treasures, Stuart asked me about the grey boxes under the eaves. What a discovery - our war-time letters!

At that very moment, I knew the letters were destined to have a life of their own. Later that year, my younger son, Capt. Hugh Egener, asked me if he might read them. Eventually he presented an edited edition as a gift to me and his sisters and brother. In 1991, I attempted to reread and edit the original letters for a wider audience. They provoked strong memories and emotions, and it proved to be too great an undertaking so soon after my husband's death. One fall day in 1994, I received a call from Maryann Hogbin of Ginger Press. She told me that novelist Joan Barfoot was interested in reading the letters and might edit them into a manuscript Ginger Press would publish. The letters had come alive again!

The result is A Time Apart: Letters of Love and War.

High motives led my husband to join the Active Service Force for service overseas in disturbed and threatening times - a time that had a lot going for us. We were young, in our twenties. My husband was launched on a promising career in law, we had settled in a house in Oakville, had a two-and-a-half-year-old son, and I was pregnant.

We both had a strong sense of responsibility and loyalty to our country and realized Hitler must be defeated at all costs. My husband knew the time had come when he must be willing to risk his life for something bigger than, or other than, himself - an opportunity to create a better world.

We had a committed relationship, but realized it would be buffeted by the wounds of war. Both of us were aware of our human foibles, fear of battle, loneliness, a temptation to sexuality, a lengthy separation, possibly death. We prayed for courage, faith and the strength to see it through to the end.

Letters were the vehicle of communication most used by the troops, since telegrams were not always available, nor did they convey the warmth of a letter. Trans-Atlantic telephone communication was not an option, and frequently, letters were lost at sea. Our letters, usually ten to twenty pages in length, were often written on the same day. It was as if we were writing a daily journal expressing our most intimate thoughts, aspirations, fears, anger, joy and love. The letters were therapeutic, and served to sustain us in our darkest hours.

The letters are about many things, but in essence they are a love story. My sincere hope is they will be read with the spirit in which they were written.

A Time Apart:
Letters of Love and War

1941

Departure, birth and death

"We will be like strangers to each other if it lasts until 1945 or so"

Waide Egener

June 16, en route to Halifax
Dearest Norah:
…It seems many days since last Thursday, but the time has not been dragging by any means. I don't think any of the lads ever worked harder than the last of the past week. Like any other person or organization there were many odds and ends to clean up at the last moment…The boys were ready to show off and marched through the centre of Hamilton with a fine swing, singing the whole way from the Barracks to the station. The route was lined the whole way and…the gallery cheered and waved and hollered.

There is nothing I can tell you about the unit's move, so will close this letter…Love to all the family, to you dearest, Waide etc.
Fred

~

June 17, Owen Sound
Dearest Fred:
…Waide, who is fine but who just breaks my heart by asking for Daddy a thousand times a day, drove up with me yesterday, Monday June 16. We intended to come on Sunday but I was too tired to drive. I am beginning to notice a slight reaction to the strain under which you and I have both been, however I will try hard to overcome it, but at present I feel so numb from the loss of you darling, but I know you will come back safely to Waide and baby and me…

I do hope you are well and do be happy. We both must be very brave because we are doing the right and honourable thing and we will never regret it…All my love dearest. A kiss from Waide and me.
Norah

~

June 22
Dearest Fred:
It is Sunday night and we were out to the beach (Sauble) today. It was Waide's first picnic of the season and he enjoyed it…

This morning, Mom and I took him up to the park from nine to eleven and he loved it. He had fun on the swing and slide and squealed when he saw the fish in the water. We walked around the paths you and I trod when we were first sweethearts. Remember? I found a picture of you and me taken up there at the park that first summer. My we have both changed a lot!…

I naturally am wondering where you are and if you are safe. I look at your picture darling every night just before I turn out the light and then I say my prayers. Waide throws you a kiss every night

too, dear. He says very plainly, "Dada gone way in car, Mama"...
Worlds of love and kisses dearest,
Norah and Waide

~

June 26, On board ship
Dearest Norah:
The most striking thing about this trip is time. Days are all askew
and hours are worse...We have practically no facts on which to go
and neither a detailed map nor instruments, but fog, cold and the
sun make you realize that you aren't off Bermuda!

The officers are well-berthed. First-class cabins indeed. It is in-
convenient that four have to share one cabin for they are...smaller
than the cubicles at Standard Barracks Hamilton. We have, however, hot water, bath etc., and a heater in the cabin and are extremely
comfortable. I might mention that I have avoided the bath since the
first night aboard, which was before the water in bath was heated.
Desperate from a long train ride, I took a cold bath (salt water). It
must have been forty degrees - shades of Lake Ontario! and the salt,
you know, prevents a lather except after hours of effort. It leaves
you with a sticky feeling and a desire to itch...
Dearest Norah:
I'll always add a page to tell you I love you and to give you any tid-
bit of private news. This time there is little to say that is at all private, still, just for the two of us, please. I am anxious for you and I
know that to please me you will take good care of yourself and especially now...Above all you must not worry and if you have troubles, let me know; you'll feel better! Love and kisses,
Fred

~

June 29
Dearest Fred:
It is about 11:30 Sunday morning; Master Waide is playing in front
with his wagon, just having been bathed and a clean new sunsuit
and his white shoes on. He is so tanned, you would be pleased to
see him looking so strong and well...

They are organizing a women's auxiliary unit to go overseas. If I
didn't have the babies, I could go with it and be near you. But I
know you wouldn't let me go anyway, would you? And watching
over your babies means more, I guess, darling. In the days and years
to come it will, anyway...

All my old friends have been kind to call me and welcome me

and have invited me over. But as yet I haven't seen anyone. I somehow don't want to and can't seemingly force myself to visit and be sociable. I'm sure the family find me a sphinx, but I don't feel like talking, so consequently don't. It is so terribly lonely without you, dearest...

Britain has not been receiving much bombing lately since Russia seems to keep the Germans busy. However, it is hard to say how Russia will fare. I miss our chats after dinner at night over the war, news etc. Loads of love and kisses and hugs,
Norah and Waide

~

July 2
Dearest Norah:
It is Wednesday, one...week and four days since...leaving Halifax. We arrived here - in the Firth of Clyde - Monday morning. I and some others stayed up all Sunday night to see us enter the Firth. It was well worth the wait. Very hilly country covered with heather and trees. The shores here are lined by small towns and estates. The Firth itself is a mass of ships...We have seen absolutely nothing of war. Apparently not a bomb has fallen on the area we are in, though Glasgow, a few miles up the Clyde, is said to have been hit. In this atmosphere this country is beautiful beyond measure.

We take a train this afternoon for Aldershot, which...is distribution centre and home for Canadians. We have had a grand time on ship. There is no rationing on board, at least in our dining room. Even oranges and bananas have appeared on the breakfast table...

I have no other news at the moment, so will close. All my love to you dear and to Waide, and to the others too.
Fred

~

July 6
Dearest Fred:
I have been busy all week. I pickled some cherries and tomorrow I am going to make gooseberry spiced relish. It is quite a task planning meals and cooking, but Eleanor and Mom help very well and Mom does a lot of baking and they always do the dishes and make their own beds and dust their own rooms. I am tiring a little more easily and "cut a beautiful figure". However, don't worry about me, I'm fine...

You would be surprised how things are going up in price. Bacon is fifty cents a pound; eggs thirty-two; butter two or three cents dearer and spices and tea. Meats are away higher...

We were out to Sauble again today. It was lovely and cool and Waide does love a play in the sand and water...He has two new double teeth, so consequently has been a little irritable and a little upset, requiring laxative and a lot of patience. It is a task raising children but since they are yours darling, it is no task but a joy.

I have been feeling a little brighter lately, simply because I have tried so hard to buck up. Don't forget, you and I have a date with the full moon tomorrow night. Waide and I will be looking at it about eight o'clock, which is 1 a.m. your time.

Tons of love from Waide and me and love and kisses and hugs.
Norah

~

July 7

Dearest Norah:

I have a job now with headquarters of the No. 1 Canadian General Holding Unit (hereafter #1CGHU) doing a bit of legal work, namely preparing summaries of evidence and applications for courts martial. I only started Saturday, so can't say yet what I think of it - army legal work, I mean...

In the mess we dine...well. Milk, sugar and butter...are available in ample quantities. There is a suggestion of...stereotype meals but the food is good and varied. We are having vegetables and fruits according to...season. It has been...strawberries for dessert almost daily since arrival but I've heard no complaints on that score! Apparently the army dines well at the expense of the civilians, which seems a shame - at least if treated impersonally...

Darling Norah:

You'll not forget the private note that is to be attached per letter, strictly confidential etc. The last few nights have been full moons...You know full well what thoughts that moon brings to me. Very, very happy thoughts of you, sweetheart, and of times shortly passed by...

Let me know what you would think of me taking up military law. I am certainly confused. There is no apparent activity in the unit except hardening up. Certainly my experience for the present is more to my benefit than what the unit is doing, but suppose I'm offered more or less permanent work in law? I shall of course have to make my own decision and probably will have before you have replied, but let me know what you say...Do look after yourself, hon,...and if you are having...a struggle to keep or get finances

straight, tell me right now so I can try to help you…
Fred

~

July 11
Dearest Fred:
Waide is fine except for the last few days. He is getting his double teeth, and they have made him miserable…But don't worry, you know how quickly he picks up. The little tyke misses you more than I think any of us realize. He talks more and more every day about you and spontaneously if anyone comes in or he goes any place. He keeps saying, "Dada gone way in car". The other night, he and I were out looking at the moon and hoping you were looking at it too, and the next night he woke up in the middle of the night and called me and when I went he said, "Dada moon". And sure enough the moon was shining in his window…

I'm sure it makes you sad to hear these little accounts and I debated whether to tell you and then I thought, it will make you glad too, to know how fond Waide is of his daddy…We won't be forgetting…that Aug. 17 is your…birthday, darling, and that you are twenty-nine. Don't forget our…anniversary, which is Oct. 10, correct?…Lovingly,
Norah and Waide

~

July 18
Dearest Fred:
…Your air mail letter which you posted on the…eighth reached me yesterday seventeenth. Isn't that fast? You can't imagine how thrilled I was to get it. It is the first time I've been really happy since you left…

I hope you don't feel by my cable this morning, which said "choose administrative decidedly", that I am trying to make up your mind for you re military law. You asked me my opinion and I felt it urgent enough to reply at once. I think it a marvelous opportunity and if you are offered it, I hope you will choose it…From a personal and selfish viewpoint, it is perhaps a little less dangerous and a man with a wife and two babies can and should think of that…

I like my new doctor and have confidence in him. I am fine and have no discomforts or complaints, except the odd cramp in my legs at night - remember I got them before Waide was born and you were good enough to rub my legs for me. Now I have to jump on the floor and they go away. I have a strong feeling it is going to be a little girl.

But dear, don't worry about me, I'm not the least bit afraid...

For a while I felt absolutely numb. It was so awful saying good-bye, and I miss you terribly. More than words can express. However I'm feeling a little brighter each day, and I make myself happy by thinking of our wonderful reunion...

Norah and Waide

~

July 25

Dearest Norah:

Time gets on. I have been mighty pleased to have received mail and telegrams from you...I was particularly glad to get word from you replying to one, for then it suddenly appeared that you weren't so far off that I couldn't consult you...

I'm enjoying my work greatly and have a pretty good time, too - not too much to sip and lots of exercise, but darling, I do miss you. I would be perfectly content if only I could transport you here, or me and job there...Will you send snaps every week or so, at least every once in a while, so I'll see what changes are coming over my little family - and how things are shaping up...

You know, of course, how much I love you and how many things I feel I could say were I near you. That's not to be for the moment, but soon, eh. Sooner than we expect perhaps. Don't spoil my little curlyhead, and spank him for me if need be, and give him a kiss nightly for me. Loads of love and kisses,

Fred

~

Aug. 3

Dearest Fred:

...I went to see the doctor this week and I'm fine. My feet were very swollen and I was worried. However, my tests are all right so it must have been the terrific heat. The weather is nice today though, not too hot and a lovely breeze. It will soon be a full moon again. It doesn't seem long since the last, does it? It isn't two months since I saw you in Hamilton, dear, but it does seem so very long. The news has just come on, and it does sound as if the Russians are doing well. But I think it is hard to know what to believe...

Every Saturday morning Waide and Mom and I get up early and are at market. Everything is so plentiful and fresh-looking. Waide carries the basket and I'm so proud when everyone stops to admire the beautiful child...

I am writing up in my bedroom with a lovely cool breeze blowing in. I have just finished doing my accounts for the month…I had to have an oil change and grease on Saturday which was an extra expense. I think I will put the car in for the winter by Nov. 1 and then my expenses will be so much less…What I am trying to do is save ten dollars every month to put aside for unexpected extras which are bound to crop up. When you get back, you will find me the best little saver ever, dear…

Take care of yourself sweet, and don't worry about me. I am just fine. Waide and I send happy birthday greetings once more and will be looking at the full moon…
Norah

~

Aug. 7
Dearest Fred:
It is just 8:30 Thursday Aug. 7 and there is the most perfect moon. I just walked home from the doctor's and I was looking at it all the way home knowing that you were without doubt looking at it too. It is very comforting, isn't it darling? I am just fine; the doctor can't get over the fact I never seem to tire and have no complaints…

The news is very confusing these days. There is so much propaganda and news not in the least authentic. There are big headlines in yesterday's papers that Mr. Churchill and Mr. Roosevelt were meeting someplace at sea.

The cost of food is going up. Bacon is sixty-five cents a pound and eggs are up to forty cents a dozen. No special deliveries on milk or cream or ice cream. They are discussing no bread deliveries and they aren't slicing it any more. Many changes are beginning to take place and things which we formerly expected to find in stores just aren't there. But no one seems to complain, nor should we…

In your letter dear, you said to be sure and tell you if I had any troubles. They are only minor dear, except for two, neither of which have any immediate remedy.

One is, I feel so terribly lonely often without you, but I do try to overcome it and swallow the lump in my throat and gradually I am learning to overcome it to some extent. I'm sure you feel the same, although you haven't said. The second is, I feel so awfully awkward and so conspicuous. However, I hope the two months still remaining will soon pass and then I'll have so much to tell you of the new babe and how Waide is reacting…
Love and kisses and hugs dearest,
Norah

~

Aug. 9

Dearest Norah et al:

...I am duty officer again - another Saturday. It is sort of fun from some standpoints. It is a change from the desk, but in the slack moments of a duty officer I become courts martial officer again...

Wednesday I took a station wagon - must have one of those when I get home, will hold the whole family, even ours when it's been collected - and I went on a trip to Eastbourne, Hastings and Rye collecting evidence for a court martial. Every bit as good as a Cook's Tour and through a part of England I wanted to see. The holiday visitors no longer throng the sea-coast towns and the lines of hotels stand empty and bare. Damage, or visible damage at any rate, is inconsequential...

You speak much of a British land offensive. Papers here do discuss it, but not with any great conviction. Undoubtedly such a move would, if successful, be A-1. There is no tenseness on that matter here - nor on any other - I should not have any worries about it if I were you, nor lose a night's sleep. It's only in the "might" class, and you know how rife is speculation...

Dearest:

...Recalling Waide's arrival, I expect that this and next month will be rather trying ones. I can see that the hot weather is wearing on you. I am so glad that you can get relief at the Sauble and at Leith. Make use of every opportunity. I think under the circumstances you should use the car any time you can get away to the beach...

Your Dad and Mom being home each night and you, Cinderella, knitting and sewing, must indeed make a homey scene. You think I'll need an armchair when I return and that my young, charming, unsatiated wife will be ready to flit the highways rather than bring in slippers and pipe. My dear lady, you are mistaken. The life I'll lead you will wear down your travel hunger...

You didn't say a thing this time as to how the house affairs are coming along. I hope that's because you have nothing to worry about. In any case, I expect a word or so, so I can form some opinion of how things go. I'm surprised how food and fuel has gone up in Canada. I cannot but think someone is jacking prices for the production is so much above needs...

I think of so many things to say to you when I am intending to write you. So many can't be said, so many escape, that the few remaining are a mite to what you should receive. I say I love you, I

17

would love to be with you. I hope and pray you will have the best and the easiest of times. It is my wish that you have happy times. I want you to know that a wall or an ocean will not prevent me being beside you when you are in need of me. You will this time be physically alone. But only that, and my love and spirit will be with you. You need not fear. Love and kisses dear,

Fred

~

Aug. 15

Dearest Fred:

...First of all, Waide and I are well. The time is drawing shorter and I really have few complaints. Naturally I am a little less comfortable each day but I have very little heartburn as I did with Waide, and my appetite is as good as ever...

Waide has been and is getting to be my real problem. You wouldn't believe or can't imagine how he is growing. I must measure him and tell you how tall he is. He weighs nearly forty-five pounds and is such a "wild man". I haven't the strength to tussle with him, Eleanor and Mom either for that matter. Dad has been busy every day, so isn't here to play with him. The result is, he doesn't work his energy off and he has tons of it and he has been very bad all week. He has been throwing his food, squeezing it in between his hands, slapping me, yelling and squealing when I correct him, running away, and just generally doing everything naughty. Spanking does no good, and besides, he is so big I can't manage it...

I have had a good cry or two about it. I feel maybe you could manage the situation so much better than I. It breaks my heart to have to be cross with him because he is so cuddly at night and looks just like an angel when I tuck him in at night.

Mom and Eleanor and Dad are paying for the maid, so that I will have help, and we are still going to have a cleaning woman, and you may say, I surely will have plenty of help, and so I will. But my duties are many, even so. I completely and entirely manage the house. I plan the meals, manage the finances, take care of the ordering and planning of meals and the cooking. It is a real problem with the rise in food prices etc...

I am explaining all this for one purpose. Would you be terribly against me sending Waide to nursery school if he still continues to be a problem? Just for six months, until I get the new baby under control and into a routine and the maid trained? The children learn to play with each other and Waide loves playmates. I know it is not comparable to a mother's personality, providing she has the time to give it...I will of course make no decision until I receive your answer. Although we are separated by many miles, I think we should discuss our problems as we have in the past, and I'm not going to keep things from you ever...

Norah and Waide

~

Aug. 20

Dearest Norah, Waide et all:

...We have changed our barracks, a move of some eighteen miles...My new room is much more satisfactory, being wider than either of the other ones were long. Pacing it off, it is approximately twenty-one feet by twelve feet. Two of us room together, the beds being about seven feet apart and between them is the table at which I am writing. In the corner near the foot of my bed is a hot-cold running water basin and near the head against the side wall is a wardrobe. Two large windows let in lots of light. I have a small lamp here on the table to write by, and yours and Waide's picture to brighten the room...

I have been on course for the last two days...Yesterday we mounted motorcycles for the first time and went riding in a field, learned to change gears, start and stop the motor, whoa and get-up. We rode for from two to three hours, and if you don't think a motorcycle is first cousin to a bronco, I can give both verbal and physical evidence that it is - physical, my dear, only on the saddle, so don't be alarmed...

Your letters to me are so much appreciated, you find so much of interest in everyday experience, and that's an art. So many persons would fail to give those little details that make it possible for me to see a clear picture. What you say about Waide, his sayings and doings, play my heart strings like a harp, but though I'm taken through every emotion, I wouldn't be satisfied with a word less...You say you pray I will return safely. I will. Do not let yourself be anxious, but be trustful. Believe firmly enough for that belief to be made a reality...

You have commented on the war in several of your letters and have asked my opinion. I have none. There are enough speculators. One thing only I have thought and still think - three years, anyway. You should expect that. A long separation, Norah, but if it's less, so much the better...The nights are dark and moonless now, but I'll be sitting by the next full one to talk with you, so listen...

Fred

~

Aug. 27

Dearest Fred:

Your third air-mail letter arrived yesterday...I have read and reread it four times and am sending it off to your Mom and Pop tonight. My own separate letter I have practically off by heart. It is so sweet, darling, and how I could ever feel lonely after reading those sweet thoughts you have of me, I don't know. Did you ever realize how much we meant to each other before? I didn't quite, and at night after I'm in bed and my prayers said, I am very near you, sweet - so near.

I must confess I'm finding it very hard to keep the old chin up these days. I mean I miss you so. But I know it is because I'm entering upon that last trying month, and you remember how trying it is. I feel and am so awkward, and this baby is more active than Waide was, if that is possible...

You are very spry and cocky re your ability to keep up with your "charming and unsatiated wife", to use your words. I could say a lot more if it weren't for the charming censorettes in Bermuda. I saw their pictures in Life. However, I'll be able to take a lot of wooing when you return - hum!...

I bought you Berlin Diary by William Shirer - hot off the press...I'm sure you will enjoy it, since it was William Shirer to whom we listened every night last year from Berlin over WKBW. It promises to be much discussed and a book I feel we will want to have in our library. I am reading it first if you don't mind...

I am sending you via air mail some darling snaps of Waide taken last Sunday. I didn't appear in any simply because I am no subject for a picture at present...I am going to have some snaps taken when I'm in the hospital of the new babe and me, and thus give you a glimpse as soon as possible of us. Eleanor will send you a cable about the third day, when we are both fine. I will write you a day or so after, depending on how peppy I feel, so we will get news to you as soon as we can...Don't worry over me, sweet - I know you're with me all the way and always. That is why I'm not afraid...

I have been asked to join the figure-skating club. It would get me out two nights a week and give me some real exercise. It would mean a $12 investment in fancy skates. What do you think? I won't have any time in the day time to ski or anything...

Night, darling, and write soon, and keep your fingers crossed...

Norah

~

Aug. 31
Dearest Norah:
...First about Waide. It is too bad he is making a problem of himself at this time. If it were at any other time I should think he'd just have to learn to stop it. Of course with his energy one must expect him to want to be on the go...I am sorry though that his age is such that he reaches this stage just when it's most distressing for you. I think you ought to send him off for the mornings to the children's school, it will be good for him to tumble with other children, and will give you a chance to give the new baby a proper start...

My dear, there is nothing I want more than to be home with you. Often I'm lonesome and don't know what to do, and can't do anything. Among the Canadians generally you will seldom find a man that does not say, "If I could be in Canada now -" or, "I'd give a leg to be back and no team of horses will ever again budge me from -". It is most insane talk, but you get used to it and I suppose that each would qualify it, if he would tell you, with something like, "But first I'll finish my job". That's the way I feel. England's a poor old country for a Canadian. Strange ways, strange people, strange customs, but worst of all strange faces and strange towns...

I am looking at the pictures you sent of Waide. He has changed a great deal from the Waide that looks out of the picture on my table. He looks like a nearly grown boy in the picture of him by himself. I am sorry I am not seeing him at this stage but will, as you said, catch up on the next one...

I hardly know what to say to you, Norah. I regret very much not being able to be with you. I will be thinking of you constantly, and of the baby, too...Above all I will think of the future and will plan for that time when we will pick up the threads where we left them and complete the pattern we began. No doubt our experience during this time will change many details of the pattern; we will weave with deeper, fuller colours and with better craftsmanship and a truer appreciation...

I give you all my love, kisses and hugs. Love too to Waide.
Fred

~

Sept. 4
Dearest Norah:
This letter tonight is just for you. Of course you may read out any

21

bits of news to the family but as I intend to write Mother a letter tonight or tomorrow, the general news will soon come along...

We were out motorcycling again on Tuesday, had a fine long trip of about fifty miles up into Berkshire. The country we passed through was quite rolling country heavily cultivated and was that picturesque type of English landscape which consists of fields that climb the hills, and hedges that straggle irregularly across your whole view. As we went along we came across a Blenheim Bomber that had just crashed and was blazing furiously as we came up. We were about the first on the scene, two men only having reached there ahead of us. We suppose that the four occupants perished. It was the first tragedy I have seen in this country...

Am eating a tomato sandwich with an insufficient amount of salt on it. Flat is hardly the word for it. At dinner the lads say, "Please pass the salt, Egener," without even looking up. They seem to have concluded that it is always in front of me, and I guess it is...

In our mess there is a tremendously long table... In some ways it recalls to my mind the table you got, if it was extended a little. I put up with it for I think that perhaps the mess had at some time a Mess Mother whose decision was to be final! Forgive my little jibe, but tonight I can't squeeze you like I'd like to...I can just talk to you. I feel as though you were encased in solid air. I can see you, walk around you, smile and be smiled at, but then there is that beastly wall that just steps in and keeps us apart! I hope we will be able to time our letters so that they will answer each other. A kind of double dialogue...Shall we see if we can work it out?...I seal up this letter with my love and my kisses and hugs and all that I can send you to make you confident and happy at this time.
Fred

~

Leith, Sept. 11
Dearest Fred:
You will see by the above that we are at Leith. Waide and I are guests of Uncle Ben and Aunt Pheobe for a week at Grandma Legate's cottage and it is simply marvelous here. Waide eats and sleeps so well because the air is so bracing and the sun has been shining every day. We have had grand grate fires every night and I undress Waide for bed before the fire and he sits on a little rocking chair and warms his hands and toes. Of course he has had every attention and couldn't ask for more...

This morning Aunt Pheob and he and I went for an hour's walk

22

down past the Flemings' cottages and into a bush to look for puffballs. Waide saw a couple of chipmunks. We came home by way of the Leith school and there were twelve children out for recess. We noticed five little evacuee children, who are living down here, dressed in Scotch plaid skirts, even the little boy had one on. I couldn't help but feel how peaceful and safe and far away from bombings it was for those darlings down here, including our own darling…

Maybe by the time you receive this, you will also be receiving a cable telling you the good news. Aunt Pheob wants to go to the hospital with me and so does Eleanor, but I am having a nurse too, since I don't want any of my family around me except to come in my room and say hello occasionally. Anyway a nurse is really needed to do the few things necessary for such a case. Naturally now and again I get a little frightened, but most of the time I feel quite brave…

As soon as the babe comes, I will have so much to tell you, won't I? Aunt Pheob says to tell you I look just like a chipmunk - a stuffed one at that, sitting at the end of the table - my face is so fat. Oh well, I'll get my slender figure back again darling before you get back. Do you ever wish we could "pitch a little woo"? I do.
Norah

~

Sept. 19
Dearest Fred:
Well dearest, Waide and I are still at Leith. It has been such perfect weather and Waide and especially I have been sleeping so well that we stayed another week…You will be interested maybe to hear of some of the things which we as Canadians are being asked to dispense with. For instance, no more aluminum pots and pans or anything aluminum for that matter. No permanent waves since the hairdressers use aluminum to wrap around each curl, no nail polish (ahum), no sliced bread…

The war news looks serious today with the reported fall of Kiev. Mr. King has been criticized by the Globe and Saturday Night for his speech the other day, which was eloquent but lacked action. He certainly will have to bring in conscription or fade out of the picture…I'm afraid I read too much about the war, too many editorials etc. It doesn't do me any good and it just serves to depress me and keep me on edge. I guess you are right when you say you feel it will be three years…I perhaps don't mention it in every letter, dear, but Waide kisses your picture every night and of course says, "God bless Daddy" in his prayers...I sometimes say, "Are you Mummy's boy?" and he says, "No, Daddy's boy."...

Well darling, I feel this letter hasn't been terribly interesting, but not having a recent letter of yours to reply to and although I am having a lovely holiday, there isn't much news. Love and kisses as always, Norah

~

Sept. 26

Dearest Norah:

...You will be getting this about the critical time or possibly a little later. I do so hope everything will go just dandy and that you will not be hurt or have too much pain. I wish I were with you, but not being able to be, I want you to know that I'll be thinking of you all the time.

You have always been such a sweet young lady. I recall just how you looked...when I found you in Owen Sound playing tennis with your cousin Jimmy - when we canoed at the park - when you "snared" me on my first visit to Aunt P.'s - don't protest!...

Those were the beginnings; soon it will be our anniversary, and that commemorates the start of so many more memorable incidents. Well, soon we'll start creating more of them. Soon I think - this bloody war will collapse...

Norah, I hope you have arranged for all the care you may need. I would like to be there to do the usual pacing, but then I remember thinking last time I might as well be on the other side of the world for all I could do. Well, here I am...

I don't know anything more I can say at this stage, just that I love you just as I have since the very first, and I use that word knowing you know just how full of meaning it really is.

Your husband,

Fred

~

Oct. 1

Dearest Fred:

...As you suggested, we should strike up a double dialogue. I hope we can and I think it is a good idea to try. I have little general news. Waide and I moved up from Leith on Sunday night. I was hardly in the door when your mom called to see how I was...I was feeling low not having received mail, and so she cheered me up considerably...

I am still waiting for the babe and tonight I'm very tired...You ask me what I'm hoping for. To be honest - a girl. My main reason being, Waide has always been so very strong and robust and has a fine pleasing personality and is so handsome, if we have another boy and he doesn't measure up in quite the same way, he might get a complex and Waide might unknowingly outshine and dominate him. A little girl is so entirely different from a boy anyway - she can go her own way from the start. Anyway, I would like one of each...

Eleanor is taking me to the hospital and is going to have the joy of first seeing the babe and then cabling you and phoning your family. She says she is taking your place this time...The next letter will be from the hospital. So bye-bye. Don't fear, I'm in good spirits and send all my love, kisses and hugs.

Norah

~

Oct. 6

Dearest Norah:

It's the sixth and no news yet. I am keeping my eyes open for word from you...

Fred

~

Oct. 6

Dearest Daddy:

I hope you got Mummy's cable telling you that I have arrived - because here I am. I came at 3:10 a.m. Monday Oct. 6 and I weighed eight pounds, seven ounces, so you see I have the edge on my brother right off, since he only weighed seven pounds, four...

I heard one of the nurses say, "Her daddy must be fair, because the baby is very fair". And then I heard Mummy say, "Well, if she is half as sweet as her Daddy, she will do"...

Love and kisses,

Cynthia Christyne

Hello darling:

Well, everything is fine and we have a daughter. She's terribly sweet. I know you would love her to death. Isn't it nice to have one of each?...I am not writing much this week because I want you to get the pictures. I know you will be thrilled. I will write you a huge letter telling you everything next week...

Good-bye, dearest, and I am fine. So is the baby and Waide.

Love and kisses,

Norah

~

Oct. 13

Darling Fred:

Can you imagine one week has gone by and all I managed was one sheet to you from Cynthia, giving you only the merest details. However I didn't feel up to it, not even to writing you, darling...

I won't go into details here except to say I came in at 12:10 a.m. Monday Oct. 6, having had only one-half hour warning at home. The baby was born at 3:10 a.m. Dr. Pollock was very kind and gave me gas but had to let me be conscious for the delivery since he thought it best for the baby. I was very good, so he said, and although naturally agonising, a marvelous experience to actually feel your own child being born and to hear her first cry. She is so very sweet and I love her like I do Waide because she is the result of our mutual love which was and is very great...

I haven't received a reply to my cable to you and I'm wondering if you got mine. If you didn't, you will be in a stew...I, like you, hope my letters of late haven't been too sentimental, because as you say we are both experiencing a separation which will only bind us closer together after you come home. I have matured a thousand times over since you left and will never again provoke you by flying off the handle, or by being stubborn and not giving in. Remember how cross I would make you? I do regret that...

All my love and kisses and hugs, sweetheart. Your family send their love and Waide and Cynthia send a kiss and a hug.

Norah

~

Oct. 15

Dearest Norah:

...I have been so happy to hear that we have a little daughter. I would like to be there with you to enjoy her growing up...A daughter, just think! Since last Thursday I have had your wire and I have not been able to write. I seem to be numb of things to say and even now I cannot tell you how happy I am about it...I just want to say, dear, that I love you, and to say it again and again. I know this will reach you quite some time after you're home and I may sound a bit daft.

I am still waiting for a letter from yourself or from someone to tell me how things are...This separation is always irritating, but how much more so during these last two months.

Still and all, I know you would not have it otherwise, for coming is the time when we must secure for ourselves and for Waide and Cynthia the full happiness of the life we will want to lead...It is not for a system or set of rules we fight, but for our own homes and for the right to determine how we will live in them and out of them, how our children will be educated and how they will live and think and to give them the same freedom and opportunity...

I hope soon I'll hear from you and in particular that I hear that you are well and the same as to Waide and Cynthia. I love you, always shall, and am very proud and happy with you in your very great fortitude...

Fred

~

Oct. 21

Dearest Fred:

I hesitate to write this letter darling, because I have felt so terribly blue and lonely since I came home that I just don't know how I can write you a cheery note. However, I'll try desperately hard, dearest. You see, it is just that I am quite weak, and just haven't got the "old punch" in me to fight yet. Because for me, with you away, it is just one continual fight. Tonight I went all to pieces and cried for three solid hours. It is the first time since we fell in love that I haven't been able to call you when I need you, and you would come - somehow you always came. So darling, I feel absolutely desperate - I'm all alone. Dearest, I'd never let you go if I had it to do over again. I could have stopped you somehow. So dear, you've got to come back to me - someday!

The baby is fine. She sleeps right through the night from ten until six, so I get my sleep...It wasn't exciting in the least for me to come home this time. The last time, you and I were so thrilled and I remember on the dining room table was a bowl of roses and it had "Welcome home sweethearts, Dad and Fred". But for little Waide, it was a great day. His eyes were as big as saucers and he sat and held her in his arms for about twenty minutes and kissed her and kissed her and kept on saying, "My baby, Mama"...

Saturday night:

I didn't seem to get back to this letter before now. However I guess it is just as well because I'm feeling so much better tonight. I hate to send you the first part of this letter, it is so terribly gloomy, but it was exactly how I felt...

The Russians are certainly putting up a marvelous fight, aren't they? If this horrible war would only end. You haven't been away six months yet, and it seems six years to me...

By the way, are you aware of the fact our daughter arrived on the

full moon? Everything important happens to us on the full moon, doesn't it dear? May our reunion happen on a full moon dearest, and a balmy night at that. Now that everything is over, I would give a whole lot for one grand glorious party and a night of loving…
Norah

~

Oct. 22
Dearest Norah:
…I have just had brought to me my night lunch - two tomato sandwiches and tea. I am becoming mightily tired of tomato sandwiches but must remember my vitamins and anyway the alternative is cheese or sardine, both of which are consistently poor examples of their breed. Food has been plentiful but tends to be stereotyped and with all the medical officers in the mess, many arguments have been had on the question of the nutritive value of our diet.

Naturally the M.O.'s are more at loggerheads among themselves than with the guinea pigs but they do seem agreed that there is a vitamin deficiency. What to do about it and whether our teeth, hair or toenails will be the first to fall out causes all the dissension. The fly in the theories is that no one that has been here since the beginning presents the aspect of hairless Joe or gumclucker George…

We have not seen sign of the Hun and I expect that he is far too busy to try a crack here…I firmly believe that a favourable end is in sight. I only wish, as do many Canadians, that we be sent to the near east and get in the scrap. Why this has not been done is strange for the English are doubtless in a position to manage affairs here, or at least a few thousand more or less could hardly tip the scale.

Incidentally, there is a complete misapprehension of the Canadians' purpose here. Whatever Englishman one speaks to, he is bound to end up, "Can't do too much for you Canadians when you have come forward so well to help us". It's the accented "us" that provokes. I honestly have concluded that the Englishman hasn't the foggiest notion of the Empire idea, but instead sees only colonies in which he might have to protect his interests. Of course, the intense Empire men haven't modernly come from merry England, but from outside, like Smuts, Bennet, Beaverbrook. The Englishman is an irritating cluck, but the tatters of many of his homes and edifices are testimonials that he has stuff…

You can see by the fact that I'm growling for an argument that I've exhausted my news…Love to all of you,
Fred

~

Oct. 24

Darling Norah:

...I received yours and Cynthia's letter today - dated sixth but posted on or about eleventh so as to include the snaps. Isn't she sweet! and does look somewhat like Waide. She too will have a long back and - I suspect - narrow hips. I think too, Cynthia, that you could be snatched up and feel just as solid and strong and healthy as your big brother who, while he may not have been as big as you, was quite a man and will be hard to manage when you become a tomboy. I'm mighty pleased you're here, for we've waited quite a while on you and you've been a mite of trouble en route.

Norah, it is splendid to have this mixed team. A well-balanced family! Your big picture is now ringed about by snaps and I just say on looking at it, "These are all mine". A proud possession!...

All my love dearest and to Waide and Cynthia,

Fred

~

Nov. 2

Dearest Fred:

...Right now I'm in a furious mood. Mother has taken it into her head that Cynthia is not going to lie and cry for a while, so she has taken her up in spite of what I say. Consequently I have blown up and generally raised the devil - but it doesn't seem to do any good. I guess I'm just in a very mad mood because the family have gotten on my nerves terribly today. I ended up by eating my supper up in my room. Which is childish to say the least. However it is just the little things that irritate me, such as Dad turning off the radio, on which was the silver theatre programme, to listen to someone shouting away about the war. However, why blow off to you, darling, you can't help. Besides, I guess I'm selfish and spoiled.

Today we told Waide about Christmas. We told him Santa was coming and he would have to hang up his sock etc. He was thrilled to death...Waide told me today Daddy was coming back soon on the Christmas tree. I think it is remarkable how he remembers you. A day never passes but he mentions you, all on his own...I have not as yet received a letter from you written since Cynthia was born. She will be four weeks old tomorrow, so I should get one this week...

Nov. 4

I held this over until today and I'm glad I did since I received a letter written by you Oct. 2 and 3 to which I will reply and then post this tomorrow…

I could see by your letter that you were trying hard to find news and I don't blame you. I find it hard to write ten pages, too. I really think, dear, not that either of us is tired of writing, but so our letters will still continue to be newsy and not depressed or a drag, we might be well advised to write only once every ten days or two weeks.

It would mean less mail I know, but perhaps more interesting mail. What do you think? If you knew how absolutely humdrum my life tends to be, you would wonder where I got enough news for ten pages. And I know it is much the same with you. I don't blame you for taking the odd bit of Scotch and playing a little poker. I've got to let a little steam off myself soon in some way or I'll go crazy. I won't do anything desperate, though…

Do many of the boys step out a little? As I told you before you left - if you do anything in that respect, it is absolutely your own business - just don't ever tell me and then what I won't know won't hurt me. I am confident that whatever you might do wouldn't change your heart, and that after all is the important thing. I am simply starved for affection and attention…

As I read this letter over, it is a great mixture of moods and sentimentality. Please read it and tear it up. I shouldn't send it but I want to. Darling, you've never let yourself go and just talked to me or told me your troubles or feelings. Have you none or do you just not want to tell me? I would be so glad if you would get things off your chest to me, too…

Cynthia is squealing to be fed and I'm tired since my day starts at 6:30 and ends at 11:30 p.m. So night dearest, and all my love and kisses and hugs from us three.

Norah

~

Nov. 6

Dearest Norah:

I am happy to know that my letters have now begun to arrive again. After all it is lucky that so many came just before and while you were at hospital. They would have to substitute for me. I am sure Cynthia is very sweet and of course I am happy and proud and will love her right from Oct. 6 and before that. It was mighty uncomfortable for me not being able to be there. I think in ways I was a bit "mad" or lunatic late September and early October and I certainly couldn't get much peace of mind until your letter…arrived. I wish I could have been home. Actually I have been working my head off, which has been a very good thing…

I'm glad to hear that you'll never be flying off the handle again nor get stubborn. My, you did those so, so often! Probably I deserved every pot that bounced off my head and the ones that missed, too.

Now you have complained that I don't answer enough of the questions in your letters nor comment on the subjects raised. I am complaining of precisely the same thing. Your letter of the thirteenth-fourteenth doesn't even mention the date of the letter you received that day; but I'll say that regardless of that complaint, your letters have been exceedingly newsy and interesting…Now darling, I am not a disgruntled laddie, and fear so many complaints may sound that way…Actually I am more than happy in my job and can say "I'm happy in the service". I have so much more interesting work than most and it is so suitable as preparation for civil practice…Love to you, Waide and Cynthia, and our friends and folks.
Fred

~

Nov. 12
Dearest Norah:
I have two letters from you to answer…They arrived at nearly the same time and have told me so much I wanted to know. They were very much of opposites, the first buoyant, the second in the doldrums, but they told me a great deal and I know that once your strength gets up you will be back in your good spirits, though mind you I know many moments of depression and low spirits too, and I don't expect you to be free of them…

I don't know whether I'll be able to send Waide and Cynthia anything appropriate. Toys here are sinfully out of the question. They are so expensive and the little tykes of England aren't getting much on their trees. If there is a collection of toys to send voluntarily as a gift to the lads and lassies here I would like to see Waide send off a few. There is such a scarcity…

Christmas has got me down already, mainly because I can't afford to send the presents I'd like to and know I'll have many to acknowledge. I wish it weren't coming…Love to all,
Fred

~

Nov. 15, London, Ont
Dearest Fred
I don't know how to write to you, dearest. You will have the cable bearing its sad, sad news when this reaches you, and we are all so

numb today from shock that we can't realize what has happened...At no time have I ever wished I were near you dear more than now. We all said, "Poor Fred, we have each other, but he has no one". And yet dear, as Don said last night, "Fred will have a lovely memory of Mom as she was when she was living". I know you will want me to tell you everything dear, painful and all as it will be to you to read it.

Last week one day, I phoned Mom and we had a grand and most happy chat over the phone and it was then she told me she had made up her mind to go into hospital probably someday soon. Yesterday, Friday Nov. 14, Bob Troloppe phoned me about five and asked me if I would like to go to London and come back to Owen Sound on Sunday Nov. 16. Something said, go and surprise Mom, and so I grabbed up Waide and we were on our way to London by 5:30. We arrived at the front door, I hiding, and when Mom and Marg opened the door, there was Waide. Mom was so pleased to see us. Then she told me that she was to be operated on today, Saturday Nov. 15, and that she was just ready to leave for the hospital. So she showed me all over the house, tried on a lovely comfy woolly house-coat which was her Christmas box from you and me and which I gave her last night, in order that she could try it on and take it to the hospital with her.

We then sat down and had the usual cup of tea, and I gave Mom the two letters I had received from you the day before. She was so happy to read them and to learn you were happy over a daughter. Then she put on her things and we all laughed and joked and Waide waved good-bye and said, "Come back soon, Mom", and Don and Kay and she drove away. As they were standing at the admitting room desk at the hospital, Mom said, "I feel funny" and fell into Don's arms and was dead before he could lay her on the floor...

Oh darling, I'm going to miss her so much. I love her like my own mom and we wrote each other every week and phoned always once every two weeks. Pop was just leaving the church from choir practice on his way to the hospital to say good night to your mom when Kay met him. Poor pop is naturally terribly broken up. Last night was a terrible night around here...I just clung to Waide all night and shook until morning. My nerves were shot before, but things are just beyond me now. However, it's life, darling, and we have to face it.

Mom died at 10:20 p.m. We brought her home today at five and she looks beautiful - not tired or worried. Her hair looks so golden and she has a becoming mauve dress on which looks so nice. She looks so peaceful and contented…Don is a brick. He has attended to so many things. I never saw him quite so sad as when he sat down to compose the cable to you, dear. He seems to miss you so…

Darling, I hope I haven't been too blunt in the way I have explained everything. I always said I would tell you the truth, and so I have told you everything I can.

If it is any comfort, and I know it is, remember you have lost a precious mother and she can never be replaced, but you have me still and I love you so terribly, dearest, and two precious lambs. It will be hard for you to keep up, but remember we are only one couple in thousands who are going through the agony of separation and experiencing bereavements…All my love dearest, and you know how I feel even if words won't come to me. Night dearest,
Norah

~

Nov. 21
Dearest Norah:
I received news from Don the night before last of mother's death. His wire was very explicit, still I am looking for his further letter and your own in regard to what happened…

I wrote to Don, Dad and Marg last night, just a short note to each. I tried to say something comforting to them. This morning before mailing them they didn't sound the way I'd hoped but pretty much like a bewildered little boy. There is no need for you and I to say to each other how we feel; expression is pretty useless anyway so I will write of other matters.

Have I mentioned before that I sent off a small present to each of the two children? They were mighty small presents but may be hung on the tree as a gesture…Love and kisses for tonight,
Fred

~

Nov. 27
Dearest Fred:
I hardly know where to commence. I am so sorry I haven't had a minute to write to you since my letter of Nov. 15, which I hope you have received by now. I got home from London on Monday Nov. 24 on the late train. Waide and Eleanor met me at the train. I think Waide was more interested in the engine on the train, though, than seeing me. He is getting to be a typical boy. Cynthia Christyne has a cold. She got it from Waide, I guess… I have been ordered to bed for a week. I'm not sick, but I didn't get much sleep in London, and the

shock and strain of everything seems to have put me back somewhat...

I'm always happy to hear that you are going places and meeting people. We all have remarked, your family and I, how you have seemingly changed since you left - you seem more mature or something. You and I will have to take a week or so off and get acquainted if you are away too long. I long so often for a grand old chat. You always kept me so happy and made life so entirely worth living; sometimes you seem so far away...

I'm afraid you are going to find me very dull when you come back. You are living in the midst of history and probably learning and seeing a great deal - my life is horribly humdrum and certainly gives no scope or chances for enlightenment, since I've even been too tired and busy to read. However, I guess I can sit and listen to you, for you will have a great many interesting things to tell me. And anyway, we will adjust ourselves, won't we?...

Do you do any military work or law only? Are you not being trained for anti-aircraft work? I can't see why you were all sent over so soon - since none of you seem to be doing what you expected to do at all? As you can gather, it is all very much of a muddle to me...

You mentioned the need for a larger army. It is slow going. The general feeling is we need conscription. Mr. King says he won't bring it in under his government unless he takes it to the country, and as someone was remarking the other day, all the men who have not enlisted already and could, having no strings, will vote against conscription and their families with them - so it might not carry...

I find it hard to write, dearest, because I'm sad because of your mom and I'm not feeling quite tip-top. But I know you would want to receive some kind of a letter rather than none. I'm not very good stuff, I guess dear. I am afraid I leaned on you too hard...

Nov. 29

Things seem much brighter today. The baby is all better and is sleeping through every night as she did before she got a cold...Eleanor has practically taken the baby onto herself, since between being away and trying to rest all I can before I went to London and since I came home, I have had very little to do with her so far. Eleanor gets up and gives her her six o'clock feeding and loves to bath her. She calls her her chicken. I feel a little jealous, if you can imagine it...

I know how much you are going to miss your mother's lovely letters. I don't know anyone who could write like she did. But I'll try hard to make up for them, but will fall far short, I'm afraid. I

have her last one to me and have put it away with yours.
Good night, sweetheart,
Norah

~

Nov. 27
Dearest Norah:
...I am glad that I waited till today, for I received your long and newsy letter dated Nov. 2; a very nice box from Kay, and a letter from Mother dated Nov. 9 - her last, I suppose...

Your description of Cynthia as a beautiful and strong baby is most heartening - how could I expect her to be anything else? Her golden-red hair and big eyes would be a glorious sight to her dad...I can see though that the two of them keep you busy. I would not worry about Waide wandering. I doubt he would go very far and he is old enough to take pretty good care of himself. Don't trail him all the time, let him get off the beaten track a bit. It will give him independence...

I've come now to where you're furious with your folks for getting the baby up and fiddling with the radio! If you ate supper in your room just to be quiet and to yourself, all right, but if to pout, then you should get a good spanking. Be careful that with the maid, the woman to clean, and your mother's and Eleanor's help, you do not get to be "lady of the mansion". Now that's not intended to be harsh advice. I can sympathize with you. Members of your family and of my own used to make every nerve in my body vibrate and my gills drain of blood when they interfered with my house and my doings...

At the present time, having been used to our own home and running it, neither of us are very good subjects for forced communal life. At times my stomach bounces with nerves, my temper quick and my tongue sharp because of interference. I have spent whole evenings being interrupted by teeth-sucking, talking and every other form of annoyance. I just, like yourself, must put up with it...

You mention the advisability of cutting down on mail. That may be a good idea. Certainly it's a long time to sit and work out a newsy letter and a job I generally don't care for. Still and all, there are few happier moments than the arrival of mail from home, and I think the same goes for you...I quite understand you when you say you're "starved for affection and attention". There's no reason that you ought not to go out sometimes, and even a little smooching isn't going to bring the house down. For heaven's sake, if you do go out, use your own good wit and sense. I want you to have a good time, but I do not want to invite disaster. I expect to have a happy home when I come home and any circumstance that would imperil that will get a quick stepping on by me. Just where that line might lie I don't know, but it shouldn't be too hard for you to realize when you're up against it...

I have wondered if your difficulty with your family is that they would take a poor view of your going out. If that is so, then tell them I approve and so to hell with it. A long-winded recital probably about nothing...

You have said that I don't let myself go and tell my troubles or feelings. Well Norah, my feelings are a hodge-podge. You will have no doubt that my heart has always been yours and is so now, undiminished. There is no circumstance that I can imagine that would change that. Both my heart and mind are as true to you as the night we sat by the old mill, or the morning I waited for Waide to be born. I have no fear either of present or future, and my whole being tells me I'll be back to give you a hug that will imperil you.

We are stuck in this bloody camp that at times gives your mind a cramped imprisoned sensation. It is an actual sensation, a mixture of depression, dullness and languor. What if I do break out on a spree? - I'd get little blame for that from you, I feel sure. The truth is that the sprees have been mighty few...

I have been to London less I think than anyone else. Why? It doesn't appeal to me, for while there is every amusement there I'd probably end up in a club with some tart or other. Now the next time I say I'm London-bound, don't get ideas. I mean merely that the town doesn't attract me particularly...

Now you asked me to get a few things off my chest, and you have some. This little tete-a-tete may not be much along the line of a blow-off, but will I hope make you see that I've lots of problems and that it's not that I want to hide them that I don't say anything, but just that I can handle them and there is no sense worrying you with regard to them. If it worries you more that you are left in ignorance of my problems, then say so and I'll take them up with you.

You too will have to handle the problems at home pretty well on your own gumption. I'll help where I can, but if our partnership can't stand a bit of stress and strain and if we can't trust each other to use reasonable judgement and precaution in what we do, then the partnership isn't going to be a very steady institution. It's built on a good solid foundation, Norah, so trust it...

One thing, Norah, that I set out to do and may or may not accom-

plish. That is to stop you worrying. I can't help but think that worry cost me Mother. It won't cost me more if I can help it…
Good night, Norah. All my love…
Fred

~

Dec. 3
Dearest Norah:
Today I received your letter dated Nov. 15…I have written you since I received Don's cable and by the time this letter gets back to you another month will have passed into the past. While you were thinking of me, I was thinking of you and the rest and of all the sorrows imposed on you by having to discuss mother's death with all the people who would come in…

Such good news to know that you and Waide took the notion to go and see Mother. It would be a day full of happiness for her and she could have quite some enjoyment from the letters I had written…Though it must have been a hard experience for Don to go through, it is comforting to know that Mother was in Don's arms when she died. I feel almost as though part of me was there, too…

Since receiving the cable I have had mother's Christmas box of fine foods and another pair of socks!…I had Mother's letter of Nov. 9…It was full of news of yourself, Don and Kay and all the grandchildren and Dad and Marg…

I want to refer back to my letter of Nov. 27. It was rather a nasty letter in some respects. I didn't intend that it should be, but some biting phrases would cut in. It is needless to say that I love you and you only. I want you to have pleasant times and as little worry or friction as possible for the duration. I seem to have had an ample heap of trouble the past bit and everything coming on top of the long wait for Cynthia has put me in a mood that jumps and jitters fairly easily. So hasty speech of reproof has its nasty beginning and sinister insinuations are made. No harm done, I'm sure? Perhaps I'm just thinking that I said more or less than I did say in said letter. You'd better check it over, but don't let it get your goat.
For now, dear Norah, good night,
Fred

~

Dec. 6
Dearest Fred:
Another week has rolled by and it is just that much nearer to Christmas. We had our first fall of snow and I must say it was quite nippy

out today. I was up early and went to market and did the weekend shopping and for the first time in weeks I felt hungry. There is one thing about me, I pick up quickly once I start. I have definitely decided my psychological attitude to a situation or problem has everything to do with my physical condition...

Waide was out for a long walk this afternoon and he came in with roses on his cheeks and an appetite. You ought to see him polish off a dinner - pie included. I've given up being fussy about what he eats - nothing seems to hurt him...He talks a great deal but not very distinctly, but nevertheless he tries everything and has a great imagination. When I get cross at him, he says, "Waide has gone away, Mummy" - meaning of course that I haven't Waide there but another bad little boy...

Dec. 10

...I had intended finishing this on Sunday, but the news came through of Japan's aggression on the States etc. etc. that I didn't finish it after all. It did strike like a thunderbolt, didn't it? Everyone over here seems excited and very concerned. This morning the news came over that the Repulse and the Prince of Wales had been sunk, also that they may evacuate the children and women from the Pacific Coast. There is now a blackout as far east from the coast as Calgary. It seems to have come to our very back door. Owen Sound might not be any too safe since the factories here are making very important war equipment. I simply can't describe how everyone seems to feel...

Strange thing! I feel calmer today than I have for weeks. I guess I'm just so angry that my fighting spirit is up. I realize darling, with a frightening reality, it probably means we are to be separated longer than ever now...You say Christmas has got you "down". It has us all down. I hope it goes very quickly, but I promise to make it nice for Waide...Loads of love and kisses, and we must both remain calm and confident in the face of every adversity.

Affectionately,

Norah

~

Dec. 9

Dearest Norah:

The only news since Saturday night has been and will continue to be the war in the Pacific. Now at last the arena is fully set. There are sure to be initial setbacks, possibly more serious than the opening phases suggest, though those are serious enough, God knows. Surely

Canadians can no longer rest in apathy. They should know now how securely the boot of war is fastened to their feet. Not from any thoughtless overconfidence, but because at last we have the threat to our home conclusively proved, defined and understood, I am glad of the new development. A hard fight ahead but one Canadians of today will be proud to have waged. I'm glad I'm in it.

So much for that. War with Japan was variously received. All seemed satisfied that the attack has not been launched without copious preparation, and consequently it is expected that for a time Japan will have a large measure of success. No one doubts for a moment that America can and will beat her to a pulp...

I'm afraid my letter doesn't show that I'm in high spirits. It sounds just the opposite and yet I am. For the first time in several weeks I'm feeling up to the bit...I've been inside such a hell of a lot since early November that I think I'll plead to be put on the parade square - just to get some of the energy floating to the top. All my insides are gummy with it and I'd better get it boiling and loose...

Dec. 10

Whew, quite a day! The Prince of Wales and Repulse! Looks like a bang-up party indeed...I've today received a very nice Christmas box from the Queen's Park War Services League with much good things to eat. Chocolate bars, cocoa, cigarettes, tea, sugar, raisins, Christmas cake, jam; writing paper, Kleenex and yes! one pair socks. I need a valise for them alone - would need to be an octopus at least, perhaps a centipede!...Love and kisses,

Fred

~

Dec. 14

Fred dearest:

...We were up to the park...It has snowed and snowed all day and Cynthia looked so cute in pink, tucked in her white fur robe in the cutter. She didn't sleep a wink the whole two hours we were out. She lay there wide-eyed and looked from side to side, taking in everything her two months are capable of. We watched the skiers at the park - today afforded the first skiing. Then we went into the ski lodge and warmed ourselves by the fire. Waide got a huge kick out of everything...

You were speaking of the cost of toys. Eleanor tried all day yesterday to buy Waide a train and there isn't one in town. Toys which are made out of any kind of metal will soon be nonexistent. However, Eleanor bought him a set of tinker toys, which he will enjoy since he is continually fitting one thing into another etc…

I am enjoying skating very much. Last night I skated nine bands out of twelve. Afterwards, ten of us went out for coffee. All married couples, but they drag me along, calling me their little "war widow". It is good exercise and I do feel so much better…

I do regret so much my letters to you of the last few weeks - they were so much in the doldrums, but as you will understand I wasn't feeling very well physically and of course it is hard to keep up my spirits. However I'm sure I won't be writing you any more depressing letters…Your letter was a bit grousy dear, but I realize we all get out of humour…

I am going to feel more lonesome New Year's Eve than any other. Do you remember the crazy time we had last year? I think I will spend it alone if possible with just the children. I hope you have as happy a time as is possible for you to have, dear. I do pray we will be reunited this year.

Norah

~

Dec. 16

Dearest Norah:

This letter should bring you better tidings and should have a better tone than its immediate predecessors. I have a new job. It is entirely different to any that I had thought might come my way and is different to my previous work to a rather radical degree…

A new effort is being made to categorize the men…Two methods are combined: first a "learning ability test" of the nature of an intelligence test, though that expression does not find favour and is said not to express the true nature of the test; second, a personal interview taking, say, one-half hour per man, aimed to reveal special qualities of adaptability, education and stability…There are supposed to be in the neighbourhood of a hundred officers involved in the field work, i.e. in giving tests and holding interviews; of those, I am one…

On Monday I assembled with about thirty-five others for a week's course of preparation. That, of course, was yesterday and it seems a long way off. Lectures began today at a nice slow gait that has not taxed either our "learning ability" nor energy…There is, of course, a lot of kidding about us already, and though "Quiz Kids" may become popular, the present name seems to be the "Brain Trust Boys".

Now the main thing for the moment is that in many ways I was very happy to be placed just at this time. There are many reasons, but mainly just that something new and different to take my interest comes as mighty good release. The last month hasn't been very happy, as you understand. This work being new holds my interest. I expect to travel from unit to unit throughout the army. Where I am any given week is unpredictable...

In many ways I don't fully realize that Mother is dead yet, and I rather hope to never come to any fuller realization. Right now moving off to new work will, I hope and expect, give me an outlet that I need at the moment. Lacking you to talk to and being unable to talk to anyone else on the subject to any extent has certainly left me on my own. Don wrote me the finest letter a brother could write. He has been a brick but, as you know, it is yourself that I look to most. You and the two children are my most comforting thought. So let me hear of you all regularly...It is unfortunate I'm not home to help you during all this long period...Since September we've both had much to put up with, and while I've not anyone to talk to about it all more than casually, it hasn't been harder for me than you...Love and kisses for tonight,

Fred

~

Dec. 23

Dearest Norah:

...You say in your letter that your physical state is closely bound with your frame of mind and I know that to be true. It is true of everyone but both you and I are particularly so made. I hope earnestly that you will try very hard to hold only happy thoughts in your mind for mulling over...You often mention that you'd love a grand old chat. Wouldn't it be great. All this history that is going by us and we in it would be so much more interesting if I could just gab it over with you, but more too, oh Norah, so much more to talk of: of you and I and Waide and Cynthia and all the folks. Imagine me even thinking I could talk for a week! But I do think so. Course, one doesn't talk all the time, I hope...

You wonder why we were all sent over so soon and say it's all a muddle to you. It's a muddle to most of us, except that you have to have so many for an army and doing law or interviewing when it has to be done is as necessary as anti-aircraft etc, so that while my English experience is not what I expected - nor you - it is a job that has to be done and I can do it...

I am surprised at the extent of the blackout in North America. I would have thought that a blackout over so extensive an area would

be more dangerous etc. than any attack that might result. Still, those who should know ordered it. I would not be apprehensive of an invasion of North America...In my mind it's not likely and ought to be disastrous to an invader. Australia is the one that may have fears and so we should first protect her...What a terrific carnage of men, women and children Russia has been, and how terrible the destruction of property...It ought to be echoed for our history how splendid the Russians have been. The country has shown itself to have one heart and one purpose and I admire them. It can't be easy to die to save a future or a compatriot, but it is so admirable. Tomorrow night will be Christmas Eve and I am as happy as I can expect to be. I think I will have an enjoyable time. All the lads have the same boots on. Good night. Love and love and love. I do love you, sweet.
Fred

~

Dec. 28
Fred dearest:
...I am enclosing a little write-up of a party we had Dec. 23 - we held "open house" like you and I did in Toronto. About 75 people dropped in...There was a dance Christmas night and the night after. I wasn't going to go, then I decided to. I had quite a bit of fun and saw all my old friends. It was amusing, nearly everyone said, "Norah, you haven't aged a day". I don't know why they think I should have.

I plan to spend New Year's at home with the children. I know if you were here, that is what we would do, wouldn't we? It is so hard to be separated, more especially at this time of year.
In your last letter, which I intend to answer in my letter to you this week, you seemed worried over what you said to me in your Nov. 27 letter. You didn't say nearly as much as you think you did. I didn't let it get my goat as you said...When you get back, which by the sound of Mr. Churchill's speech in Washington doesn't sound too soon, you can give me a "spanking". I felt gloomier than ever when he said maybe by 1943 we would begin to win.

We will be like strangers to each other if it lasts until 1945 or so. Christmas Eve as I was tucking Waide in, I couldn't keep from crying, thinking of last year and the year before, and you were home and we tucked him in together. He looked at me and said, "Daddy isn't coming home tomorrow, is he, Mummy?" The precious lamb, baby still as he is, doesn't forget you and seems to understand so much...All my love for tonight, dearest,
Norah

1942

Confessions, love and loneliness

"We can't tamper with love, for we don't know enough about it"

Cynthia Egener with her mother, Norah

Jan. 3

Dearest Fred:

...First of all you will want to know how Waide and Cynthia are...Cynthia is growing like a weed and laughing out loud. Her hair is quite reddish and alas she no longer looks like me, but is an Egener...It is no exaggeration to say, if you were a guest in the home and didn't know we had a baby, you wouldn't know from Cynthia that we had one. She is so good, never cries and requires no attention except to be bathed and fed...

Waide is getting huge...He has the greatest imagination. He has an imaginary friend, Okan KeeKee, whom he plays with all the time. He has a bath with him, he sleeps with him and he eats with him. We have to talk to Okan KeeKee too...

You know, darling, if this separation is doing you good, it is doing me just ten times more good. I have had the most confused mind ever since Cynthia was born - so many perplexing problems and situations have crept up and I am just now beginning to see clearly again. When you come home I will try and explain better what I mean. When I feel confused, I go out in the evening by myself and walk and walk and walk and usually work it out in my mind. For one thing, every now and again I get selfish and feel sorry for myself and think my lot is hard because I have to stay at home and look after the children when everyone else as young as I am is going out and having fun

Well, I went to the two Christmas dances, had fun in a way, but worked that sorry-for-myself feeling out of my system...

I guess I won't be driving the car whether I can afford to or not, due to gasoline rationing in the spring and no more tires. Mr. Churchill spoke in Ottawa last week and his speech was broadcast. Did you hear him? The people gave him a tremendous welcome. Did you hear what his New Years toast was? "A toast to a year of toil, hardship and struggle, but one more step towards victory" - words to that effect. He certainly doesn't sound as if the war will be over this year, does he?...

I am feeling better but am losing weight...My nerves are a bit jumpy but you say yours are, too. Everyone seems to be forcing an air of lightheartedness and happiness, and everyone is troubled and upset and worried underneath...

Love and kisses and hugs,

Norah

~

Jan. 5

Norah darling:

...New Years Eve was a new low. On that day Capt. Stone, who's my immediate boss, explained that he had four tickets for dinner and dance at a club of his and would I take two. Well, I'd not planned anything, and since he quite obviously was fed up and intent on partying the New Year in, I agreed. Then the hunt began for a dame. Too late to get any of the office staff...and when I searched my usual haunts I found nothing agreeable. In somewhat of a mild panic I journeyed off to Piccadilly...Finally I picked up a damsel whom I'd met in better surroundings than Piccadilly and whose presence there I dared not inquire into...We enjoyed a very fine dinner and winced at the price of whiskey, which had to be had as it was the only good thing about. Norah dearest, when I think and thought of the New Year's Eves we had, of the fun of popping corn, of games and stories and laughter, how shoddy seemed the one past. I was humourless all the while and wistful for you. How much I would have enjoyed standing with you on the porch, listening for the bells and watching the stars twinkle out their promises. Darling, they promised us much for the coming year...

Incidentally, you asked what I looked like now in one letter, which gave me quite a shock, so I looked me over. Fatter about the waist but not otherwise much different except that I fancy I've lost some of my snap...Lack facial colour, and enlarged the satchels to my eyes. Still, I do not expect you would notice any tremendous difference and I'm not so haggard as to frighten you away...All told we do have a gayish sort of life, but it is so futile without you. I have packs of friends, but always avoid seeing much of anyone or group. I don't know whether that's right or not...

Your plans for Christmas sound good. I hope you had a dandy time, though I fully realize that neither of us can hope to have a really grand time until the end of the evening sees us snuggling in together - hoping the morrow turns up late...All my love my dear, and many many hugs and kisses,

Fred

~

Jan. 9

Dearest Fred:

...Wednesday was my birthday and also skating night. I had a cake and candles and invited eight or ten in after for coffee and cake and sandwiches. We had a grate fire and danced etc....Last night there was a dance for the Polish officers and men. I and two other girls whose husbands are overseas went…as unattached females. We had quite a bit of fun. The officers are particularly gallant and kiss your hand when they are through dancing with you. Frankly, I wouldn't be crazy about the Poles. But you have no idea how the girls are running after them and entertaining them…

When I went out, I went in to kiss Waide good night and he said, "Are you going dancing, Mummy?" and I said, "Yes, darling, do you mind?" And he said, "No, but come home soon." Then he put his hand up to my face and he said with a very sweet flirty look, "You look pretty, Mummy". Imagine, the age of him…I want you to know I always put the children to bed even when I'm going out. I tell you that so you won't feel that I neglect them in any way…

I'm amused at you giving me permission to even do a little smooching. You're not doing a little yourself, perchance, with these Canadian nursing sisters, are you dear? Ahum!! It's not like you to give me so much leeway. All kidding aside, I agree we both must use our own good wit and sense and discretion. I know and you know where to draw the line, as you say…

I enjoyed the four dances I have been at lately, simply because I did let off that pent-up steam. You know me, I'm very susceptible to flattery and attention and I got it, so now I'm satisfied - no I'm not, either. When I think it over, it is just a lot of drivel and only makes me more lonesome for a settled-down existence and a rounded family life, you and I, sweet, and Waide and Cynthia…I certainly don't mind you having a little spree now and again…I do try to understand how living in camp must give your mind that "cramped, imprisoned sensation". It is a wonder you don't yell and scream at times. The poor chaps who have been over there for two years must be nearly daft by now - according to their letters to their wives, they are…Love and kisses and hugs from your three sweethearts,
Norah

~

Jan. 14

Dearest Norah:

…Snow came yesterday and continued to fall today, so that the countryside does at last look homey and you don't even mind all the skidding you do on the roads. Snow here is that damp variety that packs down on the roads and soon becomes ice…

Your letter I received Monday was very interesting, as they always are. You are indeed an expert letter writer. Waide and Cynthia's doings are so cute, interesting and gratifying...My constant hope is that I will do as well as you expect so that when I come home after the war is done, we will both be able to say we know more certainly we married the person we thought. Remember, sweet, that under all circumstances, regardless of errors or actions on either our parts, I love you sincerely as I know you do me...

With gas rationing, tire restrictions, price controls, rising costs of living and all, life will be quite a change. Tell me how you get along. Have you enough money? Are you having difficulty managing your money?...Can you manage to get a place at Leith or on the Huron side this summer? Having in mind your present income? What extra will you need? You have said little about your dad and mother lately, how are things going?...I wired you on your birthday but suppose you failed to receive it. Wires are unsatisfactory...Love and kisses and hugs,
Fred

~

Jan. 20
Fred dearest:
...It is now 9 p.m. I have just now got the two bairns settled. It is always a two-hour job after dinner at night by the time I bath Waide and get him in bed and feed Cynthia and get her settled. Waide is so strenuous lately. He is full of fun, and so energetic that he is a little hard on me. He is getting a little saucy of late and needs a firm hand...

The other day he was supposed to be asleep and when I went in, having heard him moving around, he had been pulling all the snow off the window sill on the outside and had his bed full of snow, chunks of snow all over the walls and the floor covered with snow. What a mess! And what to do with him!...

Cynthia weighs nearly eighteen pounds. She smiles and laughs out loud and plays with her hands and loves to look at the baby in the mirror. She tries so hard to turn over and to pull her head and shoulders up off the pillow. I wish I could make you realize how good she is - you would be amazed. She just never cries, and lies up in her basket for three hours at a stretch and never says boo. And yet when I change her or peek at her to make sure she is all right, she laughs and smiles...I've decided the less attention babies get, the better they are...

I have been feeling just so-so. I don't think I'll be any worse but certainly not any better until you come back...It is purely a state of mind with me. I just sort of exist from week to week, but so are hundreds of others, waiting for this horrible war to end...I received your cable dear, wishing me best wishes on my birthday, on Jan. 12. Thanks, darling, even though the cable was delayed, I did appreciate your message...

There is a new movement under way, "Total War Effort". Public meetings have been held in Toronto, London, Hamilton etc, and I presume in the other provinces too. The idea being to make the public's voice heard re conscription. There are pieces in the paper urging people to write to their member urging him to speak up for conscription.

It amazes me how many single young men, or even young married men, are still around, apparently not much concerned. However, I guess I shouldn't judge. You always said I should be more tolerant. Eleanor had a few in for the evening on Saturday night and I couldn't help feeling a little bitter at the boys who were here - three at least I know have no excuse in the world except that they are yellow. I kept saying to myself, "Why should Fred have to go first when these boys stay at home?" Oh well, you will never have any regrets, dear, and we are all so proud of you...

Most towns are starting classes to teach people what to do in case of air raids, how to put out incendiaries etc. We are cautioned to salvage all rubber, so I have a large box in the kitchen and I'm salvaging everything...

I do hope your work will be most interesting and instructive...I understand what sort of work you are doing because I have read several articles about it. Isn't the idea mainly in so many words to put the right man in the right place and so make a more efficient army?...All my love, sweet, and hugs and kisses from your three sweethearts...
Norah

~

Jan. 27
Dearest Norah:
...Well, sweet, for the first field job on this new work, it is a treat...We are billeted in a large English country house - how they did live and how did they live - It's a huge place and pretentious, but the light I write by barely casts a shadow and hot water is a real treat...The place is heated (!?!) by grates and at three paces you might as well be outside. The house has a history - be thankful for something. It is supposed to have been built by one of Nelson's admirals who, in failing health, roamed the country seeking a place to build a home.

Some gypsies told him that good health would be his lot if he built "near the five thorn trees yonder"...

Have had a busy day but knocked off early 'cause my throat's like a washboard and I have been coughing most of the afternoon...Have not determined whether this spell is a cold, laryngitis, too much smoking or that poor rum I had in London over the weekend. Bill and I went up Friday and I stayed that night with a man I'd met in Bournemouth. He had a very nice place, new and modern but subject to the English cold, as all are...I had an enormous turkey bone dinner. I wouldn't have minded that had it not been that the dashed thing cost six shillings and any good butcher could have extracted the bone for less than that and let the bird live...

The pictures of yourself and the children were most welcome and mean a great deal to me. You look in one to be a little tired, but I can well understand that when you have so much to do and everyone to look after...All my love, darling. Sweet dreams...
Fred

~

Jan. 27
Dearest Fred:
...I am so glad you like your new work and your friend Bill in particular. It is always so nice to have someone congenial with whom to work. You both seem to have things in common, with the exception that you are married and have two children. However, maybe he has a sweetheart, so probably knows what it is like to be in love. If not, I hope you will tell him it is the nicest thing in the world...

If you were only sure you would be more or less permanently selected to do this sort of work, or law, I wish I could come over and live there. However, I guess I couldn't get into the country for one thing, and a selfish act to walk out on the children, for another. Darling I must admit they are very sweet, but they don't make up for you, not by a million miles. Is that unnatural for me to say that?...

I'm feeling much better this week. I have tried to get more rest and have just generally been happier. I seem fine for a couple of weeks and then such a cold horrid feeling creeps over me - I realize you aren't here and may be away for so long and then I'm just no good for a day or so...The family is very patient with me. Even little Waide seems to understand, for he often kisses me and is very loving...I don't think there will be much difficulty in you and Waide getting to know one another when you come home. The other night it was so cute, he was standing on a chair in his pyjamas with his tummy stuck out and we all said, "Oh look at Pop Egener. Waide looks like Pop Egener." And he said, stamping his foot and looking very cross, "No Mummy, Waide looks like Daddy". Isn't that cute?

Now sweet, you aren't still sticking out for six children. I like the job, but not that well. If we have the money, I would like four. I'll be so rested, dear, by the time you get home I'll be ready for anything...

How the war changes from the time you write a letter until I receive it. It hasn't been good the last week - with Australia in such danger; Argentina holding out against an all-out break with the Axis; Rommel's army retaking ground in Libya; submarine warfare continuing on the Atlantic coast; and Mr. King insisting on having a plebiscite...

I do love you, as you said too, and I do miss you. But I must try to be happy and brave, and won't our reunion be the most marvelous thing that ever happened to us. If I only knew when. This awful uncertainty as to when the war will end. Waiting - waiting - Good night my darling, and a thousand kisses,
Norah

~

Feb. 8
Dearest Norah:
...I often think these days of how little I contribute to the upbringing of the children, and I wonder just how I could help. It is nonsense to say that there is nothing I can do for, though very limited opportunities of necessity present themselves, there must be a manner in which, the effort once being made, something can be accomplished. If you think of anything, do let me know.

It has occurred to me that possibly Waide's confusion at times over his dad not coming home may be a bad thing to happen to him, and that the more he is impressed with my existence without being able to grasp the reason for my absence may lead him into a fairyland of thoughts which may be hard to break down when I come home...

You will realize how much fun I am having with Bill Hulbig. He is a splendid chap and his interests lie in the same spheres as my own. Both of us learn from the other, as we have not learned just the same things. I find that we have much the same ideas and plans and so one of us is sure to be in the mood to instill into the other the enthusiasm to do something...

We expect to be finished this camp Wednesday or Thursday, so new adventures are around the corner...Have had tea now and it's

11:25, so must close and get this off so as to get a night's sleep. Where did the time go? It just rushed past...Love and kisses,
Fred

~

Feb. 15
Fred dearest:
...I bought some books which I am going to read and then send to you. They are: 1) Education for Death, by Ziemer - the story of the life of a Nazi in the making from the time they are young until they enter the army...2) Chateaubriand, a biography, the story of "one Chateaubriand, commonly regarded in France as the first of the Romantics", 3) Journal, An Ambassador to Great Britain, by Charles G. Dawes, 4) a twenty-cent Penguin, English Justice, by Solicitor, and Night Flight by Antoine De Saint-Exupery...I hope you don't think me foolish to buy them. I hope when you read them you will find them enjoyable...

Tomorrow night is the Rotary dance and I am going with the Dr. Whytes. Wednesday night is the last skating night, and Thursday night is a community concert affair and Saturday night I am going to a supper party - so I have a full week. During the days, I hope to enamel Cynthia's bed and houseclean the bathroom as well as my everyday jobs...All my love, sweet, and remember I'm just as lonesome for you as you are for me and it's hell!
Love,
Norah

~

Feb. 15
Dearest Norah:
Thursday we moved again...Saturday, which was yesterday, Bill and I went for a tour again to Guilford and out on the Pilgrim's Way to St. Martha's Church, which is an old landmark. Then too we browsed in the book shops of Guilford. We spent considerable time purchasing four books of the area, books on English architecture, a copy of Chaucer etc. Will never read all the stuff, but have acquisitive natures...

I do not feel you've had much time to know how much capital you can save a month. By capital I mean everything over and above current expenses. How much can you put aside a month to go towards clothing, holidays, furniture, gifts, cottage, house, saving? That has worried me continuously since I've left you in charge and I've been waiting until the few first months of Cynthia's life, Christmas, house-settling etc. gives you a chance to find this out.

When you have found out and can tell me, I do wish you would. Only then can we talk of capital expenditures or saving with any common understanding. I want you to have enough to be able to thoroughly enjoy living and for the children to have those things they need or should have. Then we can plan…As far as I myself am concerned, funds are not a problem except that I'm broke the majority of the time. That does not mean I need more, only that I will have to study the matter of selective spending…

Glad to hear how well Cynthia and Waide are doing - and, oh yes, Okan KeeKee, too…I should like to write longer for I'm in that mood, but must get to bed. Today has been the first work day with the new unit, and a hard one, ending with a pow-wow with all the officers, colonel down, about our task. So we're tired…

Love to all and all my love to you, sweet. Just about two years ago, we were thinking of going to Oakville. Remember?

Love and kisses,

Fred

~

Feb. 22

Dearest Fred:

I received your letter enclosing the snaps…I was so thrilled with them, darling, and you do look so well. They made me terribly lonesome, though. Do you sometimes get that awful realization, suddenly like, that we are separated by such a long way? I'm sure you do.

It was peculiar, I took snaps today, too. Mom and Dad and Aunt Marg (who arrived yesterday) and Waide and Cynthia and I walked up to Harrison Park. It was such a beautiful day, and the park looked so lovely, the trees shaggy with snow and the river frozen over. Waide and Dad and I skated on the outdoor rink. It was Waide's first time and he did very well…Cynthia didn't sleep a wink all afternoon, but just looked around with her gorgeous big blue eyes and took everything in…

You wouldn't consider practising here after the war, would you? I am getting to love Owen Sound. It offers so much in so many ways - particularly to children in the way of outdoor sports. We must someday ski together, dear, and skate etc…

This week is the last night for Skating Club. I will be so sorry, for I have enjoyed it. A week from this Wednesday night, I'm having a hard-time party, which promises to be fun. I have invited twenty, and everyone is going to be dressed "hard time". I only wish you were going to be here, dear.

Darling before I answer your letters, tell me one thing? You do love me, don't you? Sometimes when it seems such ages between letters, I get to wondering if you still love me as much, more or less as before. Do you ever feel the same? I don't expect you not to go out with girls, but I do pray you won't ever love anyone else. You know it may be three or four years more, and that is bound to be more of a strain each year on both of us...Now don't get to thinking I don't trust you. Hell, I don't really care if you kiss someone or even make love to someone, as long as your heart remains true. What say?...

I'm afraid you have a somewhat exaggerated idea of how well I am doing regarding my task over here. I fall far short many times. My disposition is the thing that worries me most. Sometimes I let my temper go and give Waide the devil, or anyone who comes in my path. And that isn't like me, is it?...You say your constant hope is that you will do as well as I expect. Darling, you have always been a credit to me and I know you always will be. Funny thing, I love your bad points - not very bad, dear - and often smile over one or two occasions when you got a bit tiddly...

Waide has so many "mothers", no wonder he gets confused and hard to manage. He is saucy at times. He called me a nut and a rat the other day...He yells at me sometimes and says, "Shame on you, Mummy, bad girl", and gets a face on him like a pail of worms...

I won't need any financial help to swing the cottage, dear. I am starting to save next month for it. I hope to run the car, but the family are going to help me out on that. We have a tin can into which we have all been putting our coppers all winter, and Waide puts a copper in, too, whenever he has one, and says, "That is to get the car running in the spring." Cute...

Good night, sweetheart. I love you "all the world", as I used to say...
Norah

~

Feb. 26
Dearest Norah:
...Saturday the mess had a dance and, being temporarily attached, we were invited. We brought two English ladies...two between the three of us, which was fortunate as by the evening's end I was in high shape and had lost all interest in women - a shame! Sunday,

questioning whether it was due to Saturday or the cold that had been creeping over me since Friday, I rose in horrid condition and managed a trip via bus to Aldershot - principally as a breather and "get away from camp" effort...

All of this may sound like dull times, but such is not the case. We have interested ourselves in history and topography, tactics and people, so we've been reading and seeing just as much as spare time permits. It is a small library I now carry with me and in due time I'll start sending you the books...

There are more encouraging scraps of news the last two days. Rangoon defences stiffen. Java, at bay, is defiant. RAAF take to offensive bombing. The fleets are in action off Java. British paratroops raid the French coast. The Russians continue their successes. These tidbits may tomorrow grow to real successes. That we Canadians remain inactive, albeit in a key position, is the greatest discouragement. We are glad to be here, but we must have some practical experience to make a real army. The first shock against seasoned troops is bound to be a revelation both to officers and men, regardless of the preparations...

Guess the Poles must have something, it's said the clannish Scotch lassies have gone for them, too. Perhaps a uniform is a carte-blanche, for the army seems able to get along wherever it goes...

I'm glad you had some fun at the dances etc. and let off a little steam. Get the flattery and attention you say you're susceptible to. I fully believe you when you say it's unsatisfactory. I've had lots of fun, but I'd trade it all for just you. Things will be right again when we get our home together and by God we'll realize what we have...

You wonder if a legal job is in the air. Well, I've been doing administration of various sorts and suppose I'll not get out of it, though. I'm doubtful in my own mind whether I want law or administrative work of any kind. We'll just see what happens. If there was a "show", though, I wouldn't want to be pen-pushing, you know...

I always regret signing off to you, sweet...The recompense of a hug and kiss is small in a letter.

All my love, darling,

Fred

~

March 8

Fred dearest:

You will notice I am sending this via air mail, since I have a feeling some of my letters have gone down, since I noticed in the paper where two separate convoys were attacked and some boats sunk...Your last one arrived on Wednesday March 4, and I enjoyed reading it, although there was something about it that made me sad. I don't know what...

Waide will soon be three. And he is getting to be such a big boy. He is out playing every day with his little friends Timmy, Diana and some others whose names I don't know. I looked out the other day and discovered him on the roof of a garage, the one side of which had a high stone wall beside it. I left him there and he and Timmy got down safely...The other day he came in and was rosy-cheeked but a little fagged, and what did he do but go downstairs and bring up a half gallon of sherry and took the top off and got a glass and asked me to pour him a drink...Cynthia is adorable. She and Waide are both in the same room now, each in their own beds, and they are a beautiful picture to behold...

I wouldn't mind buying a farm - imagine me saying that. I'm very serious...We might be very glad to own a little land on which to grow some food. If that day never arrives, and I pray it doesn't, it would be nice to build a cottage on it...Because darling, I really believe we are going to see much harder times - we may lose our easy way of life. And I could work on a farm if it meant food and shelter - I mean I have the guts, dear. There is no use fooling ourselves, things aren't going to be better until they are a lot, lot worse. Things do seem to be in such a mess. You have probably read where right here in our own Canada, there is now talk of Quebec asking for her independence...

You ask if there isn't some way in which you can contribute to the upbringing of the children. Darling, I can't think of how you can, at present, directly contribute. Do you forget that on you we all three depend for so much - not only financially, but our whole future depends on what you do and how you fulfill your duties etc...I only contribute to their upbringing in that I look after their physical needs. They are as yet too young to require much else. So sweet, don't worry too much on that score...

Keep smiling and be good and remember I expect the best always because you are the best...
Norah

~

March 14
Dearest Norah:

...As I suggested in my last letter, I have changed again...Here I am billeted rather than being in a camp. It is my first experience and a very pleasant one. We (Bill and I) are billeted in the home of a Mrs. Morris who is, she says, 77 years old...She herself is a keen woman whose experiences have been wide and who has never ceased to be abreast of the times in which she lived. As a consequence, we have had pleasant conversations. The remainder of the household consists of a daughter (age 40?), a young girl evacuated from London and now a student at a medical school also removed from London. A housekeeper. All have shown us kindness. I would not labour the point if it were not that this is the first English home I have entered that I've felt comfortable...

To note your comment that Bill and I "have things in common, with the exception" of wife and children. Bill has no tendency to lead me astray in any way, in case you wonder. He is not a man of excesses and is single, I judge, because of his moderate approach to women...You mention how much you would like to come over. You could not do so at present. If permission was obtainable, I could not let you because of the risk. The children could not be left alone at their age and your care of them is essential at their age...

It is hard to understand the need of the (conscription) plebiscite. It is humiliating. However, if there is so great a doubt as to the view of the average Canadian, then it should be held. We believe in majority rule and we believe in respecting the views of a large minority. If we do not, our ideas of democracy are fantastic...

I am glad to hear you are having good times and that you enjoy the dances and parties. It is difficult to picture you at them without me - if I may be so vain. They are doubtless a good tonic. You will, like myself, find them meaningless and that you carry away very little. What a party I will take you through when I'm home! A timeless whirl of mad, giddy happiness! Just the two of us at our party; sometimes four. All my love, dearest. Write soon. A pack of hugs and kisses.

Fred

~

March 29

Dearest Fred:

...We heard definite news of our cottage this week. It is a very nice cottage at Leith near the Legate cottage....$100 for the season, which means we may move down as early in June as weather permits, and stay as late in September as weather permits. So the children will have a grand summer and get lots of sunshine. Waide is excited over it and is already telling everyone we are going to Leith for the summer. So I know it will please you too…

Marg is going to go halves on the expenses at Leith, so we should manage very nicely. I manage the house (for food) on $18 a week - there are six adults now including the maid, and two children, and three meals a day. I very seldom have more than 25 cents left over on Saturday night, but I am never over my $18 and I pay cash for everything…

Eleanor went down to Toronto today to join the air force. She feels that since Canada is going on an all-out war effort, her business might have to close its doors for lack of hats to sell…and furthermore, all single women will probably be conscripted for war work, so she might as well get into something now that she likes, and work up…

Next week is the IODE dance. I am giving a coffee party (I mean coffee) before the dance. I have invited twenty-four and hope it will be nice…I have invited a Dr. and Mrs. Bonar. They are very interesting and charming. He was a former doctor of laws and economics in Warsaw and held a very high position. He is an officer with the Polish Army here…

It seems most peculiar entertaining without you, dear, and I am not going to the dance with anyone. Everyone knows now I prefer not to go with anyone, so I go with another couple and it works out fine. I feel very lonely the first and last dances, but I usually have all the rest…I was so tired tonight I just had to have a rest, so I have been sleeping until 9:30, only to get up and find the furnace out. So I have been wrestling with clinkers and chopping cedar etc. and finally have the fire going. Eleanor was away today as I said, so I helped at the store today. The rush was terrific and very tiring…

I enjoy very much hearing of your and Bill's walks, the places you see and the people you see, especially the nurses you meet. I don't blame any woman for being attentive to you, dear. I would hate to have a husband that other people didn't think attractive. But just let me get my hands on anyone who tries to steal you and - well - I guess I can't do much, can I? But I would not be gentle with her…

I for my part am a bit cynical about men now. By that I mean, I have discovered that most of them seem to show an interest in another woman other than their wife. Maybe it is just this town, I don't know. Or maybe it is just war-time. I know one thing, I have yet to see up here one couple who get along as well as we did, or who love

each other as we do...I am lonesome, very lonesome...
Love and kisses and hugs,
Norah
P.S. A year ago this month, you went active. Remember the night you came home and told me, and that you were going over soon? I felt the house had fallen on top of me.

~

April 1
Dearest Norah:
It happened yesterday, and did it make me happy! A whole new delight swept completely over me. What was it? Why your letters came, five of them all at once. I had been on a strict ration and had begun to feel on the desperate side for news of you...

Received too were the socks from Eleanor. They are keen, thank Eleanor a lot for me; your box bearing Nescafe, egg yolk, tea, gloves from Aunt Pheob...Darling, it was very very good of all of you to send such a fine array. Just a whisper in your ear: please, oh please, don't let anyone more send me socks! God almighty, I've got so many! Last time I dared to count them, I had more than thirty pair, about half of which have never seen my ugly toes...I do not wish to dampen the war effort of all the mighty knitters of Canada, so don't declare passionately my dilemma of socks - just a gentle hint to the busy needles...

I laugh at you thinking of being a farmerette! Good stuff, sweet! You mention the shore of Georgian Bay, while I had in mind Huron directly opposite. Keep an eye out and let me know...

I want to be home with you more than anything else. Sometimes feel a bit desperate about it and discouraged. I know that military strategy demands that we do not strike prematurely, but inactivity is a mighty bad thing, too. Being busy is not a full cure. Am afraid I don't find a great deal of interest in the army, though I'm by no means as lacking in interest as many.

We all feel, let's get it over with and home. It's a wrong way of thinking, for it tends to have the opposite effect to what might be expected. You would logically think that with that spirit, the attitude would be, we'll train all get out and forget everything else but our duties. It isn't. The effect is, why am I not fighting, I'm trained, let me fight and go home...

I try not to grumble. I try only to think that this army is the best ever and the way we do things is the right way. It is not so. It needs a lot more hard training and hard work by men and officers. I am not satisfied that the Canadian army is ready to go into action. If it goes in, the enthusiasm of the men will make up for a lot, but how much?

In your letter of Feb. 22, you said to tell you one thing - "You do love me, don't you?" Norah, I love you with all my heart and soul. At no time have I ever ceased to love you...This is not just talk. I do not know what to say. Just, I love you, over and over again...You say you don't expect me not to go out with girls. That's reasonable, but as a matter of fact I've not been out very often. I told you of the parties around Christmas time. There haven't been any of importance since. I've talked with gals when and where met - pubs etc. They don't mean a tinker's damn to me...

I do not object to your going out with the Owen Sound friends you have made. I do not worry in that regard. The only matter of concern is that gradually some person may become important to your enjoyment. That can be dangerous, and is for you to avoid...Norah, you do do such a good job of managing affairs at home and of keeping the children right. They sound like the happiest pair...How you do it is a marvel. Had I travelled the world, I could not have found a better, sweeter wife than you, love...It looks funny in writing, but what else can I do? Were I able to whisper in your ear, I'd say I love you sweet - good night.
Fred

~

April 11
Dearest Norah:
...Now that you've decided that children don't need any attention, you won't mind having lots around. Two are a fair start, leastways two like you have. We've been fortunate that they are so robust. I have read many little articles that make me think I'm dodging my duties to them...It is my part that I feel is wrong and lacking. I know that you do everything time permits to train the scamps...

I'm surprised about enlistment at home - ostriches - even I get bitter...I do have tolerant views, but damn, do I have to sit here and elsewhere away from you while these numbskulls and slackers are protected? It is not very easy to be reasonable about it. I won't be sorry about my own service, because I think it's just as necessary as if we were on guard outside the house, but like any man I'd like to go inside for a spell, too...

You're out a lot these nights, Rotary dances, skating, concert. Hope you have fun, but don't forget I'm a homebody...Practise in Owen

Sound? - perhaps - can't say. Doubt I'll return to law - don't know. Think I'll be a squire.

Who is giving the leeway now? I can pitch a little woo as long as I'm true? I wonder. I grant you an armful of femininity would be grand, yes, right now, if it were you. Oh, I know what you mean, I'm no prig and I don't think it matters a damn if conventions are broken so long as that's all that breaks. The mind associates loose conduct with broken love, and it's not altogether wrong...

Glad you let Waide get up and down garages etc. his own way. He'll manage - the man-child...

I do not know whether I should add this note or not, but here goes. When I read through your letters I found that you complain quite a bit of various states of nervousness, restless, unable to sleep, irritability, desire to get away, parties, and you will know probably of others you never thought to mention...Now I suggest that much of the nervousness is from lack of lovin', or desire to love, if you'd have it that way - and I think that it is only aggravated by many of the activities one pursues to cure it. Let's be honest: a dance is hardly for the pleasure of dancing. It's a type of courtship...This goes, in some measure, for other types of entertainment, too...

Association naturally leads from simple to more complex situations, and without being untrue to one's home, one tends to be, shall we say, forgetful...Now I suggest, Norah, that you are straining your own nerves by being out a lot and that dances and parties are just giving you quite a battering. Perhaps that is wrong, still I think continuous tempting will jangle your nerves more than anything else. I don't want you to stop going out, but I feel that if that's what is happening, and I know you to be honest with yourself, you will not torture yourself quite so much. I would not make you toe the line for making mistakes, as you would not criticise me, but love, Norah, is a very deep thing that we don't know too well how to handle, and it ought not to be tampered with lightly...Do not feel offended at anything said, and do not think I'm growing suspicious and/or faithless. Such isn't the case. If I should not write as I did, say so. If you have comments, give me them. All my love, sweetheart,
Fred

~

April 12
Dearest Fred:
...Eleanor is almost certain to be accepted in the air force within the next six weeks. Which means Mom will carry on the business until

she comes back. It will be good experience for Eleanor and she will be on her own for once. As for myself, I hardly know what to do. I feel more strongly every day that I must live by myself. The confusion of late has been terrific. Marg is still here and will be, I guess, until June when she goes down to the cottage with me. So you can well imagine when I say I'm confused, with six adults (including the maid) and two children around all the time…One day at lunch I said, "For God's sake, I can't stand it any longer"…

Between listening to everyone's tales of woe, I wonder if I'm sane. The point is, I've got to do something. As much and all as I love Marg and Mom and Dad, I simply cannot stand the confusion. Two children are I feel enough to look after. I never have a quiet moment with either, and Waide is good but strenuous and high-strung and I feel he needs the quietness too. I've lost so much weight and it seems to me I'm cranky all the time…The trouble is to get an apartment or house. I wouldn't be able to get out very much, but I would gladly trade the social life for a little quiet and peace…

Waide as I have told you before is picking up all sorts of things from the children…He has gone over town alone twice now. It worries me sick, but what can I do? Punishing him does no good really, for he only forgets and I can't watch him every minute. Uncle Ben found him the last time and phoned me. I said to him, "Waide, the cars will hit you," and he says, "No Mummy, I just stand still and the cars go by". How is that for good reasoning?…

It was sweet of you to assure me that Bill will not lead you astray. I haven't many fears on that score as I've said before. Is that conceited on my part?…

Mr. King spoke on the plebiscite the other night. He spoke very seriously and did not paint a rosy picture for us. He said in the past it was a case of national unity, now it is a question of our very existence. He didn't say so exactly, but he might as well have said we will most certainly have conscription of manpower. Apparently of late, the enlisting has greatly improved. People are awakening to the seriousness of our situation and to our danger…

Don't let my troubles get you down, I really believe I bring a lot of them on myself by not taking the right mental attitude towards things and also by not getting enough rest. Everyone seems to have problems of one kind and another - so I guess I'm no different.

So until my next letter, darling, all my love and kisses,
Norah

~

April 19

Dearest Fred:

...We have had a bad week - Waide and Cynthia have both been very sick. Apparently Waide caught a germ which is going around and the result was a very heavy cold with the infection settling in his ear. His temperature was a hundred and three for two days...Along with that Cynthia is sick. Luckily she hasn't what Waide has, at least we don't think so...

Along with the house, you will understand I've been busy and have little news. However, we are nearly out of the woods and they are both really all right now, so don't worry dear...I bought a bicycle, the main reason being the car situation is getting very bad and I'm sure the car won't run on the tires another year even if I could procure the required gas. I now can have only five gallons, and there is talk of reducing people in my category to two gallons...

Your letters are so well-worded and quite often philosophical. A great comfort and pleasure to read. Is it because you are in a position to see things more objectively? I feel as if I had my face right against the pane and would love to be able to sit back and see things more clearly.

I must confess I have never felt so absolutely confused within as I have the last few months. I find myself trying to hang on to certain ideals, and on the other hand I find myself becoming cynical. I feel I am personally, within myself (my thoughts) standing up very poorly to things. I'm rebellious and a quitter lots of times. I worry for fear you and I will not pick up where we left off. I'm so afraid too many things will have happened to us and maybe we won't be the same. I want to be just a little girl again and have you look after me. But apparently when one grows up one must lose those ideas. Do you ever feel this way?...But you will be tired listening to all this "drivel". My last two or three letters have been very depressing, I know. I would have preferred not to send them, but then you would wonder what was the matter. I simply must pull myself together and "buck up". I will promise to be more cheerful when next I write.

All my love, darling.

Norah

~

April 22

Dearest Norah:

...You know me so well, you will understand how seriously I ponder little thoughts and mull them over. I find I'm dissatisfied here. I do not suppose that anything else could be expected, for to be away from all that you truly love is indeed a burden...

Well, pondering all this I decided that the only truly practical thing I could do would be to develop a way of living and thinking. I've not always been content with my way of living. Though you've said little, I know you agree. Sprees and parties, excessive indulgence, lateness, unordered schedules, all bring about a hectic atmosphere. Perhaps I take myself too seriously, but I decided the first thing to control is yourself, so I am planning to do that. If I'm to be here a year or more, I will have something constructive to work on. I'm going to tear down some bad habits and build new...I believe that if by your will you can control yourself, then you can win over the other elements needed to succeed. You will think I'm daft talking this way...

I am pleased to hear that you're getting the car running. Five gallons a week! You'll have to save a month to go to London! I wouldn't get a bike. At this stage it would be silly. Shan't say you're too old, but dignity, my dear...

You suggest I accept administrative duties if offered. I have. I realize that the particular job is not what one gets so bored with, it's being away from home. The parade square, the desk, the pill box, the fighting vehicle, are all tiresome. I have no illusion that being in a front post would cure all the evils and bring lasting contentment...

I am trying to get a bit of travel education from all my moving, but I'll swear I'll not get more after this is over...

Good night, darling. Do my letters bore you? Are they too full of sentimentality? What do you want to hear? I doubt you give a damn whether Mrs. Hoare's first husband was an ambassador or what, do you? Neither do I, not a good goddamn. News seems lacking except I ate this, slept X hours, worked or didn't. Tell me what I shall write of. All my love, Norah,

Fred

~

April 23

Fred darling:

...How you write such interesting letters, dear, not having received mail, is a marvel to me. I do enjoy hearing about even your most unimportant events, it is all news to me and when you mention a midnight lunch etc., I can picture you and the others. I like to hear what you talk about and your description of the countryside...

I understand, dear, when you say I am the only one in whom you can confide. I feel if you only could, you would feel happier if you could discuss and talk things over with someone. But as well and all as I know you, I used to feel sometimes as if you were reticent about talking to me. I used to often wonder what you were thinking…

You know, dear, something very peculiar is happening to me inside. I can't very well explain it - I wish I could because I feel certain you could help. It is perhaps a battle of ideas or ideals. I seem to be struggling for a way of life that will bring me peace and comfort and help me to be strong - help me to face adversity. I can see quite clearly that having you away is the first really big problem I've ever had to face. Up until then, life was one happy song. It has been very hard, dearest. But do you know, when this battle within is over, I feel I am going to be contented, and stronger than ever before. Darling, I'm sure you will wonder what on earth I'm talking about. But I don't know how to explain myself. I'm just bewildered and confused, that is all. I refuse to say, "Eat, drink and be merry, for tomorrow we die". There will be a tomorrow, and I'm certain it is worth fighting for and waiting for…Please tell me, darling, if you faintly understand what I'm trying to explain. Are you having the same problems?…

You asked in your letter what Waide was doing these days. He still plays with trucks. But most of the time he plays with two little boys, Timmy and Tommy. He has his scooter and tricycle and wagon…This morning Mr. Fenton, the corner grocer, called and asked if I wanted something. Waide had gone to the store with a quarter. Where he got it, I don't know. He is getting to be such a boy. The other evening, I gave Cynthia a little spank and he said, "Mummy, don't you dare hurt sister". He stood up in his high chair at dinner the other night and with all the oratorical and facial expression in the world, jabbered on as follows: "Hello you folks, you're a bad boy, pipe down, darn it, I don't care, shut up" etc. etc. I guess he was just saying anything and everything that came into his head…

I do want you home so much but I am going to be patient and not fight against this awful separation. Remember one thing, sweet, I'll be waiting for you always, however long it may be…
Norah

~

April 27
Dearest Norah:
…When I last wrote I was staying at Mrs. Morris'. That has now changed. I had been there only three days when…I was forced back

to my original habitat.

Bill visited me Friday night, Saturday and Sunday...At night we went to the local dance which, despite the lack of fires, the height of the ceiling etc., was warmer than comfortable. Only a half dozen officers were there, but it was entertaining. The English girls have taught the Canadians numerous group dances and the Canadians have brought in many jitterbug steps. The way some couples whooped it up was a real surprise. Feet going like sixty, swings, kicks and whirls. To my senses, tuned to the "cheek-to-cheek" style, the dizzy pace, the stench of sweat and the clouds of tobacco smoke were somewhat repugnant. I got me a couple of potentially vigorous but momentarily exhausted partners who were sufficiently quiescent at the time to yield to my pace...

Newspapers report some bombing in Southern England, but have seen nor heard none. Only one night suspicious sounds coming from great distance indicated possible bombs or gun firing. Have been anxious to see a raid without any damage or danger. So far nothing at all either without or with risk...Nothing continues here to a late hour due to the shutting down of all transport at an early hour. I can hardly imagine Canada coming to the same state of affairs...

I haven't had mail from you since I last wrote and so have nothing to comment on. I hope you're having as good a time as conditions permit and will only exhort you to be sure you and the children have the things you need before you worry about adding to the bankroll...Good night sweet, tuck yourself and the bairns in comfy...
Fred

~

May 5
Dearest Norah:
Today is a good day because another of your choice letters arrived...I know how upset you must feel. One's own problems are enough, but to have the store, probably the same old home arguments, Marg, a maid, Pop, the children and me, all to listen to, counsel, console and worry about must nearly drive you nutty. Bet I'll get a vote from you for a quiet home...

I do not think breaking up the household would be a final solution. I think that alone, you would feel more and more lonesome. If that is the only way to solve the problem, then all right, but I hope that some other way can be found. When you go to Leith...take the summer off and quieten down. Try not to run yourself to ground by keeping at a high pitch. You ascribe some of your difficulties to your mental attitude and lack of rest. Conquer them, then. If I could put my arms around you and cuddle you, you would sleep, I know. For now, you must just believe and wait...

Glad to hear Waide has learned to stand still and the cars will pass him. Damned good policy...I can understand your being worried about him going downtown alone. No doubt your heart's in your throat, so would be mine. If he does learn to get about and doesn't lose himself completely, he'll be over a milestone, but until you're sure he's learned!?...

The plebiscite is passed, we hear. But details are lacking except that Quebec wasn't in favour. It is a shame that there hasn't been a federation of ideas. When all the rest of Canada, U.S., Mexico etc., all feel threatened, I am amazed that Quebec doesn't. If the people do feel threatened, then it is only logical that defence should be as far from home as possible...

Decided I'd see if I could shackle myself and just do what I thought best, i.e. not necessarily change habits but see if I could control them at will. Got started on the ales and put myself on a wagon for a bit. So far have been on there a month. Not desperate to stay there, just experimenting. So far so good, and one month not wasted...

I continuously think how lucky I am to have you taking care of everything at home and doing it so well. Also how lucky I am to have you. Get riled sometimes when I think of you at dances, parties etc. and pleasing someone else, but that's just normal jealousy and I know that I have your love. I'd bowl the pins out from any cuss that horned in though, so help me!...

All my love,
Fred

~

May 11
Fred darling:
...I listened to Mr. Churchill yesterday. He does sound more cheerful. The naval battle last week was encouraging but the warning is not to be too confident, since Japan may and probably will launch another attack with larger and more numerous ships...

So many people over here, the man on the street I mean, seem to feel the war will end in 1942. Oh, if it only would...I wonder if any of our cities will be bombed? It could happen here, but I'm afraid most of us feel it couldn't and are being very complacent. To those who are not directly concerned, as I am, the world goes on pretty much the same as ever. Remember it did to us, too, until you went…

Regarding enlisting - I do think it is better since the plebiscite and today Mr. King introduced a measure to amend service restriction. I don't blame you for feeling bitter at times, dear. So do I. Awfully bitter. But I, like you, when it is all over, will not regret it, I know…

It was some comfort if I may say so to learn you have had the same reactions and states of nervousness etc. as I have. And it most certainly does all boil down to a "lack of lovin' or a desire to love"…I have definitely decided that parties etc. etc. do give me quite a battering and therefore I am simply going to refuse the odd time if I feel it is best to stay home.

Darling, you know Snooks and you know with you I've simply got to be on the level. The whole thing that has been bothering me is the fact at times I have been forgetful - not very forgetful, but the whole point of it is I knew it would hurt you and that is why it has hurt me so. Now sweetheart, don't think things - I'm only speaking of a few embraces, nothing more, but it has nearly driven me crazy. And it has only been because I was so terribly lonesome for you. But if you knew how unhappy I've been. Everything seemed wrong. Under such a circumstance I seemed to separate myself from you by such a long way. I would get in bed at night and cry hours on end. I didn't let myself be kissed, darling, because I was untrue or don't love you more and more every day; it was purely and simply because I was just starved for affection.

But believe me, and this is the truth, it was only by one person, and I've put a very definite stop to it so it won't occur again. I let myself in for it and am blaming no one but myself. I guess I shouldn't have told you, but I always have and I just couldn't do anything and not tell you…The thing that hurts me most of all is that I don't believe you would do the same thing. You're much too sincere and faithful. I do hope you will trust me in spite of this, dear. Believe me, I am sorry and I'm back on the right path again. I know it won't occur again simply because it hurts too much - to be separated from you in any way is agonizing.

Darling, please tell me if I'm forgiven and if you understand. If it has happened to you, don't tell me unless you feel as I did, that you simply had to tell me. Darling, I feel happier tonight than I have for months. Maybe when you read this it will make you terribly angry. I hope not. Don't scold me too hard, please.

It has been a good experience in one way. I have found out what a wonderful thing it is when a husband and wife really love one

another. And how deep the word love is and how one must treasure it and guard it. It has taken me exactly one hour to write this last page. Talk about being tongue-tied. I've expressed myself terribly. The one thing I must know and it must be the truth - do you still trust me and will you forgive me and do you sincerely believe it won't happen again? Good night sweetheart, I love you,
Norah

~

May 11
Dearest Norah:
I'm in a recriminatory mood today. Not about anything, just being a bit listless and feeling somewhat purposeless. Have been lazy beyond hope the last few days, and I suppose that's why I'm put out...

By chance I had the radio on and on came the Canadian news for the past week. A pleasant surprise! First in interest is the coming debate on the amendment to the National Service Act. I was disappointed in the plebiscite. What in hell do these Quebecers think? Who is behind the conversion of the people to opposing common sense? I begin to think that the church is to blame. I had always opposed a hard view of the church in Quebec, believing that no group of men could be so vicious as to set one part of the Canadian people against another. Perhaps I believed wrongly. Perhaps again I've been too tolerant of their views...

I heard Churchill last night, did you? He sounded more confident than for a long time...Just be patient, Norah, there'll be a fight before we're home, but it's getting closer and so is the day I'll burst in the door again. God, what a day that's going to be! And what a night!...

Have not received a letter since last writing you, but read over today the last four received. They never fail to have interest and to give me a pep-up. Always finding new inflections in what you say. I believe I can tell just exactly what you are thinking. Perhaps that's going too far, do you think?...I sometimes wonder if we won't have harder and harder times making a go of it. Somehow we've never "needed", have we? Just that one month after graduation, 1939, remember?...Lucky us, I think in review. So musing, I cease to worry about the future. The only thing that philosophy doesn't cover is, when do I get home? I was tantalizing myself with that the other night and began to think that not one thing else mattered. You could go daft on the point...

Well Norah dear, I better hie off to bed. Keep me in mind as a loving husband, lover, and keep both sides of the bed warm, for I'll climb in again to shorten our nights.

All my love, Norah. I love you more than I can say.

Fred

~

May 15

Fred dearest:

...Cynthia is in bed but not asleep. She is kicking and cooing. She wants to roll over and over now and loves to stand on her feet. Waide was standing in his playpen at her age. Remember? She is strong too and such a bright smile. Her hair is beginning to curl and is growing quickly. She is very smart and keen for her tender seven months, and is going to be pretty. She will be so cute when she commences to run around. She is going to be a tartar, I can see it in her. Waide is a more serious, quieter child, but lots of spunk just the same...

I don't think I'm going to drive the car. There is so much talk of seizing the tires and more rigid rationing, I'm afraid I would just get it fixed up and then not be able to drive it. I already have my bicycle, and you said not to get one. I can't send it back because I have used it. Darling, I do feel you don't realize just how much use I will get out of it. Good practical use and pleasure, too. Everyone that can possibly get one has one. All the women do their shopping on them and all the businessmen, dentists, even a couple of lawyers have them. Cars are definitely scarcer on the roads. Cynthia can use it when she gets older, so I don't feel I made a mistake...

Darling, you don't know how much it means to me to hear you say, "I'm going to tear down some bad habits and build new". Most times your way of living was right, but you know as well as I that our only scraps were over you drinking a wee bit too much at times and my impatience - result, a quarrel...

So darling, I pray with all my heart that you will seek a new way of living and I know you will find one. I am seeking too, sifting and weighing things. I guess that is why I said I felt so confused and alone. But darling, I don't think either of us would ever have reached this stage had we not been separated...I agree "parties, binges, teas, excessive indulgence, lateness," are not satisfactory. Not in the least. So I feel we both can clean house...I wish there was some other way of expressing it but there isn't so - I love you, sweet. Sweet dreams...

Norah

~

May 21

Dearest Norah:

I am now at the headquarters, 4th Canadian Infantry Brigade, but will be moving within the next week...My work has been slow going of late due to intensive training program. It makes it rather bad in ways, for I don't get as much done in a day as I would like to. However, one must be satisfied.

I had hoped that this job would be done by now and that I would be able to get into a line of work that would offer a hope of advancement. That this drags on is disappointing unless they make the job permanent. I must frankly admit that I'm not psychiatry-minded and do not pretend to be able to say just what a man is best suited for. Still, I guess I am getting shrewder at the job...

I think that recently I've gotten my feet onto ground more solidly than ever before. I passed through months when I just dragged on uninspired from day to day. I had no interest in what I did and little pleasure in the doing of it. I frankly say that I warred with myself, was baffled and confused. I believe that's over; over, before anything bust...

Before I go on I want you to understand that I've not been gadding all over the country nor small sections of it, but damned if I did not think I'd blow a fuse soon. Oh I've not just looked at the landscape nor perched hermit-like in my tent, but all in all you've no complaint. I want to say tonight that I realize more than ever how much I love you; that I love you with all my heart and soul and mind and body; that nothing will change my love ever...

At the moment, we have our jobs. I owe you such a great deal for the attention that you have paid, without any help from me, to Waide and Cynthia, and for the way you have organized and kept things going. I think that there has been too much for you to do, not that you can't and aren't doing it, but just that there is more than should be reasonably expected of a young girl...If you feel that you ought to settle into an apartment or make some other arrangement, let me know and we will see how we can figure it out...

All my love,

Fred

~

June 15

Fred dearest:

...I am now at the cottage...Mom and Dad were down yesterday and took Marg back up town for a week, so I am alone with the children and the maid. It is the first time I have had them alone since Cynthia was born, and it is a real treat...

I am quite prepared to take that rolling pin to you dear if you ever go away again. Seriously though, I guess as you say we are putting things more into their proper perspective. Darling, I want you to understand one thing - inside I'm not measuring up to my problems and this awful separation as well as you might think. I resent it lots of times, hate everything and everyone, even the children...I can truthfully say I have not been really happy since you went away.

It was announced in yesterday's paper that all men up to thirty-five are to be conscripted - however it was not settled and Quebec may still balk...

Glad to hear you are on the wagon. If you fall off dear, don't worry about me not understanding. Fred dear, I'll understand anything you do and I won't blame you...

On the twelfth, last Friday, it was a year since I said good-bye to you in Hamilton. What a day and what a dreadful drive back to London. But what a day when you return!...Darling, I appreciate your words of praise and declarations of love. Many a time when we lived in Toronto, I must confess I often wondered if you really loved me. You very seldom told me - but you were always very sweet to me and loved me as if you loved me, but never before have you told me quite how much I mean to you...

Darling, in these two letters you are very depressed and lonely, as I was in a couple that crossed yours. I may be mistaken, but I have a feeling you've done something that is worrying you and you want to get it off your chest, so to speak, to me but you don't know quite how to do it? Am I right?...I understand quite well when you said, "damned if I did not think I'd blow a fuse soon". I had the same feeling all winter. I'm just now beginning to be a bit normal...

Biologically a man is supposed to be different from a woman. Remember Napoleon and his femmes du guerre? Oh hell, what I'm trying to say is, if it would relieve the tension any, get yourself a girl for a night. I know one thing though, you won't feel much better because you are so constituted that you have to love the girl to whom you make love, and the girl you love happens to be me and I'm too far away.

Seriously dear, I really don't believe it is such a terrible sin. The tragedy would come if you had more than a physical experience - if your mind and heart and soul entered into it, like it did when you and I made love.

Fred dear, maybe I'm away off the track - please tell me if I am or not. And if you have anything to confess, please do so if it would make you feel better. I've felt better ever since I made my little confession, but maybe on the other hand it has worried you...Never hesitate to write me, no matter what kind of mood you're in - I certainly unburden my troubles to you, sweet...
Norah

~

June 26
Norah dear:
Last night, at last, I received your letters, those of May 11, May 15 and May 28. I spent the evening reading them. I cannot tell you how much better they made me feel. You will have noticed how the cheer has slumped in my letters of the past month. I do not feel it a fault, for as you must well know, when the lines of thought between us fail, the horizon is buckled down tight till there is just that little piece of earth you are on that you can see. I had not been able to shake out of it at all the last week, and my last letter to you was as cramped in thought as Scrooge's Christmas Eve mind...

Well Norah, you got a lot off your chest, didn't you? I don't quite know what my reaction has been. It was not anger and it was not the indignation of the self-righteous. You may be incredulous that I was not surprised, but I wasn't. Indeed the truth is that I felt very happy. For quite some time your letters have shown that they were written under strain, and though I could not claim to know, I could hazard a very close guess. I know you pretty thoroughly. As thoroughly as only one who has loved very deeply can know. I also know myself, and I've found out what it feels like to be rigidly separated...

Both of us have treated each other's problems with understanding and, I believe, intelligence and common sense. I have told you of the codes I wanted to go by, though I've not always lived up to them, and you have done the same. We are a healthy human pair. Who said, "A man's reach must exceed his grasp, else what's a heaven for"? I do not mean that to be an excuse. When one fails to live as they feel they should, the natural reaction is remorse and disappointment...The trick comes, I believe, in winning point by point. Every time you beat a problem, you make the next easier...

Well, my experiences with women in this country have been most unsatisfactory. I don't mean that they were entirely unpleasant, but there is no bliss without love, now is there? Now pause, my lady, and understand I have had no feeling near bliss…

When I say I was not angry, I mean it only relatively. I know there is not much merit in me, but I expect you to be perfect anyway. Oh you are, Norah, you are perfect to me and I do love you sincerely. It was good to know you had not lost any of your love for me…At no time did I ever doubt you, and I do not now…

Now I intend to write you another letter, perhaps tomorrow, perhaps a little later, to deal with your letters in other respects and to tell you more views on some points. In the meantime, sweet, be assured…that I am trying and trying. That I love you as always only more. And, before closing, meekly, I ask you to believe in me and to forgive me my sins. Do you? All my love, sweetheart,
Fred

~

June 28
Dearest Norah:
I mailed you a letter yesterday in part response to your letters of May 11, 15 and 28. I had not then nor have I yet quite gotten over the ill humour and peevishness that had settled upon me the past few weeks…

I wonder if I am not too often prone to grouse, still if I do not to you, then how can I get it off? It has become evident to me that it is preferable to just write as we feel and to tell frankly what we think. Not only is it an outlet, but between us we are keeping up to date.

It is surprising - no, amazing, to find such a parallelism in the development of our thoughts. I am hopefully confident that such shall always be the case. I have at times been on the outs with myself because of the fact that I have a great deal of difficulty in making progress, that instead of making steady progress I go ahead a bit and then back a lot; it is slow and muddled going. You on the other hand seem to be able to reach a decision and to put it right into action…

One of these days the lovin' is going to be terrific. You could certainly keep me in better humour! Tonight our moon is up and I intend to sit about and watch it a bit; if only you could watch it with me. Well, I will have to be content to know you are watching it with me five thousand miles away; that still is a real comfort, is it not…

I want to be on a rather even keel, but change like the weather. Perhaps things wouldn't be half so interesting. When I'm in a good mood, I enjoy the memory of even the bad moods. We are certainly getting a lot of living in these days! When I think of a perfect scene,

I think of you and me, a warm beach, lapping little waves, a full moon, a fire warming a pot of tea. Or floating about where the river runs fast at the old dam. At times I think that that's the place I'd like to buy. A kiss Norah, a hug and good night,
Fred

~

July 14
Dearest Fred:
...The weather has changed and we are now having a bit of a hot spell. Waide and Cynthia are getting a very fine tan. Waide goes around in his bathing trunks and bare feet, Cynthia in the nude or just a diaper on. Waide loves the swimming...

Eleanor received her call to the air force today and is to report on Tuesday, July 21...

Now to answer your letters...Darling, as far as ever losing any of my love for you, I know that could never be. I love you more every day, and I have had opportunities to prove it to myself. You probably have the same feeling - I know, no matter how long we are separated, no matter what you do, I will love you until the end of time. There is only one thing I fear, that the constant association with one person, should you be in one place long enough, may gradually permit a friendship and ultimately a deep affection. It is possible, you know - it is nonsense to say it couldn't happen. But I pray with all my heart it won't. I know you are honest enough to tell me if it did, for you once said you couldn't nor wouldn't live with someone whom you no longer loved...

I haven't been to more than three parties in the last six weeks and none of them were late. I agree that I might use my time to better advantage and I have been. I've been reading and sleeping more. I have had more time with the children and I love it. Darling, I haven't been pestered with company. No one comes without an invitation...

Most of our parties are really in the long run quite wholesome and fun - everyone has more than just nonsense to contribute, since they are all quite intellectual and very often the party turns into a very interesting discussion...I realize the cottage is primarily for the children, their enjoyment and relaxation...

Before I go further, when I spoke earlier in the letter of opportunities, I meant as a young woman, shall I say reasonably attractive and gay, and minus a husband, I am naturally the recipient of considerable attention and flattery from the opposite sex. Were I not so deeply in love with you, I might be influenced - understand? Darling, words are so futile when it comes to expressing how much I love you and how much I miss you...All my love, sweetheart, Norah

~

July 15
Dearest Norah:
...I am afraid, Norah, that I have worried you by writing blue letters. I will still do it though, for if I'm not up to scratch you will want to know and if I'm bubbling over, you'll want to know that too. If I were to write just reports, you would not have much kick out of what you got, would you? You would soon just read the headlines, like a newspaper. Am I right?

I am sorry, though, that I have been so vague. You tell me you must read between the lines...My sweet, I do my best to tell you what I think, I do not know how I can be more specific. At times I feel that I am far too blunt. Perhaps I am wrong in trying to paint up a picture without showing the characters...But I do feel it difficult to express myself, and when I do get breezing along in my narrative, my grammar all goes to pot and I often wonder how you can read my letters at all...Nearly all my similes and parallels need trimming and rearrangement and my nouns and verbs, whew!...

You know, there is not one item that I could name as being the reason for loving you or home, just a sum total of so many little odds and ends. My darling, I know that you understand what I say, for you feel that way about me, too. I look myself over and wonder what anyone finds to like about me, and when I give that up in despair I admire you all the more for being able to find something to hang on to.

It is partly because of this fact that I said once well back that we can't tamper with love, for we don't know enough about it...What gets me is that we've heard the story time and again, books, movies, pulpit and stage, and we try it out for ourselves and run the chance. I realize that either of us can have an affection for another person - an outsider - and that such a romance can be very pleasant and that for a time, it might be dominant. Would that hurt us? Well, all the story books say yes. Do you wonder I'm vague, though, when there are thousands of feet of library space used up in just nibbling the subject? Here is the situation, Norah. I love you very deeply, passionately; you stand for everything I love and respect; your beliefs are my ideals; your actions are proper; you believe in and want the kind of a home I want; you love children; you are honest. Hell, you're the finest thing in the world! Now for that, for your love, I am happy and, of course, selfishly so…

But if you change, what then? If you should get to treat your kisses lightly. If you should dance more than sweep. If you should think more of a tea party than a swim. What then? Would you have changed that part of you I love? How do we know? Still vague, eh? You try it!…

I used to think love letters were nonsense - just for poetic adolescents - but not now. You see I'm trying to say I have always loved you as I do now, only never before did I have to tell you or be told in return. Your actions, your interests, your body told me. I have to give expression in a way I didn't have to before…

I will be frank with you. I have not had a shadow of love for any girl here. I am not above reproach, though. I have fornicated. I must confess I did not feel like an evil viper…I almost think you would laugh at me if you knew what I thought at the time. Now that's off my chest, I do feel better, yet I wonder if I should have said it.

Norah, I expect you will be somewhat angry, though I don't suppose you will look on me as a particular rotter, either. I do feel that by telling you, you will know what is behind some of the lines I wrote, and that you will have less worry about me. I mean that you won't think that anyone else means anything to me. I honestly do not think I've been untrue to you - is that a strange thing for me to say? Do you think differently? I want you to tell me…I want you to understand my vagueness, for I lack the skill to express myself. I feel that such acts as mine are wrong because of their emptiness and also since they affect not only me, but you and other people. I need not press the point, the number of ways are infinite…

I do believe that we are going to enjoy life more when we are together again, for we will know better what is important. Do I say too often, Norah, that I love you all the world? I do wish I could really show it…

Fred

~

July 16

Dearest Norah:

I wrote you a long letter…In it I told you more frankly than before my doings. Tonight I have a couple of things to say that I feel should be said, and if in saying them or if they themselves are untrue and I thereby offend, forgive me…

Norah, I have had the chance to ruin everything I value by having a woman for the duration here. Cut my ties and sail along easily until I would cut them again. Let myself value a relationship that would not stand for anything and that would harm what is important…That we have been bandying back and forth letters of frankness is evidence that we have both had a tough time but have come through.

Perhaps we each think that it has been by the merest bit that we have hung on, or that chance or accident has sided in with us. I do not think that that is so. Though I hope that we will not ever have to endure the experience, I think that the plumb line might sink deeper and deeper still without finding a limit to our endurance. I think that each of us has, by belief in and trust in the other, even beyond the dictates of reason, shown that we are a justification to our heritage. I think too that simply by those means we have kept solid both our personal front line and home front, and I think that, regardless of our realization of our weaknesses, we ought to be proud of ourselves.

I leave the thought with you. Good night and sweet dreams. All my love,
Fred

~

Aug. 2
Fred darling:
I'm terribly happy tonight, all because of a radio broadcast I heard. It was to the effect that sixty-five personnel selection staff officers were slated to come back to Canada to do the same work here. I'm hoping and praying that you will be one of those selected. Oh dearest, wouldn't it be marvelous? Words couldn't possibly describe how happy I would be…I know I shouldn't build up my hopes, but I've been almost jumping up to the sky since I've heard the broadcast…

The children are fine. Cynthia is getting her third and fourth teeth. She is creeping all over. I have her in cute blue overalls and she and Waide were playing yesterday with my supply of canned goods. Waide is very gentle with her…

I hate to hear you say you're bushed - it is hard, but remember dear, we both knew it wouldn't be easy. You ask how you can help me - well, this is how you can help. Every morning when you get up, resolve to make a success of your day. Work hard, make a good job of whatever you do, smoke less because you know it is bad for you to smoke so much, drink less, try for a better position - your captaincy for instance. Keep your eye on the ultimate goal and keep me and Waide and Cynthia before your eyes.

I find if I keep you before my eyes and the future and remember that this day lived well will make future days happier, it is so much easier…I once thought it was easy to be a great person inside, but I find it is very hard, the biggest task one would ever want…

Thank you for your words of praise for me and my efforts. All I can say is, if those are the requisites I need to make you love me, I'll try still harder…

Aug. 7

Dearest: It is some days now since I wrote the above. Your dad arrived on Monday night and is going home tomorrow…I received two airmail letters from you on Wednesday, Aug. 5. In it you mentioned a boat letter which was on its way to me telling me in full about your experiences with someone in England. I will commence another letter to you on Sunday and talk to you about us etc. then. I can't think when Pop is here.

I have this to say: all that matters to me, dear, is that you love me. If I should lose your love ever, I will of course carry on, because I would still have the children's love and they come next to you. I would prefer not to discuss the matter and not to tell you of my experience and what I think until I receive your boat letter. Be assured, dear, you have more of my love every day I live. And I feel we both have had somewhat similar experiences and have both made the same decision because of our great love for one another…

Norah

~

Aug. 6

My darling Norah:

…By now you will have received all that I wrote during several weeks, at least I very much hope you received it all, for I do not think part can stand without the whole if you are to understand me.

I had hoped that my letters would in some measure reassure you, though just why they should is impossible to say. At least I told you honestly what I thought and how I feel and, as for me, I think that the bond between us has never been stronger…You will perhaps find that hard to understand, but could I be with you to review the ten years of ups and downs we have seen together, you would…

Perhaps I did not say that the actions recounted occurred some time past. It is not of great importance. I believe it foolhardy to make promises the breaking of which would be as wrong as the wrong itself, but I do think it would be totally unfair for me to ask that you put up with a sense of uncertainty and hold trust on an insecure foundation.

I think, too, that while you have not read more between the lines than you ought, that there is much too great a chance of misconstructions and that particularly now, a very innocent incident might raise questioning it ought never to have engendered. I do not believe such a situation would be easily bearable to you. I do not believe you would be happy in it. Finally, I do not believe it warranted. Unless you totally disagree, I will tell you frankly of any conduct. I can call a spade a spade and would prefer to do so than to suggest…

It has made me very happy to find our thoughts running so parallel that our letters bearing the same kernel of an idea are continually crossing. You said, "a friendship and ultimately a deep affection. It is possible you know - it is nonsense to say it couldn't happen". I clumsily tried to say much the same thing. We must not fail to realize that we are the same sort of human being that are all about us - though damned if the rest aren't unimportant!…

Norah dear, I just must close this and do some work, though I should like to just chat on with you…All my love, Norah,
Fred

~

Aug. 19
Dearest Fred:
…Cynthia is coming right along and is so dear. She has a mind of her own and makes her own demands in her own way. She and Waide play and play together in the playpen. Waide was so sweet the other day. He never forgets you. The other day, some chap went by in uniform with a Glengarry on like you wear. Waide quick like a flash said, "I wonder if that is Daddy?" So he is always looking for you, dear. The other morning he got out of bed and pulled down his pyjamas but not far enough, for when he went to pee-pee it shot all over, so he exclaimed, "Darn that penis". Isn't that a scream? He noticed the other day that Cynthia was different than he, physically I mean, so I showed him and explained as well as I could and he was very serious and most interested.

The news is now on announcing the commando raid this morning - it is most heartening. Apparently the losses were heavy on both sides. Now to answer your letters.

Darling, you were very sweet and so honest with me to tell me of

79

your experiences during the past year. Dearest, I don't feel you have done wrong, why I don't know. I guess I love you too much…I don't think any the less of you for it, nor do I love you any the less…

I have read your letter many times since Monday, and darling your expressions of love for me were so sincere and made me so happy…As long as you love me as you do, I can carry on indefinitely. It gives me something to work for - to know you are proud of me and appreciate what I am trying to do is all I ask…

Imagine you saying you wonder what I find in you to love - darling, I love every bit of you, even your faults if you have any. But as you say, it is hard to put one's finger on the reasons. Darling, I do realize we can have an affection for an outsider and it is pleasant and maybe it is dominant for a time, but it does hurt you because in your heart you feel a traitor and you feel that you are hurting someone who is the most precious thing in the world to you, even if they aren't aware they are being hurt. I know you must have felt that way, for I did. I was so terribly unhappy, I felt like a sick person…believe me, I was never so unhappy as I was for a while last winter…It was the weaker part of me, and the stronger part, the part you love and respect, is in operation again…Do you feel I have done wrong, have I gone down in your estimation, did you expect me to be bigger and stronger? Please tell me honestly. I don't regret my experience because it gave me a fuller understanding of how important our love is and how precious it is…

One thing I want you to believe and that is that my reason for wanting an apartment for myself was solely to be alone with the children and have more time to enjoy them. It was not to put myself in a position to entertain someone or my friends in general…

Darling, I do know you are starved for me and Waide and Cynthia…But it will be worth the struggle, and when we get our arms around you, we'll never let you go. Never…
Affectionately,
Norah

~

Aug. 27
My darling Fred:
…The Dieppe raid got me down and I wondered how brave I would have been if…you were in it and if I had lost you. Most of the time I feel you will come back, but sometimes I have a horrible fear you might not, and then I am almost paralyzed with fear and sadness.

Darling, I don't know what I would do or how I could go on

without you. Why does one person have to mean so much? I mean, one could go through this life so much easier if one didn't feel so deeply. Before you went over, looking at the whole thing objectively, I felt if I lost you, I might someday marry again. But I know now I never could...

Russia is doing better today and there was a joint RAF raid and Russian raid over Germany last night. But I'm afraid it will be a long time yet.

I don't seem to have much news this time. I seem to be thinking mostly of the future and what we will do when you come home. If it is in the summer, we will certainly have to go up in Muskoka, where we can swim and canoe and play tennis and lie out under the moon...

It makes me very happy, too, to know our thoughts have run so parallel. It is almost unbelievable, isn't it, Fred?...Waide is getting to look like me, but Cynthia is not, dear. She is like you and Mom - and so beautiful. I think you will be more like your mom as you grow older. You have her great sincerity and honourableness. I hope our children inherit those qualities...

My love and kisses and hugs, darling, as ever.

Norah

~

Sept. 24

Dearest Fred:

Goodness, look at the date darling. Soon we will be married six years, and soon Cynthia will be one year old. Can you believe it? I loved you very very much six years ago, dear, but I love you worlds more now simply because we have done so many, many things together, had so many experiences, pleasant mostly but some trying ones which, all added up, give the reason for a deeper, fuller, more understanding relationship.

Cynthia is a beautiful baby as she nears her first birthday...She is so pretty and strong and so smart and loveable. She puts her little arms around my neck and hugs and hugs me. And Waide is a prince...

Now to discuss business...I didn't have one cent reserve from the summer to outfit the children for fall. Maybe you will feel it was poor managing, I don't know. However I sold my bond after worrying over it for a couple of weeks and spent $30 just like that on their shoes, underwear, overalls, sweaters. Waide had grown out of his last year's suit for outdoors, so I got him a new coat and leggings and cap, $9.98. He takes size five now. It has been quite chilly this last week and they need warm clothes. I don't need a thing, thank goodness. You know, there is a class up at the school in sewing and I feel I should join it and learn how to sew - I could save money - much and all as I hate sewing...

When night comes I seem so unsettled I can't sit still. I'm much better, but still restless and upset, simply because I'm lonely. Don't you find you're the same way? Now dearest, don't worry about me, I'm not restless for male company. I know that will never happen again, just as you probably know the same...

The BBC news is on now. They are speaking of the convoy to Russia recently which was protected by seventy-five warships...

I love you sweetheart - I miss you just as much as ever, but ever since we exchanged confidences or confessions or whatever I should say, a very great peace has settled over me. I'm more patient and more willing to wait, because I know nothing could ever part us...
Norah

~

Sept. 24
Norah darling:
...This letter will reach you, I hope, before Oct. 6 and 10, both such important dates. Do you remember your incessant error in your marriage date? You would continuously say it was the eighth or the sixth - if the latter, you were tampering with future events!...For the time being you are the patron saint of both days, for on both have you brought happy news to the world. Give Cynthia a kiss for me - a big lovin' one...

I've settled down to some sort of routine here in London. So far, I have been out a lot for there is much of interest. Generally go into the local. The particular one generally visited seems to get the pick of the district - that isn't any hell. Seem to meet there lads from units I toured. Every time I have gone, I have met someone I know and of course meet new people...

Got into a banter-argument with a mite of an Irish nurse and wound up by walking home with her, her Scotch chum and an Irish lad. His friendship with the two girls, it developed, was through his fiancee, who he had lost, her boat being bombed on its way from Eire...They were a good bunch, out for fun...

What I am somewhat in need of is to find a person whose talk and interests lie in some speculative direction. I presume I need to do a bit of reading to get into the mood for arguments dealing with the prosecution of the war or my own immediate work. I have no desire to be an arguer on current news only, and while I have no intense theme nor have a clear and certain mind on subjects of permanent worth, I do feel that in these days, thought of the less tangible of the events and experiences of life is most important.

Regarding transfer home: I have no reason to feel that there is the slightest prospect. Certainly if the newscast you heard was official, it is not even known by the lads here and no one had even heard the report…All my love, darling, and just keep remembering that I love you more than anything in the world…

Fred

~

Oct. 4

Dearest Fred:

I am writing this seated before a bowl of red roses, with two other bouquets of the same roses in the other room. Darling, I was so thrilled when they arrived. The flower shop phoned me and said there was a cablegram from England for roses for me and did I know from whom they might be. So I said, my husband, of course…

I will be thinking of you on Oct. 10. I think of you every hour of every day anyway, but I will be thinking of you more especially and remembering six years ago. It was a Saturday then, too, if you remember. Remember the church and how quiet it was, but very solemn and beautiful…Remember the first thing you asked me to do was fill your pipe. Remember?…

Monday night I made ten thirty-three-ounce bottles of grape juice to serve this winter instead of tea or coffee if anyone drops in. It is very good and Waide loves it. I had to hide it on him. I also made fifty cookies, also having to hide those…So after all my work it was 11:30 when I finished. If you recall, I often worked in the evenings in Oakville waiting for you to come home from the armoury - I wished the other night I could hear your familiar hello and I could run to meet you…

Waide prefers now to play with his friends or else take them all with us when we go. I can see his point. He's a real boy and I don't intend to keep him tied to my apron strings, I intend to give him lots of rope…If I master him this year, I will be fine for he is getting more able to reason things out instead of having to do things without a reason, as is the case when they are very small. But he is big and wilful and a regular boy. If he gets ahead of me, I'm sunk. When you come home I'm sure you will be so glad to see him you won't want to be the disciplinarian right away and I don't blame you, and I'm sure Waide would resent it until he gets to know you again and understands your place in the home. We could have a problem on our hands if neither of us had control. Let me know your views on the matter. It is hard for you to advise, not having seen Waide for so long...

On Thursday, as an anniversary treat to myself, I went to Toronto by car for the day with Kay Middlebro, Billy Henderson, Jean and Mary Wilkinson, to see the Russian ballet. It was a grand day and a jolly outing...To our disappointment the ballet was cancelled, since the government would not let them cross the border. So we shopped and went and had tea at Simpson's Arcadian Court and then went to a lousy show, Manhattan Tales. In spite of our disappointment, it was fun...With you away, I want more than ever to have real friends, not acquaintances...

You no doubt saw the list of decorations for Dieppe gallantry...You of course will be following as we all are the battle at Stalingrad, and also have your opinions pro and con on a second front...

I am not going to fuss over Cynthia's birthday. She is too young. She will of course receive a gift from us all. She took two steps the other day...Good night, my dearest. Be of good cheer and patient and hopeful. We will be together again sometime - soon maybe...
Norah

~

Oct. 5

Dearest Norah:

...Saturday night we had a house-warming party out at the major's house. He and two captains, heads of our staff, have taken a place together. It was a bang-up party. Pretty schnappsy...Sunday I went to the Officers' Club dance, 4 p.m. at the Grosvenor House, Park Lane. It is held in a very large room, larger than any I can think of as possible comparisons. There are a multitude of tables, each presided over by a lady hostess who supervises the young hostesses...

My hostess was Mrs. Ryland, who was indeed very charming. I had a long chat with her and have been invited to her home, which is in Park Lane - London's swank society - will have to have a look-see! She has a son in the Middle East - so, is that age, is very active in organizing benefits, Red Cross etc...

You answered the letter I wrote...about my personal experiences. You were sweet and so fair. I think few would be as frank, honest and understanding as you have been, but then I did expect it of you, for it is a characteristic of you that I have always known and admired. That we love each other more than ever before is marvelous...

I believe both of us have felt much better since we got down to facts and were frank. You asked me in a more recent letter if I sensed your own conflict before you told me. I did. I wasn't suspicious, and I tried not to be jealous or nasty, but instead I felt that it would be best to let you work it out and that was why I encouraged you to go out, make friends etc. I believed that if you were knocked over the brink a bit, you could swim back and you rewarded my confidence a hundredfold...

Well sweet, it has all been worth the price. The experience has been a very good thing, grand in fact, for it has developed an insight in us that we could never before have had...I look forward with every hope to our early reunion. I do not know when it may come, whether during or till after the war. I feel much calmer and happier now than I have before. Ready and willing to go right through to the end. I am sure of myself and of you, of our complete love and of it enduring. I cannot say I ever had the slightest doubt about these, but now, I do not know why, there is a certainty that has an endlessness to it, that gives calmness and repose. Understand?...

Tomorrow I have arranged a trip to a field unit to look around a basic education school (for illiterates) that I am charged with finding the students for. One must choose men that are trainable and have some notion of language if possible - and principally a desire. People without enthusiasm or hope or urge are indeed the truly untalented, are they not - animated clay...

Now it's after twelve and so Cynthia's birthday. Did you and she get your flowers?...Hope she has the happiest of birthdays, though she'll likely let it pass without a thought this time...All my love, Norah my sweet...Good night,
Fred

~

Oct. 11
Dearest Fred:
My darling, I'm lonesome - lonesome as -...I'm so low this week, if I wrote a long letter it would only depress you. Between warding off a cold and receiving no mail from you for two weeks now (where is it?) I'm really in the depths. Your lovely flowers were so sweet, though, I couldn't be entirely unhappy. Cynthia had a nice birthday and took twelve steps just to prove she could do it...She can now paddy-cake and kiss and say and wave bye-bye and say peek, Dada

and Mama and then the rest is gibber, and gibber she does…

I saw Mrs. Miniver during the past week and loved it but wept buckets. Be sure and see it. It isn't so sad, it is just that it made me so lonesome for you. I know I'm giving in to my lonesomeness lately, everyone is noticing it…I have been marvelously patient and cheerful with the children, though, and they respond to me much better.

I should be so thankful you are reasonably safe, though - oh, I've got lots to be thankful for, but sometimes I forget…Darling when you get this letter, just don't let my mood worry you. Please think that maybe tomorrow I will get a letter…I always have the impossible hope you might just walk in some day. It is funny, but sometimes our marriage seems almost unreal. Do you ever feel that way? I say to myself, "Did I ever have Fred with me, did I?" But then when I get mail or flowers or a cable I'm jerked back into reality and know as well as anything, you are probably hovering over me at that moment.

Darling, have you still a moustache? I have meant to ask you for ages. I hope so, because I liked it so much…
Good night my dearest,
Norah

~

Oct. 19
Fred dearest:
I'm in the seventh heaven because I got two letters this morning. The first for three weeks. You don't know how awfully happy they made me. Three weeks is such a long time…

Tuesday night was our French class, which we hold at a different house each week…We read in French in turn a page aloud and then Mrs. Bonar, in French, questions us on what we have read and we reply in French. It is very interesting. Mrs. Bonar says in her frank way that I am too methodical in that I always want to write down the verb, its root etc. and idioms and the gender of nouns etc. She says I'll never learn to speak French that way…

I heard Mr. Churchill announce England could expect more bombings this winter. I do worry about you, dear. Be sure and go to a shelter at nights won't you, dearest, if London is raided heavily. Don't risk yourself needlessly…

Just as I finished the above, Eleanor phoned. She tried her exams today, written and practical, and stood highest…She was almost in tears, poor kid. She is posted to Newfoundland …Mom is quite broken up over the break and I am too, but it's silly because it is just the thing we have been wanting and she too, I believe - to get a little experience and travel and broadening...

Do you look any older? Have you the odd grey hair? I have two. Don't chuckle, I'm too young to get even two. Are you still a good figure and physique? I'm a little too thin but still look pretty much the same, I guess...

Personally I don't feel you will be able to find a woman friend who can forget sex and love etc. and just be pally and talk on interesting subjects. A woman is either fond of or in love with or not interested in the man. Her heart naturally has a say, whereas a man's doesn't necessarily. I find I can't have a man friend because I'm just not interested. I can talk all I want to to women.

Now don't think I don't want you to have a woman pal. It is fine as long as you can find one. I trust you and know I have all your love, so don't worry about me...All my love dearest, tons and tons of it and worlds of kisses...

Norah

~

Oct. 22

My dearest Norah:

...I have resolved time and again to make my letters to you a sort of diary expressing each day items of news and talking the day's thought or commenting on some very ordinary thing that may have little inherent interest but help to build up a scene of the England I am seeing. You know that I often think that the most trivial things are what might be the most interesting reading, and I've thought for example that I probably have under-described such things as the pubs, the people, the conversations, the canteen, the food, the office building, the bus, the street, the taxi cabs etc. etc., which are so commonplace to me that it is only on occasion that I think of their news value to you who are so far away. What do you say?

You have been so very very good describing your routine household tasks, your friends, chats and in particular the children's everyday acts, and I have literally munched the news eagerly and looked forward for more of it, while being less intensely interested in the record of happenings on the world scale.

Waide sounds like a very independent and healthy boy and my hat's off to you, sweet, for the job is a big one. Particularly big when a girl has only two children to hang tightly on to...You were worrying in one letter about him blaming KeeKee for his misdeeds. I understand your questioning the wisdom of letting it go on, but on the whole I think it's a very good thing - not to be excessively tolerated or indulged in, of course, but I reason this way: He knows perfectly well that it is only a figment of his imagination - he's not fooling himself, and from there in, it's safe.

It helps to develop his imagination and to develop a sort of play act all his own that will test his ingenuity and initiative. Better that he be mischievous or gay about his wrongs than that he develop any inner shame. Is it not better that he say, "I have a counterpart that is Mr. Hyde and he is the fellow I wrestle with", than that he bemoan his nature and cry, as so many, "I am a sinner, I am unworthy and a disgrace to God and man". I rather like his lively human way...

You talk about the second front, as do we all. I personally doubt our ability to open one with any hope of success now, or in the immediate future, but of course I am as ignorant as the dog on the street as to the true military situation. I would say that we must secure Africa first, but then, just being superior in that region may be enough, though I would not have thought so. We were superior once before...

I must mention how happy I was to know that you got your anniversary flowers and that you enjoyed them. Such a small gift, but then we are both most happy simply at the remembrance, is it not true?...

All my love as always,
Fred

~

Oct. 25
Fred darling:
...On Saturday I took Waide to market and shopping with me. He promised to be good and he was...He is quite thrilled over Hallowe'en and Christmas this year. I have such a limited selection of toys - there just aren't any. I think I will buy two goldfish and a bowl and I think he will enjoy that. What do you think? I have carefully saved several things from his tree last year which were too advanced for him, such as paints and paint book and crayons and plasticene etc. So I'm going to put them on again this year. He has forgotten them, I know...

Some day the four of us will have lots of fun. Darling, when I say four, what are your feelings about the size of our family? Do you really want more, or do you feel two are sufficient? I'm undecided. It is a case of what you want, with me. If you would like one or two more and we see our way clear financially, I'm willing. But I really and truly want a whole year with you when you get home and then maybe, eh? Pregnancy has its drawbacks and discomforts and I want us to be able to do things and go places when you come back, if it's only on picnics and swimming.

Another question. How do you feel about practising here in Owen Sound after the war? I am getting to love every aspect of it and have made so many friends and Waide is getting his roots in, it would be a bit of a break to leave. But as before, any place with you would be heaven, but if you were interested here, I want you to know how I feel...

Saturday afternoon, unbeknownst to me, there was a parade...Waide came in with five-year-old Peter Connelly and wanted to go...I had to stay with Cynthia and couldn't take him. I remembered you saying, let him be a man-child and don't baby him. So I said to myself, here goes. So I gave my consent. Off he went with drum and sticks and Peter. He had a great time and I later learned that he literally "stole the show". Peter forsook him in his eagerness to see things, so Waide wandered over to the band and ended up by parading at the head of the band, beating his drum, serious-faced and totally unconcerned over the people lining the streets. So your son is a real soldier boy and an extrovert of the first order, don't you think?...

There is talk of rationing butter - oh dear, how I love my butter! I manage to make our tea and sugar ration do. It is a bigger problem every day to plan meals. There are so many things one cannot get...

The war does look better - the offensive spirit seems to be in the air. With Stalingrad holding and on the offensive and the 8th army launching an attack on Rommel, Italy bombed four times in the last forty-eight hours and the U.S. active at Guadalcanal, it does help to make one feel one step nearer victory and the end of the war. But it is a long way off yet, I'm afraid...Love and kisses and hugs,
Norah

~

Oct. 26
Dearest Norah:
...Since Saturday we have all been keenly following the few tidbits of news coming out from Egypt. All of us are full of hope that this will be the time...

I expect you would like to know what is the usual, around-the-fire talk in Britain today. It seems to me that whenever you pull up a few English for a gab, you invariably get into "the world after", and primarily the discussion is based on reconstruction and related topics. England is sold on a "planned" countryside and town…You will be familiar with the type of project - scientific homes; dispersal of factories; clustering of communities; trunk highways; and city green belts.

War has of course directly assisted the planners in a variety of ways - by destruction of city centres, by dispersal of factories, by development of materials (plastics principally), by the creation of complete underground factories on totally new principles…

The Americans are quite numerous, flooding London on their leaves. "Flooding" is a gross exaggeration of course, for this mighty city can absorb a country's population without bulging. The Yanks are getting over their first enthusiasm and now replace the Canadians as the butt of criticisms regarding poor deportment and also replacing them in the crime items of news. I perhaps haven't mentioned it, but there are rather numerous prosecutions for rape and kindred crimes, robbery and assaults which involve soldiers…

You are talking about sewing classes. Probably a good idea, for there will be an increase in the tearing as time marches on. I'd hardly expect you to make a hobby of it, for your talents are more called for in other spheres of more importance…

I miss you very much, but like you, feel that we have now strength to go on in the knowledge that if not tomorrow, soon we will again have ourselves together in body as we are now in mind.

All my love, my darling,

Fred

~

Nov. 1

Dearest Fred:

…Six of us are going to meet once every two weeks to learn to sew…Imagine me sewing. However the girls are all nice, we accomplish something and have a cup of tea and cookies and much conversation. I seem to see such a varied group, but it is refreshing not to see the same ones all the time…Tuesday night was French class…After our lesson,which lasts for an hour and a half…we launched into a discussion of morals among young children, kids in their teens, married couples etc., the war, Poland and its sufferings and reconstruction. Mrs. Bonar is a graduate in economics from the university in Warsaw and is most interesting. It is quite enlightening to learn the Europeans' point of view, which does differ from ours in many ways...

The tea dance at the Officers Club at the Grosvenor House, Park Lane, must have been very nice...Have you gone over to Mrs. Rylands whom you met yet? I'm glad to hear of you going to such things. A certain amount of "swank social contact" is an advantage. You always had finesse, but I think one can always have more and I am more convinced one cannot be too well versed on the little niceties of social conduct...

I had never thought of our position facing things as individuals before rather than as a couple. Thinking it over, I believe you are right when you say in these wearing times maybe it is easier. I often think when the children act up and are cross and demand so much attention and I'm tired, in a way if you have to be away any time during their childhood, it is better now, for it would worry you and worry me that I might not have as much time for you as I would like. Maybe we would be impatient and on edge etc., so as you say, maybe we are getting off lightly. Certainly, Fred, we would never have discussed half the things we have or come to such a full understanding...

I had so wanted you to like my Aug. 19 letter, and you did. I've never been dishonest with you and if you felt I was deceitful for a time, it was because I felt I shouldn't worry you or couldn't tell you in the right way so that you would get the proper slant on it...
I couldn't love anyone else but you and I never have. I was infatuated, but what is infatuation but a physical experience? By that I mean your physical self says someone is attractive, but the mind and soul do not enter in. Love is such a hard thing to define, isn't it? Have I explained myself?...

You mentioned your trip to a field unit to look around a basic education school (for illiterates). I didn't suppose you would have enough illiterates in the army to warrant such a school. Your work has great scope, has it not? I suppose you can tell me very little about it. Fred, don't you feel that someday, in spite of it meaning our separation, you will probably feel your work in England very well worth the sacrifice?...
Love,
Norah

~

Nov. 10
My darling Norah:
...I haven't had mail from you for quite a long while. Neither have

others received much. I suppose it is the diversion of ships etc. to Africa, and if so we will be tolerant though lack of your newsy letters is depressing.

I have received a tin of "Club Chewing Tobacco" from you. Did someone pull your leg? Or are you educating me to better habits? I'll have to grow a moustache again for I think it grand to have whiskers to slurp through and to catch the drippings...

I suppose it will be on into December when you receive this, though the time of closing Christmas mail is not near yet. It will not be long, sweet, before you'll be decorating another tree. Even wee Cynthia will be able to take an interest in this one... Purchasing things here is a bit of a job. I intend to see what there is, but may just send you the value and let you be judge. You're best at that anyway. I do feel somewhat guilty shopping here when there is little for the children of the land...

My activities of late have been very limited. Indeed you might say I'm living a sedentary life. The cause is not hard to find - darkness is "down" by the time I leave the office, additional transport cuts have been made and altogether there is not much amusement for the resident Londoner...Have found myself lacking in any form of inspiration recently, not being capable of stirring in myself an original thought of any kind whatever. It makes for a dull existence when even your own thoughts provide no amusement...

The news that the 8th Army is again in Tobruk is headlined today. They certainly are driving on apace! When these attacks developed only a few days after I wrote you that I could not see how anything but a clearing of Africa could be attempted, I decided I and the generals agreed and decided they ought to have me on their strategy - harumph!...All my love, a big hug and kiss. Sleep tight. Fred

~

Nov. 22

Fred dearest:

...We had snow Monday and Tuesday so Waide had fun sleigh-riding on a hill at the end of our street. He is out every morning and afternoon, so is really in very little. He has a huge appetite these days and the result is, he is as fat as butter and really huge-looking. He has never looked so well...

Wednesday morning I did the household shopping...I went to the Kinsmen dinner and dance at 6:30 with Bob Dyment, Peggy Hammond's brother...I didn't really want to go and I was certain I wouldn't have fun or Bob wouldn't like me. However I put on a very pretty white crepe dinner gown which Eleanor gave me and put a white flower in my hair and away I went. The dinner was at the hotel and I would say there were a hundred there. When I got there I found I knew nearly everyone, an entirely different crowd from whom I generally meet but all nice...

Stopped for the 10 p.m. news - major victory of the Russians around Stalingrad, having driven them fifty miles from Stalingrad. The British, French and Americans are closing in on the Germans in Tunisia. It does make one happier to hear nothing but good news from all war zones for one solid week...

Your letters are very interesting dear, but I do like your suggestion of making your letters a sort of diary expressing your thoughts. I'm sure you would seem closer to me...I'm glad I have succeeded in giving you a true picture of Waide...It must be hard for you to imagine just how he looks. He is getting quite handsome - his face has developed and his eyes are more of a personality. He has rosy cheeks most of the time. He doesn't talk very well and thinks things and often tries to express them but can't...

Cynthia is a great chatterbox, all jib-jab of course but she understands a great deal and will talk one of these days...She loves to laugh and loves to cuddle. She is at the stage when I can teach her and discipline her to do a great deal...

I've hardly left space to say I love you. Fred, it is maddening to have to express it the same old way and in a letter, isn't it? But dearest, I do. You're my sole reason for living and being happy - you're sweet. Good night dearest. A kiss and a snuggle very close.
Norah

~

Nov. 27
Darling Norah:
...Like yourself I've been on the downs for no other reason than lack of mail. It is most wondrous what a letter can do and what the lack of one may do!...Norah dear, it is so good of you to write so completely of the children. I would only know I had a daughter if it were not for you, but you have told me so particularly of her that I have seen her grow and know her every in and out. It is great to feel that I could dandle her on my knee and talk to her of what happened and what interested her with full confidence of knowing her thoroughly. This you have given me and more no living person could have given. It has been a tremendous boost to me and made me feel

a nearness to the family, and could not otherwise have experienced...

I feel you are worrying about Waide...His tendency to boss I do not feel to be undesireable, although it should be curbed within measure. A boss can be a bully or a leader, but a follower can be neither, so of the two it is eminently desireable that he should be the first and that he ought not to have it ironed out of him in the interests of social harmony...

Am certainly without any "girl friends" although I have lots of acquaintances among the sex at the P.A. (Prince Albert, the local). And among these many that are nearly good friends. They are good drinking and gabbing companions, at least. No entanglements though, sweet, you may rest assured...

I was brought up at a start when you enquired what I now look like. On reflection I thought, well, in a year and a half, changes take place. I'll write my specifications in detail at some other time, but I will say at the moment that your husband does not fear his ability to retain some charm of manner, some form or shape or some guile at the art of love and will hope not to disappoint you in these respects. All my love, Norah sweet. A big hug and plenty of kisses.
Fred

~

Nov. 29
Dearest Fred:
It has been a very upsetting week. Mom has been sick, her same trouble, low blood count, Waide had another attack similar to the one last summer...There is nothing one can do. Cynthia has been cross and to cap it all, I have a low blood count, too...So I have to rest more and have medicine and pills to take. So isn't that a tale of woe...

Isn't the war news cheering? I listened to Mr. Churchill yesterday. Today the news is mostly of Italy and the announcement that the Italian underground have asked for civil disobedience throughout all Italy. One wonders, will Italy make a separate peace, or can she?...

Skating commenced this week. I went and skated a few bands. I do hope I will enjoy it this year.

Darling, if you were here, I'd cry and cry tonight. I'm not a very good soldier, I'm afraid. I want you so much. All the medicine in the world won't help that awful lonesome feeling - I'm so tired, dear - war news, war news, trying to smile and be gay, people around me. Oh I must stop this. I promise to pull myself together, dear, and write you a big long cheery letter. For every day has its cheerful moments and I'll smile again.

All my love, dearest. Please don't worry about me. I love you worlds and worlds.

Norah

~

Dec. 4

Dearest Fred:

...I was or now am ashamed of my last blue-air-letter to you sent about Dec. 1 or Nov. 30. It was a great tale of woe and I was tired and feeling very lonesome and sorry for myself. Since then I have managed to get a little rest and things look different and happier. So please excuse and forgive the other...

It is going to seem so queer I imagine at first when you come back, Fred. Waide is more grown up and talking and Cynthia running around. We never will again have each other just alone like we did in Oakville, with Waide off to bed early. It worries me for this reason. I never did want the children to come between us, to spoil just your and my pleasures together, and now more than ever I don't want them to. I guess we will work things out, won't we? We will have so many adjustments to make. Do you feel you will be a little restless at first, having to settle down to a more or less routine family life?

Not that we won't both be so happy, it isn't that, but we both, whether we want it or not or realize it, have more freedom than before we were separated. I mean, I come and go when and where I please. I make the decisions instead of consulting you and you do the same. Do you see what I mean?...

The war news is still good. However we hear little of what is actually going on, I presume. The minister of finance spoke last night announcing a lowering in the cost of living in several respects. The consumer is naturally to benefit, but the seller or wholesaler or producer will not suffer. They are going to reduce the cost of tea by ten cents a pound, coffee four cents a pound, milk two cents a quart cheaper, oranges are to be cheaper too. In order to do this the government will bear some of the burden of the taxes and tariff on some commodities. We will probably have to pay for this in some other tax so there will be no difference except maybe we won't notice it so much. A hidden tax seems easier to pay than a perfectly obvious one, eh?

I have been reading The Street of the Fishing Cat by Jolan Foldes, a story of refugees. It is all the more interesting since I have met…Mrs. Bonar and now have a little idea how these people feel, away in a strange land, strange customs and language, away from all they love…

You mention the happy times we will have when we are together again. Darling, I often feel like you do, that we will be strangers - I feel frightened, just a little. Darling, do you realize our first meeting and night will be just a little strange, but romantic. All initial newness will wear off when we come home to the children, don't you think?…You will have to be introduced gradually, and yet young Waide has a very real sense of your place in the home…

Letters are so inadequate. These one-sided conversations with an answer coming back in three months are so unsatisfactory.
After the war, I'm never going to write a letter. I think you feel the same…
Good night dear,
Norah

~

Dec. 9
Dearest Norah:
…I am off on leave. I started away Monday after having spent a hectic morning and afternoon getting everything arranged and settled, and left by the seven o'clock train. It brought me into Aberdeen at 9:15 a.m. Tuesday…Being a night trip I saw little, though the latter end of the trip was made in early dawn and the sky was a treat.

Felt very seedy on arrival as might be expected. Went to the station restaurant and had breakfast beginning, of course, with porridge…The city is most amazing. All buildings are built of a grey granite quarried nearby and the greatest uniformity exists throughout the city. The solidness of the construction is marked and you get the impression of walls of granite lining the thoroughfares…

Friday has brought me away by the 10 a.m. train, aiming for Glasgow. Will pass through Perth and due to arrive Glasgow about two or 2:30.

Darling, I am having a pleasant holiday but it is so empty. Nothing whatever really rouses my interest except via curiosity. There just seems to be nothing in anything that I am keen about. I sometimes feel so disconsolate that I can find so little in the present. After all, day-by-day living can hardly rely solely in dreams of the future. That is all I have. Present activities are simply time-spending, meaningless, void. It is wrong in principle I know, yet I cannot change it.

I love you so very much and I want to be with you and the children and nothing else seems to have any meaning. You will excuse my pouring out this mournful plaint, but I cannot feel joyousness, not with you absent…You have all my love. More than you will ever know.

Fred

~

Dec. 14

Dearest Fred:

Well darling, another week has gone by and no mail. It is four weeks tomorrow since I received my last letter…

I have been very busy this last week. I have completed my Christmas shopping and did Eleanor's too. So I had a big job on my hands, had I not? I have been feeling so much better. I have been taking my medicine regularly and I have almost stopped smoking, just one a day, and really I can work all day now from eight to eight and not feel fagged. Christmas and New Years promise to be gay and full of fun. We have lots of snow, which makes it seem more festive. I get a sick feeling now and again at the thought of you not being here. My second Christmas without you, sweetheart, but there will be other Christmases and we will make up for it, won't we?…

I went up to French class which was at Jean's house…We discussed children and both Jean and Mary said they felt I showed Waide considerably more attention and affection than Cynthia. As a result Cynthia was bound to develop a certain independence, which would hurt me later on since I wouldn't be as close to her.

I realize it is true to a certain extent. I have always felt Cynthia was hardly my baby. Everyone else has had her so much. She has had no need to be entirely dependent. And then too, I didn't get the thrill out of having her since you weren't here when she was born.

Another thing, while everyone else was making such a fuss over Cynthia, I didn't want to see Waide's feelings hurt, so I clung to him and stuck up for him. So this past week I have devoted more time to Cynthia and picked her up more and loved her and kissed her and she has responded. She runs to me to be loved and then Waide comes running and says, "You love me too, Mum, don't you?" He isn't jealous but he does look hurt when I kiss Cynthia first etc. But I do think it will be good for both of them and for me too. Aren't children a problem as well as a great joy?…

Wednesday was uneventful during the day except for housework and shopping. Oh no, it wasn't either. Mr. Radcliffe, who is the manager of CFOS Radio station and himself an announcer, interviewer, violinist etc., called me and asked me to drop down to the station, he wanted to see me. So I did. He had an interesting proposition. He said he had heard I was a good speaker, had good social connections and was a diplomat - ahum! - and wondered if by any chance, if after an audition and my voice was good on radio, I would like a full-time position on the staff doing all phases of radio work, announcing, interviewing, selling advertising to companies and firms and stores in town, writing my own "spot" ads etc., even being in plays.

It sounded too good to be true, something I've always wanted to do and right in my mitt. However I realized you would never agree to it in a thousand years since it would mean putting a practical nurse over the children and seeing very little of them. So I refused. However I am to have an audition this week and Frank said maybe I could at least pinch hit occasionally.

I must admit, darling, I wouldn't like to have anyone else over our babies. I realize more every day I've got a big job and an interesting one and as important as any job in the world. I must make a success of it and I'm sure these rascals will pay dividends. And if you succeed and they succeed and I've helped you all in any way, I will be content. I realize it is my great love for you that makes me feel satisfied to be in such an unobtrusive position, since as you know I've always wanted to be doing something spectacular...

I love you, sweetheart, and I miss you worlds and worlds. But I am feeling so much better and more like fighting it through...
Norah

~

Dec. 18
Dearest Norah:
...Dec. 29 the Lorne Scots are having a get-together. I am going to try to attend. It will be a big party, as you may surmise...I haven't decided what to do Christmas. The proprietors of the Stanley Club, to which I belong, are having a small dinner party to which I've been invited, but I don't know as I am keen to go...Think I'll let the Lorne Scot party suffice for the mid-winter festivities...

Darling, I've never written you a Christmas or New Years letter. I mean I had intended to write a Christmas letter to reach you about the 25th. Somehow I've never been able to get into the mood - in a way I'm just as glad, for I am not at all anxious to get a Christmas mood...If I were to try to make something of it, I know it would be a ghastly failure. There isn't anything in the season, all by yourself.

My letters lately haven't been successes, I know that. There is no hidden reason - no women or anything, though I feel sure you will never wonder on that score since we straightened out our problems...

Nothing seems to buck me up and I confess I am completely buffaloed. I want only to be with you and nothing else, work or play, has any meaning. It seems such an eternity since I held you in my arms, and yet it is only one and a half years. Likely it will not be more than one more. Sometimes that seems such a short time, at others so long. It is worth any period, but the going is slow.

Well sweetheart, don't let my grousing and blues get you. Have to get it off my chest, and it's best to tell you...All my love, my love, to you.

Fred

~

Dec. 24

Dearest Fred:

...As you can see by the date, it is the day before Christmas and I am so busy. There are so many little things to attend to and to buy and salads to make etc. etc. So darling...I will ramble on as fast as I can and disregard the composition.

The most important thing is that I love you, sweetheart, and miss you so much. Everything I do I think of you, and wish with all my heart that you were here, but we are both going to smile nevertheless, aren't we?...

Where will I commence? I will tell you about the tree. It is a very large one and is in the dining room, and has lights and tinsel and balls on it but no balloons, I couldn't buy a one. There are lots of parcels on it, mostly for the children of course, but it will be fun tomorrow morning to see Waide's face. He is so excited, he can hardly sleep...

Several people have said to me, "Norah, you are a very lucky girl, a nice husband with a good profession and one who gives you everything your little heart desires and two nice children etc." And I realize I am lucky. The most important thing of all though, dear, is that you really love me...And I am so happy even with you away, for I know that you mean more to me even away over there in England than most men do who are right here living with their wives.

By that I mean, dear, I feel you can go out and have fun, perhaps like other girls, even sleep with them, but I KNOW that I am the only one, and if ever I am not I know you will tell me. And that applies for me too. But I know we will never have to tell each other that it is someone else, will we?...You know, Fred, I am at the stage where I can actually laugh at your two "affairs". Especially when you said if I knew what you were thinking at the time I would probably laugh. I am not the least bit cross nor jealous. Not that I would want it to be a regular occurrence.

Though you know, I don't know what the dickens you or all the rest of the men think we poor women do without our loving...I feel like tumbling into bed right now. Gosh I am lonesome! I really would give all the money in the world to have you cuddle me tonight...I love you with all my heart. I always will...
Norah

~

Dec. 28
Dearest Norah:
...I received your Christmas parcel Saturday and it was lovely, thank you dear, very much. I got out the desk photo case right away and put into it the darling pictures of Waide and Cynthia, and of Cynthia and yourself. I had quite a smile, for the picture of Waide and Cynthia makes both look very angelic, and I know they are imps - good imps of course...

Christmas Eve I went out with the staff on a party. About fourteen of us started and gradually diminished to Bill Wallace and I and a bevy of girls - thereupon we broke it up and sent them off on their trains.

Christmas I went to the Stanley Club for dinner. The club is small and about fourteen were seated. Very good dinner, but hell, just acquaintances. At night I went to dinner with some party (I was invited as a fill-in) got tired of it and wandered off. By this time I was wandering, and wandered home. It's a good thing I have an instinct that takes me home when I ought to go...

It has been a merry Christmas, but how short of being home with you...It will be grand when the four of us can gather round the tree and have Santa open the presents. Waide will have been excited about Christmas, won't he, and you too should have had a pretty good time. Cynthia will be quite oblivious of the goings on, I expect, but the bright lights may catch her eyes...All my love, dearest. I long to see you.
Fred

~

1943

Grit and depression

"It takes a powerful lot of love to carry on and stick sometimes"

F. T. Egener, England

Jan. 10

Dearest Fred:

...I was up skiing today from three till six with Jean and Les and Mary and Lois and Peggy and Peter. I am by far the poorest skier, but enjoyed it and learned to come down and turn either to the right or left without falling...

Pearl was away sick Thursday afternoon, Friday and Saturday, and I might say I was very busy. Last night (Saturday) I washed and ironed and made pie crust and worked until twelve. This morning I made two pies and hung the washing in the attic and generally tidied up. Pearl was back today and I welcomed her with open arms. The children are so active and are into everything and demand many many little attentions...

Friday night Jean and Les and Bob Dyment and I sat before a grate fire and listened to my music. It was very restful and enjoyable. I refused to go to the show with Bob on the grounds it might cause talk. People in this town, not your friends of course, are very ready to criticise, as many of us war widows have learned. So I dunno. As I told Bob, you have given your permission for me to go out if I wish, but then again it may be best to limit it to parties and dances. What do you think?...

I feel you can trust me and I feel I've been very sensible ever since my own little episode, and I feel therefore I can tell you where I go and with whom etc. and not have you suspicious and worried. I know I feel that way with you. Of course I never did even faintly suspect anything out of the way ever - I honestly have always felt I could trust you and I can say this, that if I ever felt I couldn't or lost your love, my heart would be completely broken, and I mean broken...

I don't know why, but I've felt more contented since Christmas and New Years. I do know why - I have a strong feeling I'll see you, dear, in 1943, and I'm living every day with a song in my heart because of that...

Norah

~

Jan. 22

Dearest Norah:

Today is a mild January day, relatively bright although clouds obscure most of the sky. It has been a quiet week and my activities have been of the most limited variety...The January financial doldrums are in part at least responsible for my quietness...

From your letters, you seem to collect a lot of confidences, and I know I do, too. Is it that we're over fool's hill, more mature, recognized as members of the kindred of lonesome hearts, or what? I seem to get many a peep of insight into the mechanism of people that I never got before. Sort of a bird's eye view. It's damned interesting, entertaining and an eye-opener...

Don't worry that the children might come between us or spoil just your and my pleasures together. They will give us far more happiness than they take away, and we will always have our pleasures together as well. As you say, we will live together as a unit with consideration each for each. I had never hoped to live otherwise, nor am I happy with the complete freedom that separation gives me...

I think long thoughts till I turn to thoughts of us together and then the pictures flood through my mind: a glimpse of spring, a garden of flowers, blossoms fluttering to the ground and you flitting through it all with a gay laugh and a twinkling eye, tarrying to be caught. And oh so many other visions of complete happiness...
All my love, dearest, and oceans of hugs and kisses,
Fred

~

Jan. 26
Dearest Norah:
...Tonight I'm invited to a bridge game which I will attend with some apprehension since I've played so little the past few years and the opposition sounds keen - probably can tell you the result before I close.

It is "tomorrow" now. I did a very strange thing and failed to go to the bridge game. The reason is very complex - that's true - it wasn't just chance that I became more interested in the thought of pubbing and so phoned to excuse myself. Mainly, I suppose, I did not relish facing three women for the evening particularly since (it's not a boast) one of them has designs upon me, which so far I've carefully prevented her from executing largely by avoidance, which method is the most effective I've ever discovered.

The lady in question is the wife of one of the proprietors of one of the clubs I frequent, has a very beautiful year-old son and is of buxom beauty herself. Confined within the four walls of the club she is a fine lass and there all's well. Outside would be a different proposition, I fancy...

I regret that your note showed you to be depressed by my lonesomeness - of course I'm lonesome, but I am not down in the utter depths that you seem to imagine. I do not intend to deny that there is little or nothing in this life that is attractive to me. I admit that essentially I'm a home bird and that my pleasure is bound up with family life. I long ago realized I had to make the best of a bad pudding, and have tried to be interested in many things that otherwise would not attract me...

I think that once we lapse into the attitude that the present is meaningless and that some utopian state will exist or has existed in which we will be or were utterly content, we seal our chance of ever being satisfied, but on the contrary ensure that we will be forever malcontents. We should find something in every day that is a pleasure...

For you and I, life together we know was richer than it has been separated, but it would be quite wrong to say that this life is poor. We look forward to that richer life, but we must not abandon the present. We have learned a great deal since June '41, and in retrospect the experience has been one we would not have missed. That is true regardless of the yearnings and trials...

Have finished reading Europe to Let. The book left me with the uncomfortable feeling that Europe doesn't deserve anything better than she is getting. With the antagonisms that existed before the war quite probably ready to reassert themselves after this is over, what hope is there of a cooperative Europe?...Often I am inclined to think, "to hell with Europe, let it rot in its own filthiness". It is because Europe has failed to develop anything but tight little loyalties and so become an incomprehensible puzzle that we cannot look for leadership to it.

This is one reason why I deplore the tendency at home to snipe at the French-Canadian instead of amalgamating both races' ideas. We need to be drawn together, not wedged apart...So much for politics. I certainly ramble...You have been such a very good girl, doing your job and keeping all the threads in hand and untangled. I am very proud of you, just as everyone tells me I should be...
Fred

~

Feb. 12
Dearest Norah:
...Tuesday night took out Bobbie Ellis, her friend going with an air force officer name of Brookie. Went to a fashionable west-end restaurant for dinner and dance. The floor was about two feet by two

feet, so can't say I had a wild time, but since both Brookie and I started out the evening with a quart of Old Angus, I must admit I wasn't asleep.

Last Saturday night I went on a pub-crawl to Putney, and Sunday went to the officers' club afternoon dance with a Joan somebody, who wandered into the club I was pepping up in. Besides the show and dance, I've not done anything this week though I did drift into the pub for a while the other evenings. All of which must sound like a lot of binging, and indeed it is, but don't be alarmed.

One reason for my furious activity is that I'll be leaving C.M.H.Q. in a very short time. This is at my request in accordance with the intention I outlined to you last fall and with which you concurred...

You certainly had many parties during the festive season, and sound as though you had a good time. Incidentally don't be afraid to say that you have a good time when you do. I understand that you want me to realize that you feel the lack of my presence and that you could have more fun if I were home.

I admit I'm envious of those lads who may enjoy your dances and company, but I am glad when you have enjoyable parties and fun. You realize, I'm sure, what I mean.

If ordinarily I make no comment on your remarks re your friends etc. or the odds and ends of problems you are presented with or the conduct you should follow, it is not from disinterest but because I am fully confident of you and of your ability to make a sane and reasonable decision. I trust you implicitly and do not feel any need to interfere.

So it is with your question as to whether you should go out with Bob Dyment, as distinct from going to parties with him - or anyone else. Darling, I know nothing will ever come between us and am not fearful that any thing or body will. What you should do, considering all the factors that exist about town and family, is much more easily determinable by you than by me...

As for me, I do go out, as you know. Perhaps that's different; at least no one starts whispering campaigns etc...

All my love, Norah...

Fred

~

Feb. 13

Dearest Fred:

...I remember Mrs. Ellis and I remember you saying what a nice person and a good sport she was. I am truthfully happy you enjoy her company, and it is nice to have a good pal. I would not say though that I would be honest if I did not confess I feel envious of her enjoying your company and just a little jealous. But that is only natural, isn't it darling?...

I didn't want you to know, but I ran $60 into debt on my summer cottage venture. It was just beyond me financially, that is all, what with carrying on home expenses, running the car, my share of the cottage etc...Then Christmas took another $40 just on presents and extras. You know the extras at Christmas...So by addition and subtraction, I have about $100 left in the bank...

I am sitting in the kitchen...There is a great coal shortage in almost every city and town. Coal is rationed, one ton to a house at a time. We have had our order in for four weeks now. The roads are blocked and have been since November, so we have not been able to have any more wood drawn in...I bought a little Quebec heater with pipes for $10. It heats the kitchen and Cynthia's bedroom. So I am very cosy here just now.

I have been asked to take a district and canvass the first two weeks in March for the Red Cross and Navy League. I also expect to help fill out the new coupon ration books. I wish I could do more to help out. As yet I haven't managed to get to the Red Cross rooms one afternoon to help make dressings. I'm quite tied during the day...

Thursday night, Lorna Elliott and I got together to discuss taking a few tap-dancing lessons, just for fun. We have secured a teacher and have had one lesson. We are going to get up a dance or two to do at a party or maybe even up at the Y some night when the IODE entertains the soldiers...

It is only human when I say I have few worries over you when you are at the work you are, and I hope you will remain there since you were selected to do that work. Your work is necessary, I know it is; and as you said once, winning or helping to win this war isn't all done looking down a gun sight. So I pray most earnestly you will remain. I'm not big enough darling to say, "I'm willing to lose my husband if it means winning". Nor does anyone else feel they can say it.

Pearl is leaving for sure this time the end of March. She says she hates to leave me because she is so fond of me and the children, but she would like to get into war work and away from Owen Sound...So I have decided to have my tonsils out in March, probably the second week. I confess I'm as nervous as can be, but I've had a couple of severe attacks of tonsilitis since the middle of January...

Love and kisses and a hug so big,
Norah

~

Feb. 23
Fred darling:

...Wednesday night, Lorna Elliot and Jean and I took our tap dance lesson over here. Waide is crazy about tapping, so I let him stay up and he sat in a big chair and watched. He tries it and tries it. He said, "I wish I were a girl Mummy, so I could tap". So I assured him boys can learn to tap as well as girls. Mom said this place was like the house in the show You Can't Take It With You that day...

Monday afternoon Mary and I took Waide and Dian to the rink skating. Waide did very well but of course cannot as yet skate alone. He was very keen, and I plan to take him two afternoons a week for the next six weeks...

I brought him home and bathed him and got dressed to go out to dinner at seven, the occasion being the Kinsmen birthday dinner and dance. I had received your Jan. 22 letter that afternoon and was in a very lonesome mood and very wistful for you. I wore my new black velvet dinner gown and Bob took me. Just before he came and after I was all ready, I sat down and had a cry. Mom cheered me up though. Bob is nice but so very, very far from being even a millionth as nice as you, dear. I was in no mood to go...

Friday night, Lorna and I went to the C.C.F. meeting. The speaker was a local chap, a graduate in sociology from Varsity. He spoke on "why I am a member of the C.C.F." After the meeting, the president and the speaker came and spoke to me. We talked for quite some time on this and that, and last night, the president, Mr. Elliott, brought me over a small book entitled The Socialist Party in England...

Don't think I'm going to plunge into some party or other, dear. It is just that I have heard so many people denounce this or that party or programme etc. and I am determined to learn a little about socialism and also about the C.C.F...

I love you worlds dear, and I'm a real good girl and have been trying hard to live each day to its fullest possible enjoyment.
Affectionately,
Norah

~

March 3
Dearest Norah:
As you see I've returned to the reinforcement unit...I arrived here

Saturday afternoon. There were no Lorne Scot officers about, and indeed there are only two of us here...We partied Sunday and then went to the afternoon tea dance at the supply column mess, which developed into an evening party. I spent some time there and some at the Queens Hotel being a stag; both were "dampish"...

I have been left in charge of the company. As the whole unit is in the process of settling down into the new organization, there has been plenty and more to do. There was nothing laid on and I've been laying it on. Tuesday and today have been as busy as I should ever like to be, but it has been a pleasure...

I shall not trouble you with the odds and ends of activity that make up the day's work, but I do not seem to have settled till now...I am going to like it here I feel sure, since all the regiments are "Scottish" and they all seem anxious to get together both at work and play.

For the time being I'm doing administrative work again - as usual! - but hope to get in a spring and summer largely outside. Already I've had more exercise than when in London and that is a very happy actor. I feel better even though I anticipate a great physical ennui to set in. So my love, wish me well...

Fred

~

March 8

Dearest Norah:

...Last week was a very busy one, least I thought I was busy. Running up and down from one company officer to another and otherwise from hither to yon. I still have the company all to myself...There are PT parades, night training, arms training and first-aid training all to get under way at once...

Had a good afternoon at the club - I was glad I'd gone as I was surprised to find such a comfortable layout. There are several ante-rooms in which tea is served, as well as the dance floor which is ringed by tables. After six the bar was open in another part of the building and when the dancing finished at 6:30, most repaired there before breaking up...

It was nearing one o'clock when I finally arrived back in camp, not because the pub stayed open so long but I was restless and it was a grand clear night out. Just as I was wandering about the company lines to check up on the blackouts, there was a raid far to the south. It was such a clear night that you could se the flashes even from where I was, though the distance was obviously considerable, and you could hear the various crackles of the guns. I saw some explosions in the sky which looked like a star had exploded. A solitary plane passed overhead several times with a large dull-red light showing. It was one of our night fighters, I presume. Its red light mixing in among the profuse display of stars was quite a picture...

All my love sweetheart, give my love and kisses to the children.
Fred

~

March 11
Dearest Fred:
...The weather has been nicer this last day or so, so Waide has been out. He is too full of beans when he can't get out and work off his energy. He is cute. When I get very frustrated and things get beyond me, I will sometimes say, "I could just scream."

Well, the other evening just before dinner he had made a fort out of blocks and Cynthia came along and mussed it up and he said, "Oh, I could just scream", and he got a face on him like a meat axe. He was so funny I had to laugh and as a result he laughed. Tonight he was in the bathroom waiting for me to help him undress and he called me and said, "Mummy, you had better hurry, for I'm not in a very good mood today" - imitating me again.

Yesterday afternoon I met him over town with three other lads riding on the back of a coal sleigh. He came home okay but was very black. What would you do? Let him go? He gets such a kick out of it. Cynthia is cuter every day too. Her quick observance is the most remarkable thing. She has to see a thing or hear a thing only once and she has it...

I am still missing practically a month's mail. As a result I don't know how it happens you have left the personnel selection staff and are back at the regiment. I was shocked to hear it and had a wonderful cry all morning. I was eating my breakfast and reading the letter and the tears were falling down and Waide said, "Never mind Mom, Daddy will be home soon". Poor little kid, he is so sweet and understanding.

I felt so secure about you when you were at the personnel selection staff and I have a strong feeling you asked for a field post now that things are shaping up. I have never, I feel, interfered with your decisions and I don't intend to now dear, but naturally I am much more anxious about you now, if you are going to be more active...

Maybe when I get the mail still missing it will clarify things a bit. I don't know how I could ever live without you dear, if anything ever happened to you. I'm going to try to be brave and hopeful and trusting because I believe it is only right that I do. I fear this next year is going to be a difficult year for all of us...

I'm having my tonsils out Tuesday morning next...I so much wish you were here to be with me - I'm silly I guess, but I'm really nervous about this pesky operation. It probably won't be bad at all...
Affectionately,
Norah

~

March 16
Dearest Norah:
So another anniversary has come round, Norah, and I am sure both of us are thinking of our run down to the hospital and young Waide's first cries and all that happened that day. You have never looked happier, regardless of your night's work, and I'm sure never had more cause. I always remember on today your courage and buoyant spirit...

The countryside is coming to life with spring and is much the same as I described to you last year. The profusion of flowers and the variety of species never fails to surprise me. I had a spare hour this afternoon that I filled by climbing one of the many rolling hills about, from which I could see all the surrounding country and the sea, too. It was a grand scene, and on so fine a day one could spend all their time just taking it in...

I've no night life to report...I get up about 6:30, woe is me. Tomorrow it will be earlier as we're off to see a demonstration to which we march some eight miles; oh yes, back too...
All my love,
Fred

~

March 18
Dearest Fred:
Just a note dear, for I'm so dopey I can hardly see the page. I had my tonsils out at nine this morning and I got along very well...I can't swallow, little less drink or eat. All I have done all day is rinse my mouth with peroxide. I'm not fooling when I say I would rather have two babies...

I received your Feb. 12 letter today. I am not at all happy about you asking for a field post but I guess I mustn't interfere with your decisions, must I? It is just that I will worry about you constantly...

I am going to bed soon, to sleep I mean. So will close. I hope I dream about you, dear. One dream which I don't want to have and which I often have is this: You come home and are not a bit glad to see me, in fact you don't want me nor want to cuddle me etc. I introduce you to my friends and you don't like them and they don't like you…We quarrel and you leave me. Then I waken in a cold sweat. It is so silly, but I have dreamt it over and over. Do you ever have any dreams?

Darling, in some letter soon tell me just how you feel about our separation. Do you feel it will take long for us to readjust? Have your ideas changed much? Do you still think we'll have fun, care-free fun together? Do you feel you might get home on a furlough or course?

Saturday 3 p.m.

…I am sitting in front of a lovely grate fire. I have been reading and dozing and now writing. I've got a case of the blues today and have found it hard to keep the tears back. It is unavoidable and I'm trying hard to convince myself by this time next week I will be tip-top. My throat is so sore and it took me one hour at noon to drink a little tomato soup and one glass of milk, a cup of tea and the filling from a pumpkin pie…

Don is not at all pleased with what you have done re going back to the unit. Nor is your dad. I still feel numb about the whole thing. I've learned that you will do exactly what you feel is the right and honourable thing to do, regardless of what anyone else thinks. You know you can count on me to carry on in any eventuality, and of course I can and will. Perhaps if you had to consider what would happen to me or the children a little more, you wouldn't be quite so free to put yourself in more danger than necessary.

I can see only one attitude for me to take and that is, if you are to come back you will, and if you don't there is no amount of worrying will help. If I let myself worry I will go simply crazy…I am quite provoked at you, dear, and must say it. If I didn't love you so much, I wouldn't be so concerned…But it does no good to talk. You've done it and it is useless to say more.…

It hurts me to have to be cross at you and you'll probably be cross at me when you read it. You know I love you to eternity and beyond no matter what happens.…

Norah

~

March 21
Dearest Norah:

...We moved again yesterday, which has brought us to a very fine old country home surrounded by ample grounds. The quarters should be quite comfortable except that the rooms are somewhat on the large side both in floor space and height so that one's few pieces of equipment hardly relieve the sense of barrenness and at night all heat goes to the top...

Wednesday we were out to see a "German" demonstration. They had clothed and armed about sixty-five men as Germans and these carried out tactical exercises as prescribed by German instructional pamphlets. The exercises done with live ammunition and well-practised were very interesting, and one knew the men were keen to see them as they were thoroughly attentive...

Listened to Mr. Churchill's speech, which I found considerably less interesting than I had hoped. There is far too much time and thought and talk being expended on the "days after". Damn it all, let's get home first! We've still a long way to go and no extra time to spend. Seems to me I can best listen to what everyone wants to do in the perfect world when I can recline with you in under one arm before a few crackling logs. Hell, they can talk then for days at a time and I'll listen to the whole of it...

All my love, darling,

Fred

~

March 24

Darling Fred:

I've been going to ask you what you think about this idea for a long time now - here it is:

Truthfully I get so terribly fed up with Owen Sound. I have scads of friends, a social life etc. etc. But what I would really like to do is go back to school. Here is what I have in mind.

Move back to Oakville, I love it so because we had the happiest year of our life there. Get Marg, who would come in a minute I know, to live with me, and go to Osgoode. You know how I've always wanted to take law. I could commute by train, the children would be fine in Oakville and Marg could look after them in the day-time. I would have my evenings with them and the weekend.

I could have something to fill my mind and if I ever needed it, I would be fitted to earn my own living...I love school as you know, and the chances are you will be away another two years, maybe three. It would give Marg a definite interest.

I'm really keen about it and have felt I must mention it to you, dear. Please consider it and let me know. I could commence this fall coming if you agreed...Tell me truthfully, do you think I could do it? The course at Osgoode, I mean? I promise I wouldn't neglect the children. I am sick to death of parties and I'm not interested in any other men, as you know. Can you understand how I feel, sweet? I feel sometimes I'll smother or scream here, and I get so frustrated. Please darling, let me know what you think...

Norah

March 26

Fred dearest:

I posted a letter to you on Monday last. I am afraid it will be a morbid one to read. I was feeling so low and also upset over your move. I also mentioned my Osgoode idea, with which you will not agree, I feel, because it will, if I did it, take me away from the children too much - and I guess you would be right...

Really Fred, the more I read lately the more confused I am as to what I think, believe etc. I often, oh so often, wish I could discuss the various topics and problems with you. I feel so inconsequential in this big world. Is that the word I want? I believe so.

For so many years life was so good to me. I was always enthused. I still am. I refuse to be otherwise, for I feel if I live long enough and grope long enough, I will work out a philosophy of life.

Right now I don't know what I would teach Waide and Cynthia. I'm confused in regards religion, politics, everything. Probably you feel the same...

Darling, your letters of late have been a little impersonal. There is nothing bothering you, is there? You would tell me, wouldn't you?...

Remember always dearest, I'm with you in my thoughts constantly. I'll love you for ever and ever and there could never be anyone else but just you and I. It is such a magnificent feeling, isn't it?...

Norah

~

April 5

Fred dearest:

...Pearl left last Wednesday and I surely find a difference. Up at seven and going until eight at night without a minute's rest...Meat rationing starts in May. Meals, the variety and planning and procuring of the food and delivery problem is one bug-bear, especially when I can't get out to shop unless I take both children and then I can't carry everything and push a go-cart and watch Waide...

I realize, Fred, when the offensive is launched, things will be in a great turmoil and am fully prepared to go minus mail or any word for weeks at a time. No news is good news. As long as I don't get bad news, I can stand it. Darling, I don't want to be alarming or always mentioning the worst, but we must face facts. Would you, for me, in case anything should happen, sit down and some evening write a personal message to me and the bairns - telling us of your sincere devotion to us, expressing some of your wishes, what you expect of me and of Waide and of Cynthia, your ideals, your beliefs, etc. etc. Would you please, dear?...

Waide is talking ever so much better and is increasing his vocabulary fairly quickly - he is becoming grammar-conscious, and will say, "Is it can or may?" or "Is it her or she?" I find they learn at a very early age. Dad cut his hair again, a real brush cut, and he certainly looks more like you and a real boy. Cynthia is cute, dear, but becoming very difficult to handle. For example, I had an occasion to spank her today. She got as stiff as a board and red in the face and slapped me back as hard as she could. So I then put her on a chair and isolated her and she was much better...

You will be following the war news closely, as are we. It is hard to say what will happen and when and where...I long for you, dear, but am waiting patiently...
Norah

~

April 13
Dearest Fred:
...Today was one of those hectic days. Cynthia has the croup and was pettish...This afternoon I was trying to iron with Cynthia tugging at my skirts and Waide was playing on the washing machine when all at once he pulled it over. Luckily he wasn't hurt and it wasn't broken, but it just seemed to be the last lap...

Waide said tonight when I was bathing him, "My goodness you've been cross today, I don't know what I am going to do with you." He also said he thought he would pack up and leave because baby cried too much. On Sunday I had occasion to spank Cynthia and she flew to him for sympathy and threw her arms around his waist and he hugged and kissed her and said, "Never mind, we'll go to England and see Daddy"...

Today I filled out our application for sugar for canning. One has to estimate how many quarts of canned fruit and jam and jelly one needs or will likely do and then allow one-half pound per quart for canned fruit and three-quarters of a pound per quart of jam. It is said, regardless of what we want or need, we will be given only fifteen pounds for canning...

Do you know by any chance that strikes in Canada are becoming more prevalent and the situation is fast becoming critical? Norv Hipwell, who is president and general manager of Russell Bros., who do nothing else but war work, boats, forty and eighty-foot diesel engines, radio detectors, Cummins engines etc., spends half his time in Ottawa over labor problems...Tonight another strike is threatened in the aluminum plant in Quebec...

I know so little about it, but I have been talking to a few men who are intimate with the situation and it is alarming. I do notice most members of the C.C.F. are labour men, who are all for unions and "agin" the government and the capitalist etc. The other members are theorists who feel the C.C.F. is the medium by which we will arrive at socialism....

I feel I can't even run my own home smoothly any more, nor do my friends seem to do any better - everyone is worried and frustrated, the whole world is in a turmoil. I thank God, Fred, you are over there sometimes, because I have observed how frayed the nerves of everyone are and I'm sure ours would be too and then there would likely be discord etc....

I should be shot for complaining. I do hope you are as happy as ever in your work...I'm wearing my hair a new way - up now, and everyone says it looks very smart and makes me more dignified...Just to let you know dear, I'm not too bedraggled-looking for you to come home to. I'm hoping it might be this summer?...

Norah

~

April 19

Dearest Norah:

...The concentration of the Lorne Scots has been completed. As laid down, it will be for approximately one month. We are in a beautiful location and in good spirits to see each other again. The training promises to be rigid but will be a change from platoon tactics...

I am glad to know those pesky tonsils are out and to feel that you will be well recovered by now. I am very sorry, Norah dear, that you felt so sick with them, but am sure that the benefit will be a full reward. I must say it was good going and I commend you for taking the bit and doing what had to be done even though you knew it would be painful and exceedingly uncomfortable, if that adequately expresses what you went through.

Tonight I want to talk to you on another note that I felt to be in the letters. You seemed worried about our relations. You seemed to wonder about how much we had changed and how difficult might be our readjusting period. You seemed more worried than usual about current conduct.

I don't think you should be worrying at all. I do not think I've changed, that is to any extent. Both physically and mentally I'm precisely the same as when I went. Oh yes, a few pounds more in the waist or this and that other normal change; probably a bit more convinced of how I intend to live and work and play, but still pretty much in a state of mental flux as to those matters as to what beliefs and convictions moral, political or otherwise I am going to hold to...

As regards you dear, I've not changed either and I've been truer to you both physically and mentally than I imagine you think. I do not feel a stranger to you now nor do I ever expect to...

Now old dear, have you a picture of where I stand? As I've assured you time and again, I love you and you alone. I don't see that the coming year is apt to be a hard one for us in any way.

You also wonder about my safety...I'm not going to get hurt. You must stop thinking I might - it all will be tramping around here with only our feet hurting for long yet. Those away from the scene are too second-front conscious and too inclined to expect the direst of results. If I get banged up, then I do and that's that. It not only looks a remote possibility, but I believe it is. So must you.

Regarding your going to Osgoode. No. You have a big job on hand. So have I. We must do them. During these times the only work I'd agree to you taking would be some actual work contributing now to war service or the conditions needing to be met at home, as Red Cross, social services etc.

Regarding a summer cottage. I hope you can arrange to go for the summer months. I would prefer you to go to Goderich, but then that is one request of mine you have always ignored. It is of course one of the few I've ever made. Still and all, I hope that you and the children can get to the water for the summer and get out in the open lots...

Both you and I find it hard to keep on a budget...I don't object, I love to spend too, and do, and therein lies a problem. We must guard that we do not over-spend...So as one spendthrift to another, let's be more careful. All my love, darling,
Fred

~

May 2

Dearest Norah:

...The week was full of training which I'll not bother to detail though it was interesting. Day and night we were "cracking" - night schemes of the military kind is what I refer to though as you'd expect there was great getting together among our long-separated Lorne officers...

It was a good show and as things turned out especially fortunate for me, for I cease, for the time being, to be a Lorne Scot...We go in and become part of the Saskatoon Light Infantry...We had little forewarning of this changeover and it was only actually on Friday that I learned we were to move out of the Lorne Scot concentration. Somewhat of a disappointment...

Hope all this isn't boring. I know that the organization of an army unit isn't of much interest to one not right in the throes of it. Everything is cracking, though, and there's no sitting around. We all speculate on how soon the sitting around ends for all, and who doesn't. We keep thinking in terms of day after tomorrow, and one day we'll be right...

One thing puzzles me. Your recent letters keep saying you think this year will be the toughest of all for us (you and I). Why? We know how and where we stand, we're sure of ourselves, we're certain. We've had our times of stress. We should sail through this one effortlessly. In one letter you said mine had a tone of the impersonal. There was no reason for that, if it were so. You need not imagine I will develop any commanding interest in anyone but you, dear...

Should you have thought that Bobbie Ellis was the cause, I'll scotch that now. Bobbie is by far the nicest girl I've met here. She's a solid-headed lass though, and an honest wife. There's no fooling about with Bobbie, which is one of the reasons I like her. She's full of good fun and devilment, but just the same she is essentially a pally girl. She carries on in the way I expect and believe you do at home - good fun...

If on the other hand you have just been on the worry about me and action and all, I can only say I wish you'd quit thinking anything might happen to me. Hell, it simply won't, so stop your worrying. You'll wrinkle your brow and that'll be all the damage to either of us.

Don't take all the speeches etc. so seriously. Of course we'll see action, but you needn't think everyone's going to be bopped off...

I love you all from top hair to toe tip, and I always will.

Fred

~

May 15
Dearest Norah:
I'm writing this short note to you tonight since for the next few days I will be busy and will have little time for my personal affairs...

I had the pleasure of learning to drive a carrier the other day...If it ever looked to you like an easy job, may I tell you differently! After an hour my arms really ached. We were driving on broken ground, up ravines and down and through woods. It was sport as a novelty, but I certainly have a new respect for carrier drivers...

Took the officers of the company out to teach them motorcycle riding last night and travelled a road that was both historically and scenically very interesting. It led along the sea coast, sometimes down close to the beach, at others high up on cliffs that permitted a broad view over the low-lying adjacent country which is beautiful at this time when each little field, parcelled off as they are only in England, was of a different shade of green...

If this letter sounds a bit cryptic, it is only that there is almost nothing I can pass on to you of the many interesting events of everyday doings.

It's grand to be really busy, outside and working with equipment of all sorts, vehicles and weapons and all. I really like it immensely and it is so much more enjoyable to me than the blooming office jobs I've so often tumbled into.

Tomorrow we start for two or three days vehicle travel, i.e. convoy practice, and will route over many new roads...To be on the go is, I guess, in my blood and I am looking forward to the move...

Moon's getting full, sweet, and my, how I'd love to be sitting beneath it with you. It's a link, though, isn't it? I never do look at it without thinking of you...
Fred

~

May 16
Fred dearest:
...Today I received your April 19 and 25th letters respectively. After a lapse of nearly five weeks it was a marvelous feeling and lifter-upper - even though you did have a warning note about my spending and a sarcastic remark to make re me never going to Goderich for a summer...

The children are in bed - Cynthia is asleep but I still hear Waide.

He developed mumps on one side this morning. He isn't a bit sick, and his appetitite is perfect, but of course I have to keep him in bed, which is a tremendous task...The gas has been shut off for over a week now. I managed to borrow a two-burner electric plate, but even so it is no easy task to cook meals or make varied meals without an oven. We have had plenty of salads and sandwiches, which is expensive eating this time of year...

The news today was that the air force had bombed the two great German dams in the Ruhr. And of course last week the allied victory in Tunisia was announced. It does make one more joyful and yet we still have to face the awful casualties of an invasion and the uprisings in Holland, Belgium, France, Norway etc...

I appreciated your talk re our post-war relations. I hope you will realize when I'm sick and down physically, I also get down mentally. All the problems possible but not probable leap before me and I get worrying and fretting, so if I sounded more so than other times, please understand why...

One criticism people seem to have of me (my friends and my acquaintances) is that I idealize you too much and underestimate the job I'm doing and worry far too much whether I'm being a good enough mother and wife. As they point out, if I keep on idealizing you as much as I do, when you get back, wonderful and all as you are, you are human...

Regarding a summer cottage in Goderich: admittedly I have made no attempt to get a cottage either last summer or this one. When you went overseas you said in so many words you wanted me to be happy while you were away and live where I would be happiest. Am I not right? So going on that assumption, I have preferred to summer at Leith.

To say I have ignored your request re Goderich entirely is, I feel, unfair. I did offer to move to Goderich and live in the old home with Marg for the duration...but Marg did not accept my offer or suggestion. It was made for one reason only, and that is because you love Goderich so. Goderich means very little more to me when you are away than Owen Sound would to you if I were away...

I will be more careful in the future regarding my spending. I realize a lot of things I have bought, such as my bicycle and my black velvet evening gown, and furniture, could have been dispensed with until after the war. I feel on the other hand my tonsillectonomy and my trips to London and the odd other expense, e.g. clothes, were necessary. I have very definitely something to show for every ex-

penditure...
Love and kisses,
Norah

~

May 23
Dearest Norah:
...I often wonder what I've learned or accomplished in the last two years and I'm afraid the record is quite negative. Surely though, we both must have gained a wider outlook, a greater appreciation of what counts and a fuller and readier sympathy for other people. There are many pages of literature that have meaning now where they had little or no meaning before.

I am not sure that I don't think it has been worth it, i.e. to gain insight into the aches and pains of separation. I wonder if we would enjoy life as much if we lived the serene, complacent and relatively emotionless life that we call Victorian. I believe for example that the trust we have developed for each other, the willingness to carry out our pledge of standing together through thick and thin, is more than a mere accomplishment of fact, I think it is a milestone toward a fundamental contentment with life and living...

I'm interested in your joining discussions with the C.C.F. group. I've never studied their platform, but it does no harm to talk. Frankly I think that there is much too much talk and far too little action in all spheres. Everyone wants to bang off their chest about what they'd do about this and that and waste hours (I mean it) daily in the self-lauding occupation of having their say. Man's a funny animal. I've wondered just why I'm fighting and just what I aim to accomplish. I've been going to set it down, but never had a clear-cut complete picture.

Stripped of all else I think we can agree that the sole true reason for fighting is simply belief in the principle of collective self-preservation. That's always been my own reason, and the arguments that have raged re the merits of various political systems don't mean a damn...

I don't want tight control of people and enterprise by government organizations...I believe it dangerous to put power into government, to force it, in point of fact, to assume more and more jobs. Hell, the process is vicious for it grows weed-like and eventually the burden of keeping the employees of the country's largest "non-profit" organization functioning would have all the rest of us sweating our heads off.

The more one sees of government and army (which is a small edition of the same thing) methods of functioning, the more one realizes that they are doddering and lacking experimentation, over-cautious, inefficient, unenterprising and far too restricted by the number of hands between the job and the person capable of making decisions...Well that, Norah, has been a long digression...I love you Norah, all the world, and send all my love to you. Love too to Waide and Cynthia.

Fred

~

May 26

Fred dearest:

...Monday night I persuaded Dad to go up to Lorna and Fred Elliott's with me. Lorna and I had jointly arranged a discussion group...Jack Stevenson and his wife, both grads from Varsity and Jack is very much interested in the C.C.F., Peggy and Peter who belong to no party but who are very well-informed on many subjects, Lorna's father who is a lecturer and a great admirer of Russia, Grace Pollock who is interested in C.C.F. as am I but who is sceptical. Well, we had a great evening. We started out with C.C.F. and branched off to Russia, China, labour problems in England, Europe (pre-war of course) and C.I.O. and unions in general, religion, the teaching of religious knowledge in schools, Quebec, private ownership versus public ownership, e.g. CPR and CNR and the history of the Canadian National Railway, etc. etc. We ended up at 1 a.m...

Since meat-rationing commences tomorrow, May 27, I bought a lovely roast of beef. Mary, who lives around the corner and up the street a wee way, said I might roast it in her oven, which I did...

Darling, the only reason I said I felt this coming year would be our toughest year was because I felt it would be a year of great anxiety if the allies invade. It is only natural that I will worry over you when the invasion begins. No matter how confident I am that you will come back, and I am confident, there will always be a very real fear in my heart until I can once again hold you in my arms. Understand?

I wasn't worried over Bobbie Ellis. I know she must be a very good head for you to admire her...

Another thing I meant to mention was the fact Waide weighs forty-seven pounds and Miss Cynthia forty. She is absolutely huge and has a bigger head and face than Waide. Waide is more the image of you every day and is very sweet like you are. Cynthia is adorable, of course, but I feel she is so independent and has so much confidence even at twenty-one months, I won't ever feel she is quite so close to me. But believe me you will adore her and be as proud as punch of her...

Affectionately,
Norah

~

May 30
Dearest Norah:
...It is apparent mail at both ends has been delayed and tangled. We both must realize the situation and take it for what it is. In between times the no news is good news adage must be our guide...In the coming year there may be times I will be unable to write as often as I have, but it's unlikely that there'll be many periods like that, so sweet, chin up and bear with it...

I'm doing work now with the 4.2-inch mortar. It is a valuable weapon and the handling and management of it is very interesting...Packs quite a wallop, I can tell you. Fires a mile or two with ease, so you see I'm practically an artilleryman!...

Your last letter showed the concern you felt over the possible consequences of me being in a scrap, and you suggested I write a wee note to you and to Waide and to Cynthia. I understand how you feel, darling, but I could not do that. I'm as certain as anything that nothing will ever happen to me and I certainly have no expectation of death.

What I think and believe in, I think you know, if not for a word-by-word description, at least as a general picture. I do not think I could clarify it...Like yourself I find myself quite confused in regard to most of the problems and I suppose we will continue to be so during the duration of our lives.

Probably it was much easier in our grandparents' days to live when rules of life were quite standard. We have liberty of thought and action today, but has it been a real benefit to our enjoyment of living? Perhaps being dogmatic would be less trying...

I suppose we are lucky to have to be separated for the times certainly create nerves etc. that cause estrangements, but I do not think you and I would be much different than before the war. You will remember the jittery days we spent grabbing up the news and how the outbreak of war was actually a relief. We didn't fly at each other's throats then, so I don't suppose we would now.

I am intensely proud of how well you have managed each problem and especially how well you have done in bringing up the children. It is much the heaviest load that you carry, and I'm truly sorry that I cannot help you...

At the moment I should not like to come home. I want to see the beginning of action and have some experience of active service, for I would not like to just come home for a month or six weeks and then be off again...

After suffering a separation of two years, I would not be content and I do not think you would, if I were withdrawn to service in Canada...Possibly Germany will be defeated within a year. That's the first goal.

If I should die in the accomplishment of that, I know you'd be left a long, bitter struggle. I've tried to leave you as well off materially as possible, though I know the inflation threat is very dangerous to your security. Still, we can't plan beyond what we have...

I'll mail this off to you tomorrow and hope it reaches you real soon so as to make you happy for another week - it isn't much for a week's satisfaction, is it dear?...

Fred

~

June 1

Dearest Fred:

...With no help now and house-cleaning in full swing, I seem too tired to sit down and write for three or four solid hours. I'm sure you are very busy too these days...

Tonight it was eight before I finished the dishes and nine before I got the cherubs to bed. I am still cooking with a two-plate electric, and such a nuisance it is. On Monday I put on a furnace fire to heat enough water to wash, and by five at night I was still washing, having had to change the water and wait again for the furnace to heat me more water...

It seems years ago, and yet it is two years ago the 12th of this month since we said good-bye...

In case you feel a little irritated with me for spending...here are a few expenses I met: $50 debt on my last summer cottage venture; $60 for my tonsillectomy and hospital bill...$35 for your watch; Christmas time with its extras and admittedly a little splurging such as sherry and roses for my table etc. took $30...I know you don't begrudge it to us, but only naturally would want to know...

Last week was fairly quiet. On Saturday night, Pat and I and Capt. Findley went over to Mary and Murrays and Art Marron and his wife were there...This Friday night Dick Sutherland is taking me to the nurses' graduation dance at the golf club...

It's no fun really without you. I do feel surely by this time next year I will have you home. Everyone is very jittery and on edge, running to the radio and expecting every morning to hear the allies have invaded. It is very hard on the nerves. Everyone talks about it every place I go, and people make speeches on the terrible aftermath until I could scream...

All my fondest and complete love, sweetheart...

Norah

~

June 3

Fred darling:

I wrote you the day before yesterday and such a lot seems to have transpired since then...This morning I got a letter from Bobbie Ellis. She intimated you were on your way, and perhaps bound for North Africa. Naturally I was very startled...So - are you tonight in the Mediterranean or perhaps in North Africa or not? Bobbie said you had hopes of contacting her husband out there and I remember you saying he was in Africa. It is a strange world. All morning I felt stunned. I went over town with the children and seemed to be in a daze.

But this afternoon while I was ironing from three till five, I commenced to think. It shocked me because I never somehow thought of you going to Africa. But then I realize you will see just that much more of the world and have that many more experiences. So I'm behind you, or before you, whichever way it is, wherever you go my dearest Fred...Did you ask Bobbie to write me and tip me off? It was a very nice letter and I intend to answer it real soon. She said she hoped I would write and she would be glad to do anything at any time for me if need be. She spoke of you as my very dear husband, which was sweet...

There are about a thousand troops here waiting to go overseas and every day a group of two hundred or more goes by our corner on a route march and Waide gets out in the middle of the road and marches behind them. We are to have a blackout on Monday June 7, and Waide came in today and told me we must shut out all the lights because the Germans were coming to bomb us. I had quite a time to convince him it was only a practice blackout and that we were not going to be bombed really...

Darling, you know my thoughts are with you constantly, don't

you? For me you are the most important reason for me living, and I love you and admire you more and more every day. Someday soon we will be united.
Good-bye now,
Norah

~

June 12
Dearest Norah:
Hello sweetheart, do you remember what today is? Second anniversary of our leave-taking. Not a day to be celebrated exactly, is it? Still, I always think that as the time goes by, the day of our reunion comes nearer, and so mark off the anniversaries with pleasure...

We moved since I last wrote and have remained busy. There has been lots of interesting things to do and I'd like very much to keep a diary of them all by writing them down in this letter, but then I am not allowed to say much of that sort of thing, as you know...

You know, Norah, that I understand quite well how easy it is to spend and I wasn't irritated...You brought the matter up in one of your letters, so I am just assuring you that I wasn't surprised that you needed it. Money goes quickly, what? You listed your expenditures and I must say your spending was more rational than my own...Cynthia must be quite a lass from your description - 40 pounds! She'll be a full-rigger for sure! I can't but laugh at her independence and single-mindedness - reminds me of a girl I know...

By the way, Norah, one thing I would like you to soft-pedal. That is what you think of me. Now first off, I'm quite sure you are blowing me up too big. You are bound, you know, to be a bit on the ideal side when I'm not close enough for you to see my faults close up. I don't want to come home and find your friends think I'm something entirely different than I am. Hell, they have to like me, not something I might have been.

That goes doubly for the children. I'm happy that they have a good opinion of me, but I do want to be me. You know, it has really worried me a great deal and on those black days when the world seems pretty grim and you think yourself one of the lowest forms of humanity, I've sometimes thought it would be better not to come home and spoil the imaginative picture that the children may have formed of me. Now darling, understand that's not normal, but please don't put me into a picture frame. Let me be as bad as I am, and just as good and no more as I am...

Glad we straightened out that question of a tough year coming up. Every letter that you mentioned it sort of confused me, for I couldn't see what you were driving at. Since it's only the alleged coming invasion risks, I'd stop your worrying. Perhaps it will come, perhaps not, in any event it's best to let the events shape up on their own without anticipating too much...

Good night and sweet dreams,

Fred

~

July 9, Leith

My dearest Fred:

...We moved down yesterday and are pretty well settled tonight...I'm feeling better today after a good sleep. I don't feel like seeing anyone or going anyplace. I've felt like that now for three or four weeks. So if anyone calls on me it will be fine, but I don't feel ambitious enough to invite anyone down. I'll probably pep up, but I'm happy at present.

I feel now you may be home in a year and that instead of forcing myself to go a lot and be gay etc., I can be a bit of a recluse and I won't grow stodgy before you return. I simply can't force myself any longer to be gay when I'm not...

Ever since yesterday morning when it was announced Sicily had been invaded by Canadians, British and Americans, I've been concerned as to where you are, dear. Then today it was announced thousands of Canadians had been landed in Africa. It is a desperate feeling dear, wondering, wondering and still trying to be one's usual self and gay with the children. I've been somewhat dazed ever since yesterday...

Waide has been a bit out of hand the last day or so. He is so determined at times, and if I'm strict, very strict all the time, he's perfect but if I relax, he is out of hand and sometimes I get so tired and feel like an old shrew. Cynthia is at the stage she squeals for everything. I am having my times with her - cute as a bug but a tartar. It is no easy job raising a family with a pappy away...

You know more than ever dear, my thoughts are with you. I'm really very optimistic. Somehow I feel you will be home to me and not so very long, dear. It is hard not to cry, though. I love you so and want only you. I'm really so very lonely and fearful...

Good night, Fred dear.

Norah

~

July 11

Dearest Norah:

We are reading the paper avidly and listening to the radio for fuller news of the Sicilian landings. Good news, isn't it? Into it at long last...Naturally we all knew something of what was going on, though no more than the next when or where, but even what meagre knowledge we had couldn't be written home...

Have little or no personal news. Was over to another unit's mess last night to a dance they had. Didn't dance, but helped hold up the bar a bit and felt like a steam roller had hit me when I wakened this morning. In off hours have been reading much about post-war planning - not that I think we're close to that stage - but simply that it's the only constructive thing going these days and as such is stimulating and at the same time restful...I suggest you read on those lines rather than war books...

I'll bet a plugged dime you're a bit bewildered, especially in view of Bobbie's letter, which was true and yet as you will know not quite true. See?

All my love dearest, and a hug and kiss for each of the bairns.

Fred

~

July 14

Fred dearest:

...I will be interested to hear the right of it someday regarding the letter Bobbie sent to me. Evidently you have my letter telling you I suspected you were either on your way or slated to leave soon for Africa. Tell me by answering yes or no was I right. Just put "Bobbie's letter - yes" (if you were to go but didn't) or no (if the contrary)...

Every morning about 10:30, Waide and Cynthia and I start out in our bathing suits and go down to the sandy beach on the other side of the bridge. We all have acquired a nice tan already. Waide looks like a young god...He runs through the water and is the picture of health and happiness. Cynthia looks sweet too, with her sun-suit on and her lovely curls sticking out under her sun-bonnet. She plays in the sand and likes to dabble her toes in the water. I think you would be very proud of us if you could peep at us...

Friday afternoon we went swimming...I swam across the river and back, and when I neared the shore Waide ran in to meet me and fell into the deep water and of course it frightened him. He is now quite timid and doesn't want to come out with me. I don't feel I'm a strong enough swimmer anyway to teach him, and I'm so hoping you'll be home next summer and can teach him...

Saturday morning Waide and I went to town with Mary and Murray. I had so much shopping to do. I bought black currants, forty cents a box, and red currants and last night down here I made jelly. We were all owed sixty pounds of sugar for preserving. So I can preserve until that is done. Food is really scarce and expensive. Eggs were forty-eight cents on the market and I had to stand in line twenty minutes to get even two dozen at Walkers, where I buy my fruit and vegetables. It was a jam. It took me thirty-five minutes there to get what I wanted.

My butcher had saved me some bacon. Meat is so scarce that he is going to close up for two weeks and take a much-earned and needed holiday...

I do feel somehow you will be home before many months. I so hope so. I'm feeling better, dear, and not so down...
Norah

~

July 23
Dearest Norah:
...Regarding Bobbie, the answer is yes. I believe now that it will be in the latter part of August, but then it is so hard to tell about those things and I've not been told...

Dearest Norah, I would so much like to be home with you and the bairns. It seems such a long time since we played and loved. At times I find welling up in me a deep resentment at being so separated these two of our best years, at others I just feel helpless. Helpless that is to get near to you. Feel then like a straw aimlessly shifted by a strong and relentless force...
All my love, sweetheart,
Fred

~

Aug. 9
My dearest Fred:
...I've been writing blue airmail letters for some time now, in the hopes they will be faster. This is the first long letter I've written for three weeks.

Your father is to be married, in fact will be by now - high noon today...I feel rather queer about the whole affair. If I stop to think of Mom and how sweet and gracious she was and unselfish etc., I feel sorry about the whole thing...Howsomever, I plan to be friendly and give them as nice a time as I can while they are here. Which doesn't mean we will ever forget Mom, who was so inherently good and wise...

Major Rainer has just left, having dropped in for ten minutes to say good-bye. The whole staff leaves...tonight. I appreciated Vert's visit. I purposely haven't been going to the mess of late because I decided it was a waste of time and energy and a foolish way to spend Saturday night and Sunday afternoon. Today Vert was very sweet. He said he felt I had made a wise decision and one that more girls should make. He said he would always remember my kindness and lovely face and sweet children.

I'm telling you this dear, because many times of late when I'm lonesome and nothing to do and I know the others, some not all, are up at the mess having fun and I know I have been invited and could have fun, did have the few times I went and was popular too, if I do say so; I feel after all it is a right decision...It doesn't relieve my loneliness and it takes me away from Waide and Cynthia...

It is ten days since I had a letter. I'm of course wondering if you are still in England...The next of kin of casualties have recently been informed re Sicily, but no lists in the papers. Oh gosh darling, in spite of your optimism and mine, I worry myself sick over you sometimes. I truly feel I would simply die of a broken heart if I lost you, dear...

Norah

~

Aug. 19

My dearest Fred:

...Your father and Evelyn were here from Saturday morning until yesterday (Wednesday) afternoon. So you can imagine how busy I was. Evelyn is a very nice person and you would be pleased to see your father so happy and attentive. He couldn't, in my opinion, have found a nicer second wife. She isn't a bit like your mom, consequently there is no cause for us to compare the two...

I felt like the old lady married for a thousand years because they were so gay and happy and loveable and I seemed so out of it. But I tried hard and I know I succeeded in giving them a grand time. And they just raved about the children, how obedient and well-mannered they were and how beautiful Cynthia was...

I have had no mail for nearly three weeks. I'm naturally wondering why and where you are etc...The other day I let my imagination run away with me and I really was crying and laughing with joy at the thought of having you home again...

Take care of yourself, sweet, and all my love and kisses and hugs.

Norah

~

Aug. 23

Dearest Norah:

...While I arrived here last night I was officially taken on strength as of this morning. Consequently it is rather surprising that I am leaving again tomorrow morning. It is for a course, duration approximately one month, and is on mortars...

What I'm so aggravated about is that by all the twisting and turning I missed that Mediterranean cruise. Damned if I'll forgive them!...

Outside the above matter, I've spent a pleasant summer. Could not say where I was nor much of what was going on...

Incidentally have seen absolutely nothing of the fairer sex this summer, except of course for casting appreciating looks at them from a distance and the odd time I had to drag myself onto the dance floor or let someone sit as wallflower all evening. It has been singularly a stag summer, which I suppose is a good thing. Afraid my outlook towards the women is pretty cynical. It would be for sure if I had not your perfection to bear in mind. Your amorous letters the past two months were more than a pleasure. They kept me going when I hit one of the lowest and most prolonged ebbs I have ever experienced.

I did wonder if it was to be permanent. Since said no, but I'd never known week after week of it like that. It's not all gone by, but the worst, I think. It wasn't natural but largely generated by deep disappointment.

From planning to leave London I had directed every change I made insofar as was possible toward getting in on this summer's show...Damn it, I'd not have budged at all if I hadn't thought that one way or another I could get into it...

Will close now for tonight, Norah, hope my rambling doesn't put you to sleep before you get this good night...

Fred

~

Sept. 3

My dearest Fred:

Well there was news today, wasn't there, with the announcement that the Canadians and the 8th Army had invaded Italy. I was eating my breakfast when the news came on. It was a queer sensation, dear, to say the least. Of course for all I know there may have been another hitch and you may still be in England...

Maybe you think I am a bit cracked to imagine you in Sicily and maybe in Italy, but what would you think if first you get a letter telling me in so many words in reply to my letter, "Yes, the latter part of August". Then I get a cable with a new address and no regiment on it, so I conclude you're off, then a few nights ago it is announced that the Saskatchewan Light Infantry is in Sicily…

It was very warm yesterday. It passed uneventfully. In the afternoon, Waide and Cynthia and Dad and I went swimming. It was dull but warm, and the water was grand. Waide will now come out right up to his neck and while I hold him, try to do the dog paddle. This winter the pool at the Y is to be all done over and they are to have an instructor. I think I will take him over and give him four or five lessons. It is said a child his age can learn in four lessons.

I believe in learning in the beginning how to do things properly. I never seemed to accomplish that. Of course you don't agree with me on that point, do you? If I remember correctly, you maintained one should swim, for example, for the pleasure it gives one, not to excel. And there are arguments pro and con. I maintain if one learns how to swim or golf or play tennis properly, one can enjoy them more.

These one-sided arguments aren't much fun. I miss you in so many ways, but probably one of the ways I miss you most is our discussions and arguments. I'm afraid many a time you wished yourself far away from my babble, but I so enjoyed it…

My fondest love dear, as always.

Norah

~

Sept. 9

Dearest Norah:

…It was yesterday morning that my batman reported that the morning news radio 8 a.m. had announced Italy's capitulation. Everyone knew the news was good, but it was surprising how little comment was made…At night Kit and I and some four or more others went some four or five miles to a local pub; not a single word or comment did I hear all evening!

And so the news was received. I expect there are many who won't know it yet, if the reticence here displayed is general…

Time now to pile into bed and slumber, need it too, for we had a long day all in the open and I have that blown feeling. How are the bairns tonight? All my love to you and to them.

Fred

131

~

Sept. 11

My dearest Fred:

...We enjoyed the summer so very much dear, and it has been devoted almost entirely to the children. I really dread going back...I of course would love my own apartment, but I really can't see how I could do it...I made ten quarts of chili sauce today, Sunday and all, which took me all day - I had some job trying to sterilize jars first and then cook the chili sauce on a two-burner electric...Tomorrow I'm going to make two baskets of apples into jelly, Tuesday I'm packing, and Wednesday Mrs. Morrow, my cleaning woman, will be down and we will clean the cottage and move up to town after supper or just before, whenever the truck can come...

I understand how you feel about missing out on Sicily, dear. There is not much I can say, it is over and done with now and I was in the dark about everything so could not cheer you when you were so depressed...Never mind dear, maybe you'll get out there yet, or some place equally as exciting and interesting. From a purely selfish viewpoint, I wish you would never get any place, but that is silly and almost cowardly. If I were you, I would want the same as you...

Noticed you said you have seen little of the fair sex. Now darling, you mustn't become cynical about women and don't you go putting me on a pedestal or I'll fall off for sure when you come home and you'll be disappointed...

Darling, it will soon be our seventh wedding anniversary, and on the sixth of October Cynthia's second birthday. This will be our third anniversary apart. Do you realize out of seven years of marriage we have only lived together under the same roof for two-and-a-half years? I hope for every two-and-a-half years together we don't have two children or we will be swamped...

I feel there are going to be many many unhappy homes after this war. Not every girl will be just bursting with joy to welcome her husband home, nor will every man be eager to get back. And of course once couples are together again, most of us will have to relinquish some independence and freedom. Now I'm independent and make decisions for myself and have full authority over the children etc. You have your freedom, can come and go at will etc. It may be a little hard to readjust; it would be harder if we had not the children...

If possible I'll always be a homemaker, dear. And yet when you read about the Russian women who are not only homemakers but captains on ships and meteorologists, scientists etc. etc., one wonders if Russia has not a lot to thank the women for - maybe we should be able to do more than make a home and bear children...This isn't a very loving letter, dear - much too impersonal, but it is just that I feel depressed and can't seem to get into the swing of it...

Love and kisses and hugs galore,

Norah

~

Sept. 27

Fred dearest:

...I wonder sometimes whether the summer is worth all the hard work one has to do when you move up and get settled. With the exception of Mrs. Morrow helping me for one day and a half, I've house-cleaned every room, cupboard and drawer, even the fruit shelves and made twelve jars of grape jam and eight pints of pears since I wrote last, and today I washed from 9 a.m. until an hour ago, 8 p.m., four weeks' washing. Of course I had several interruptions and meals to get in there too.

Frankly I am so g.d. disgusted with everything and everyone right now, I could boot even you. No, I couldn't really, sweet...Guess what - I have gained twelve pounds during the summer and I look a scream in my skirts minus a jacket with my tummy and fanny sticking out...I feel as well and better than I've felt for eight or nine years. And sleep - just like a top or log or something.

After so long a time not being able to sleep, it is marvelous. It is a combination of many things, really. It is really just the last few months that I've got adjusted to you being away. For so long I fretted, fought it, tried to overcome my loneliness in various ways, but I'm all right now and I'm nearer to you and you feel nearer to me than ever before.

Please understand dear that I've always loved you terribly, but now because of these awful two years I love you more than ever. It takes a powerful lot of love to carry on and stick sometimes, and I have great sympathy for couples who blunder because maybe they haven't the love to fortify them. And by "blunder" I don't mean only or necessarily the sexual angle at all. There are so many problems and situations to meet...

Fred, you and I are so lucky, even though we are separated. I have said before and I'll say it again. You are missing a lot of fun with the bairns, but you are also missing a lot of confusion etc. which in wartime is hard on the nerves. I have all my time to devote to them and they need it. When you get home I'll have them trained, I hope, so that I can devote some time to you.

But dearest, you must prepare yourself for this: no matter how much we will want to be always together just you and I, it will never be quite that way again. We won't even be able to talk as freely, for Waide's ears are long and I think Cynthia's are going to be even longer...

She has started to talk in sentences now. She can butter her own bread and even tries to cut her meat. She is very progressive and aggressive...Tomorrow I'm taking them to the fall fair. Waide is greatly excited and I'm sure Cynthia will love it too...It is now 11:45 and I must tumble in. I've had a lovely evening talking to you...
Norah

~

Oct. 8
Dearest Norah:
I received today your letter of Sept. 28. Not bad delivery for long air mail. You sounded as though you wanted to send a rather tarty letter - said you were disgusted with everything and everyone - still you didn't hold your mood, for your letter was sweet and on the up. You have been working hard!...

You were talking of how much better you are feeling, and of how in the past while you've had some relief from the struggle of adjusting to being separated. Confess darling, I've never truly adjusted and have grown somewhat bitter as a result. Find myself on edge, unable to settle down to a contented, purposeful and consistent life. Get so damn mad at myself...

From Thursday last to Monday I was umpire on a scheme, then got forty-eight hours' leave which I spent by visiting London for the first time in months. Getting to be a worse spot than ever. Prices are so high that you tip-toe down the street for fear that to step out will cost you another quid. Got some odds and ends I wanted - a sleep with an honest-to-god mattress (- no, not mistress!), a rather hefty binge and so home...

Am going on another scheme starting tomorrow. Promises to be a strenuous one and I look forward without enthusiasm to a week in the open with rather chill conditions. Umpire again. At least that means I ride...Will likely be unable to write till the scheme is over, and after that may sleep a couple of days if previous experience is a guide.
All my love, Norah darling. Give a big hug and kiss to the bairns.

Fred

~

Oct. 15

Dearest Norah:

...The children must be developing rapidly. I can detect major changes in Waide...Is his sense of "being bad" a bit intense? I mean, is he so anxious to be the good boy and not displease his mom and dad that he isn't being bad? Naturally he can't have his way about every little thing he wants to do, but I should not like to hear of him thinking before he does a thing, "Is this good, is it bad?"...

I'm thinking of the rules etc. as methods and items by which he must canalise his activities and within which he must guide his thoughts. It is somewhat amusing to sit and think just why one has to learn to curb one's natural desires and to fetter one's energies. It takes you down to the fundamentals of gregarious living.

When we say "right and wrong", don't we mean this is how you must act to live with other people; this is how you must conduct your activities if you are to earn your living among other people; this you must avoid if you are to preserve your life, your health and your happiness.

Today it's more important to know the way in which a thing may be done than what may be done, for what may be done is beyond any man's imaginings, but how is his everyday problem.

I laugh when I think that I am somewhat convinced that method is the thing to know rather than the end...Never in my life have I looked at the way to do a thing, but just what do I want to do, and then did it. An original red-tape cutter. I suppose the smart person learns how to do it all through the right channnels. Not me, and for myself I doubt I'll learn now...

Quite some time ago, one of your letters said, "I had to stand in line nearly twenty minutes to get just two dozen eggs." Nearly every time the question of queueing comes up, I repeat it as a story and never fail to get a hearty laugh.

I've often seen yards of a queue standing a couple of hours just to get a bus. Waiting for service is an expected call on one's time...The two-dozen part also amazes, you'd need to have about twenty children under five to get all those eggs at once...

Your letter of Sept. 2 started off under the impression I was likely in the Mediterranean. I'm sorry about that. I made the mistake of hinting where I was or might be, but must only have confused you. Certainly I didn't know much myself and as things turned out as they have, could not have but misled you.

It's a mistake to have made any hints and I wouldn't do it again, for it all worried me more or as much as you, and then my well-founded expectations did not materialize...

All my love, dearest,

Fred

~

Oct. 21

My dearest Fred:

...I've been successful in getting a good reliable girl of 30 to stay with Waide and Cynthia while I go away for a few days. I hope you will understand dear, and not feel I am pampering myself. I'm not going to London because that is just as bad as being at home...I think I will go down to Toronto...

Waide and Cynthia are fine. Cynthia is the life of the house. She has your bombastic ways and is so cute and full of fun. Waide is running around with a false face on already...

It is a relief in some ways to reread your letter and hear you say you find yourself on edge sometimes and "unable to settle down to a contented and purposeful life", because I get so provoked at myself too for the same reason and often think it is a weakness on my part alone. I've done more cursing inwardly and more grumbling etc. than I've ever done before in my life...Have you had a photo taken? If so, send one please...

Love and kisses,

Norah

~

Oct. 22

Dearest Norah:

Had some mail today...Your letters dealt principally with Dad and Evelyn's visit...It is apparent that you found Evelyn good company and I judge you like her. I am glad it is so. I have wished Dad happiness and I mean it. I hope to like Evelyn but feel it will be very difficult, particularly difficult to act normally towards her at any gathering of the family or indeed in her and Dad's home where she would correctly be "hostess".

You need not think I've set up a flinty hostility towards her, for I have not and will try to make things easy for herself and Dad when we are together...

Two weeks ago I won about sixteen or seventeen pounds playing poker, but have given most of that back now, which is how it goes.

Find myself very nonchalant about money, i.e. it seems to have lost any value. I, having as a youngster been quite a saver, find my present attitude somewhat surprising…

I do love your letters dearest, they bring so much cheerful news and are my only link to what I most want and desire, home with you and the bairns. I sometimes wonder whether we'll woo as we did before, especially just before, or will we be too mature or too shy etc? You seldom have said, what say you now? In fact you've never said how you like to be loved, have you?

All my love, dearest,

Fred

~

Nov. 2

My dearest Fred:

…Jean Childs was just in and we are all set to go down to Toronto a week from tomorrow and back the next day. Mary Wilkinson and Kay Hueston are going too, and we are going to see Blossom Time at the Alex in the afternoon and invite a few of our friends down to our hotel room on Wednesday night and have a little fun…

Fred, I'm so tickled to go because it does brighten my days. With you away, there is so little that interests me - you know what it is like. I do enjoy Waide and Cynthia, of course…You will be amazed and pleased when you see how smart they both are…

While Dad is away I have the furnace to look after. We are burning wood, coal being so scarce and rationed (practically). It has been mild and we are very cosy…Lots of people have no wood or coal, and tonight new coal restrictions were announced due to eight thousand coal miners on strike in Alberta - no settlement is in view yet…

Sometimes I wonder how things will be when you return - things are so different and so changed. When you left, you and I seemed so young and inexperienced and immature and carefree - when you return, you will be more mature. You're bound to be, I am. I actually feel old sometimes. Isn't that silly, dear?

You will have two more or less grown children instead of a baby boy. But I'm sure we will work out any adjustments necessary, and we will be so happy, won't we?…Do you ever wonder what I look like or wonder what my voice is like? Sometimes I can't remember your smile, for instance, and yet most times I can see it as plainly as if I had seen you yesterday.

Tomorrow night I'm going to the hotel for dinner - the hospital aid executive are having a dinner meeting. I didn't know I was on the executive, but apparently I'm on the ways and means committee and the Christmas dance committee...

Tell me dear, have you been writing as often? The only reason I ask is that if you have been, then I'm missing a great deal of mail; if you haven't been, then I won't worry about it or be wondering...

I wish you had time to sit and write me a gabby sort of letter. It's ages since you have, and I think the last one went down because I never received a long boat one you mentioned in August...

Well dearest, this letter is no "wow", but it is more cheerful than most of late. It was a down period for me for a while, and I should hide my depression from you, I know...

Affectionately,

Norah

~

Nov. 8

Dearest Norah:

I have been away on another scheme. When I arrived back Saturday your blue sheet was here dated Oct. 21, also the four photos you sent separately by boat. The pictures were grand...What grown children we have, dear! Cynthia reminds me a lot of you. I think she looks like you in many ways. Why you have said she's like me I can't fathom, for she certainly is your image...

Plan to go to London a day or two, principally to see Bobbie from whom I had a letter a week back saying she had scads of news for me and was bubbling over to tell it...Plan then to visit about for a bit and to go to the south coast on a hospitality ticket - like when I went to Aberdeen...

I have received three enlarged snaps of myself which are destined one for you, one for Don and one for Dad. In a way a Christmas present, but remember they are only enlarged from a snap and I don't like it myself...

You did say something of Waide going to school this year, but do not suppose you meant it. He's too young, I think, and can learn more at home unless he's under your feet. I intend writing him a Christmas note. I expect it is time I addressed him a letter now and then. Do you think so?...

Amuse myself day-dreaming about what we will do and have and work at after the war. Have already created a law firm, a trust company, a Muskoka camp, a farm, a bush and a couple of small subsidiary businesses. So far they are all flourishing, wonder what will in fact?

What do you think of a return to Toronto? If it meant living out; if it meant living in the city? How about the small town?...

Do you realize that it is now just about two-and-a-half years since I left? Too damn long. I am dying to get home to you and to love you up and argue you down until you're sick of seeing me about. How long will it take, I wonder, for you to think, "I wish he'd get out from under my feet", or "When's the old man going to take a week's holiday and leave me to myself"...

Big hug and kiss and all my love.

Fred

~

Nov. 15

My dearest Fred:

...Waide has the measles but a very light attack. He broke out last Wednesday and by Thursday night the spots were gone. However, I have to keep him in bed until this Thursday and in the house for a week after that. Cynthia got measle serum today...

I went to Toronto via Hamilton on Wednesday last with Jean and Kay Hueston and Jean Harris...We went to Toronto and got to the Royal Alex at 2:20 and the curtain went up at 2:30. I hadn't seen Blossom Time since I was ten, so I thoroughly enjoyed it. I had forgotten it was so funny in parts.

After the show Jean and I met Kay Hueston and her sister in the Royal York tavern and had one beer and the tavern closed - no beer...However, we went to the Park Plaza and had three more...Finally the Park Plaza closed too, and I got my dinner...

Somehow one feels when one does get away, one should break loose and have fun, but when you get there you're not interested in having fun, in fact I wanted to get home as fast as possible. Silly old me dear, but seeing so many men in uniform made me twice as lonesome for you...

There are a new bunch of officers here and I was invited to the mess last night but did not go purely and simply because I had no interest in going - don't think I'm making a martyr out of myself dear, or shutting myself away from temptation. I'm not. I'm just not interested, so why go?...

I'm certain being a sensible, considerate and co-operating husband you will agree, a large family is fine and a great joy if the mother has help or, if the bank account won't finance help, then if Dad will occasionally help bathe the bairns or amuse them and say their prayers or read to them while Mama does the dishes, in order that both Mama and Papa can sit down and relax together.

That is the one thing that worries me most, Fred. I simply won't be able to spend as much time with you in the evenings as we will both want unless you do help me, and you didn't like to do dishes before, now did you? And in spite of the fact you love Waide and Cynthia, will you want to bathe them some nights and read to them or take them for walks? They take a lot of one's time dear, you will find out...

You're probably laughing at me by now, or provoked because maybe you feel I'm not treating you as a mature dad, but darling, how can you be expected to be all at once when you've seen so little of your bairns?...

I suppose I should wish you a merry Christmas in one of these letters, since by the time it reaches you, Christmas will be around the corner. I think I will blow a fuse if you're not home by next Christmas. For Waide's sake especially, I must make this Christmas a happy affair...

I don't think Waide is too conscious of right or wrong. I'm glad he is as conscious as he is...I disagree with you in that I believe one should consider, "Is this right or wrong for me," before doing a thing...

I think one must discipline oneself in all things. A person is like a machine almost. It is most effective for its own good and the common good if controlled. But you know me, I like to plan everything and have a plan. I like to see a well-organized piece of work or play which signifies an organized mind...

If I make a mess of training the children and you aren't happy about them, it won't be because I haven't tried dear, will it? I have many faults, but I believe I'm dependable and work most of the time as hard as I can at whatever I'm doing, which is something...

I must close and toddle off to bed. It is 12:30 and I'm so tired. Good night dearest.

Norah

~

Nov. 24

My dearest Norah:

It is a shameless hour of the night to be starting a letter to you, but I just felt I had to say a few words to you before going off to bed. They ought to be lovey-dovey words really, for that's the way I feel and I want most just to say again I love you...

I found a pack of mail waiting me, largely mail that was posted in July and August that has finally reached me...Received too the parcel you sent containing shirt and the photos. They are grand, dear. All of you look so very beautiful, and they make me want to be with you...I've been thinking of you all day...

Went to London Friday afternoon and returned Sunday morning, had some fun though not much, the usual round of pubs etc. Saw a show and had some good meals and that's all. Didn't see Bobbie as I had intended, seems she was on a week's camp duty...

When you say that at times you feel old, I cannot but grin - but I know what you mean and I agree we are bound to be more mature when we are again together. Not so mature, I trust, that we'll never be silly or too staid to forget all for a few moments of bliss. It's a hell of a long time, is it not, two-and-a-half years now! Got a lot of time to make up. Can you stand crowding four or five into two or three, overtime on the night shift?...

You girls! The hospital aid committee meets at the hotel for a dinner meeting - what a glorious aid to conviviality are these committees...

I feel now that I shall never see more action than I am, and have finally accepted it and concluded, "well, hell". I'm not at all happy about prospects, but just sit and let it slide...

Saturday and Sunday I will have to take a mortar range firing practice. Have been busy organizing it. Will be away. Plan to spend the night on the grounds we used this spring for the Lorne Scot concentration. Should be an interesting outing.

In the meantime, have to train enough men to fire the damn things, and tonight have to lecture eight or more officers on the elementary lessons of observation post duties, ranging etc...

Closing time, dearest. Hope you're happy when you get this. All my love as usual, and an extra special little bit to boot.
Fred

~

Nov. 26
My dearest Fred:
...Eleanor is home and leaves in the morning for her new posting - the RCAF station which is a convalescent hospital out Bayview...She is simply thrilled. She will be driving the ambulance and station wagons again, having been in charge of equipment at Borden...

One thing I notice, everyone seems overworked, tired, on edge, and confused or frustrated - especially the women who have had the full burden of the children since their husbands have been away.

I won't go into it, because I'm definitely "down" all the time any more, and it doesn't make happy reading...

I made arrangements to have Waide have his first swimming lesson on Monday. He's so thrilled, and I do hope he is not nervous and is as keen for his second lesson...

I'm reading a very interesting book, Father Abraham by Professor Hardy, head of the classics department at the University of Alberta. It is really a book. You would be amused at me. There were parts of it made me feel so desirous for you and amorous that I had a hard time to get to sleep, and then there were parts that made me so cynical about men I almost hated you dear, because you are a man. It is a book which, if you were home and we both read it, we could discuss and discuss...It's the devil not being able to talk to you, dear...

Norah

~

Dec. 3

My dearest Fred:

...Today I got your picture - I was so excited, for it is two years since I got those two snaps of you when you first went over...You look older and your face looks set. To be honest dear, I had a good cry over it, because knowing you and your disposition, I feel you have suffered a lot more than you've told me in regards loneliness and mental conflicts etc., and it shows in your face.

And yet as I studied it, and I did all day, your former boyish vivacity, shall I say, has been replaced with something else very fine - you're more mature and look every bit the man.

What did you think of my pictures? I've changed too, and maybe you felt just a little sad to see an older girl, did you? We can't grow younger, and I would love you as much if you looked ten years older. It is just that it is hard to believe we aren't children any more, or even young carefree people.

Waide was terribly thrilled with it, and Cynthia kept saying, "My daddy, Mom"...

Fred, I'm so tired. Seems I'm always complaining, but not only work tires but loneliness and the humdrumness of everyday living, which if you were home wouldn't seem humdrum...

I was to two teas this afternoon...There has been nothing doing in the social way for ages, so it was sort of fun...

Love,
Norah

~

Dec. 8

Dearest Norah:

...Sunday afternoon I went to the Queen's with the intention of having tea - believe it. Happened to sit beside a lady who turned out to be Lady Beecham, wife of the orchestra bloke by that name, on tour in the States. Asked me to her home at Oxford. Must be some place, since she claimed some four hundred had a Christmas party there last year...

Introduced me to her son, who arrived late. She claims he's a more talented musician than her husband, and if conventional mind-image of musicians is a guide, he's better than many...She herself was a sharp-featured, plumping woman, dully dressed...

For all the above, I enjoyed myself quite handsomely, had a good chat and a pleasant time. I confess I hadn't the haziest what or who Beecham was in music, so had to do the diplomatic dodge...

Got that one-sheet airmail from you in which you expressed your confusion as to whether you hated the male sex, and me as one, or loved me for being of the male sex. I had a good snorting laugh considering your probable expressions of face and tongue had I gotten the blast direct!...

You said you think we were maturing in the art of making love. Believe me, I'm anxious to make some before the maturing goes too far...You seem to expect it will be hard to "domesticate" me. Nothing is more unlikely. What is going to be hard for me is to find my niche. I never found it before the war, nor has any experience I've had indicated it to me. I fear I never shall, add that I'll be fated never to know happiness in my work...

My sweet, I do think you're a bit browned off just now and a bit overanxious about running things "just right". You never would let a thing slip, would you? Have to re-educate you, I suppose. We are at different poles, aren't we? Funny, for we are so exactly alike in ways, too...

I know we disagree in regard to methodicalness, being best etc., and that we would not teach the children precisely the same things. I'm quite content with your way of teaching and happy about it. I do feel Waide's a bit like me down under, and for that reason think perhaps I could help him avoid some of my own errors. I don't know. Perhaps your more methodical ways will be a profitable counter-balance for him.

I quite often think of the things that most influenced myself. One can hardly know them in truth, I suppose, or so we are led to believe. From two of those, I'd like to see him relieved: 1) an over-consciousness of wrongs and rights; 2) a belief his work is not valuable because he is small and young and his capacity little, comparatively. I am most anxious he should learn to carry his jobs through to the finish and learn that now. Let the rest go if you like, but I should like you to agree with me there. In fact, think that is your creed anyway...

All my love, dearest,

Fred

~

Dec. 21

My dearest Fred:

...I was amused by your encounter with Lady Beecham and you saying her husband was an orchestra leader, not knowing what orchestra. Darling he is, if I'm not mistaken, conductor of the world-famous London Philharmonic Orchestra, he being Sir Thomas Beecham. He was guest conductor not so long ago of the Philadelphia Philharmonic.

But my sweet, it is for just such things as that that I love you - you are always interested in the person for themselves, not for what or whom they are or may feel they are. I, on the contrary, would probably have been quite pleased to meet Lady Beecham, and I hate that trait in me, but I really don't feel fundamentally I'm a snob...

Tomorrow I am going to make a Christmas pudding and seven dozen cookies and pie crust and get the London parcels off, besides the regular work...I'm feeling some better, and if I did not feel I should get to bed for a rest, I would sit up until one or two and answer your letter....

Frankly, I think we are both getting pretty desperate for each other in a physical and mental way both. Do you feel there is any hope of a leave, say next June? Even if this European show isn't over, I mean. By the sound of the papers, radio etc. etc., the invasion from the west must be near at hand...

Affectionately and kisses and hugs,

Norah

~

Dec. 26

My dearest Norah:

Both Christmas Eve and Christmas Day I intended writing you. Instead I just sat reading over papers and books and set no word on paper…Mostly I thought of you and home and of how we will spend our future Christmases together…

I think you see me in more danger than I am, or that you expect coming events to place me in such danger. It is not so.

Naturally I can say practically nothing of my jobs etc., and I learned this spring and summer how misleading and erroneous it is to do so, for if I ordinarily talk of work and then at some time for security must not, then the change could only be worrying to you. So all I want to say is that you should have no worry of me, that I am not nor likely to be in any sort of danger, and in particular that I expect to have nothing whatever to do with the much-heralded western front.

I know dearest that this forced separation has of itself much to do with you being on edge. Me too…Having come through the past two-and-a-half years, we can, I know, take the next few months in our stride and come together again in pride and happiness…

Friday night we sat about a huge grate fire, sipped a few Scotches. A couple of times some song got going, but the party spirit didn't seem to overtake anyone. I may put it myself this way: I didn't have any sense of the season. I felt neither happy nor sad. I simply could not think of it as Christmas Eve. Other Christmases here I've felt pretty horrible, the being-away-from-home feeling being magnified. Did not have that mood at all…

Tomorrow night we have our dance. I've already invited three gals, none of whom I know but simply because in the search for conversation they said they'd like an invitation to our dance. I'll have to hide!…

I realize I'm not really very worried about your having been upset. I think, darling, it has made you do what you knew you should be doing, getting more plain, honest-to-gosh rest…In a way, that you should be nervy puts such an emphasis on your love as to be a plum to me. It makes me pleased to know that a letter from me buoys you up so. That's how yours are received by me. I'm right up in the air when I get each and every one, whether they record troubles or not.

In fact I like the letters less that are written when everything is smooth. I suppose I fancy I can help fix up difficulties. One feels useless if he doesn't see a way to be a part of the family…

I can't but think this past year has been a particularly hard one. It has been for me, in that the strain of being away has been more than ever noticeable…I pray I'll be home with you by this time next year.

How grand it will be to hug and kiss you again, to sit and talk, chop in the yard, be bawled out for tardiness to the table. To push you out for wearing socks in bed!

It's all not far off, dearest. All my love for now...

Fred

~

1944

Danger and determination

"I feel certain you are in action"

11 PtN. 'B' Coy, Perth Regiment, Cattolica, Italy

Jan. 1

My dearest Norah:

This is a short letter composed solely because I've been sitting here and thinking of you and the children and wanting to take you all into my arms and tell you how much I love you all.

I am lonesome for you, painfully so. I think I'm a poor soldier in that often I feel, "is this life worth it? Can anything justify this horrible separation?...Can I possibly put up with this another year?" Darling, you mean so much to me.

This new year dawns bright with promise. The promise that I'll soon be home. We all see now how victory can be ours. That it may still not be just months is true, but there is the end in view on the horizon at last. What a marvelous thing that is to you and I in our little personal life! What an inestimably grand thing it is when you sum it up for all the countless others!

I think back over the years of our married life and remember how the threat of war jangled our nerves and spoiled our enjoyments, and then how its coming brought to us the realization that the fight had not only gone against us, but that we were face to face with possible defeat.

I think how insoluble it looked, how when I left you, we could not see the path to victory, only the means of staving off defeat. I know that after only two and a half years, to be able to look forward to definite victory is a miracle...

I feel proud that our own sacrifice has been a part of that success, and that gives me resolution to see it through to the end. I am sure you, too, feel just the same.

To the New Year then, dear, with great confidence and the real hope that it will bring us together again, never to be separated.

Fred

~

Jan. 3

My dearest Fred:

...First of all, we are all well and have been. I'm feeling my old kipper self again. I think at Christmas time when I was convening the Junior Hospital Aid dance and had to phone so many people regarding it and discovered that everyone seemed depressed or sick or overworked or something, that did more to make me snap out of my depression than anything else. Really, people seem to be so frustrated or something. The strain of the war is definitely telling on people...

Waide and Cynthia were up Christmas morning at 7:30, so we all came down in our dressing gowns and opened our parcels. It was such fun. Your picture, your latest snap, is on the table in the living room, and so you were looking down at us all the time...

Sunday (the next day) was a quiet one for we were all tired and as far as I can remember, it passed uneventfully - oh, I remember one incident. Waide went to Sunday School and left in the middle of it before the collection was taken and went over to the dairy and bought an ice cream cone. So of course we had a very serious talk over that...

I try to impress on him that there is a right way to live and a wrong way - and never do I want his incentive to do right to be what so and so may think of him, I want it always to be the fact that it is the morally right thing to do. Do you agree? In other words, as he grows older I want his conscience and his intelligence to tell him what to do. The more I think about things, the more I realize the mind rules the mind, not the heart or some other influence, and if you tackle a problem or situation with your mind, you can't go far wrong...

Friday I spent the day busily and by 10:30 p.m. when I finally sat down all dressed and everything, I felt tired. The house looked lovely with a grate fire and candles burning and the table was pretty with red roses in a silver bowl and candles...The folks commenced to arrive by 11 and by 11:45 some forty-odd were here, so we served sherry and at midnight joined hands and sang Should Auld Acquaintance etc., and then everyone kissed everyone else and wished them happy New Year. I felt very sad for a few moments, dear, but then I felt very happy because I'm so confident you will be home before next New Years. Don't think I didn't miss you every minute, dear, just because I was happy, because I did. But my sweet, I couldn't stand many such depressions as I had two weeks or so ago...

On New Year's Day was our municipal election. The C.C.F. made a strong bid to get the four men of their and labour's choice elected on the council. There were sharp editorials in the paper accusing the C.C.F. of interfering in municipal politics. The same thing was true in Toronto, where 22 C.C.F. candidates ran. There was a record vote in town and the four C.C.F. candidates were snowed under...Toronto's 22 C.C.F. candidates were all defeated, too...I stand and look at your picture every night and I love it more and more...
Norah

~

[Censored]

My dearest Norah:

...I've very little news for you, yet I wanted to write as starting to-morrow I'll be mucking about the country on a scheme and in all probability unable to write even if I were in good humour to do so, which I probably will not be - damn this January weather! But I shall as soon as I'm "bathed" again...

I send my love to Waide and to Cynthia. I pray that under your excellent guidance they will continue to grow into strong and sensible girlhood and boyhood. I send my love, too, to all the family. All my love, Norah darling. Love, hugs and kisses galore.

Fred

~

Jan. 13

My dearest Fred:

...I was greatly relieved to read your words in regard your work and your future role in the army - it did relieve my fears. It isn't human not to be afraid, and when one's prospects are that the person whom one holds most dear in all this world is soon to face death and the horrors of war, it is enough to almost send one crazy.

And yet I used to reason, why should I expect my Fred to come back ahead of others? They all can't. I've reasoned and prayed and fretted and discussed it and I have only a hazy solution...I guess it boils down, you've fitted into your niche and so do a good job and the sooner it's over, the sooner you're home, my sweet.

As for my rest - I will try, I promise. But Fred, it's my nature to drive myself, or better, to be driven by a force within me. My incentive is, "Whatever you're doing, do it with all your might and make a good job". I'm inherently enthusiastic and ambitious and take those qualities away and you haven't got me, have you?

Before I met you, I wanted to be a career woman. What in heaven's name I wanted to do or be I didn't know, but I was always, always working like all get out towards some intangible goal. Now I've got my goal or true incentive. I want to make a good job of being a good wife and mother and always have your and the children's love and respect and admiration, and that is my only ambition. And it is a big job and a full-time job, and there is no letting up...

Darling, we can come together in such happiness and we can be proud - not of everything we've done, but mistakes and experiences are some good if one learns from mistakes. I can only say I hope I never have a harder three years as long as I live.

But now my thoughts are happy ones, my feelings and sensations comforting ones - I'm just waiting now almost patiently, for you. I'm not frustrated any more, like at first. I'm not fighting it. I'm most of the time not even lonely, because you're really awfully near me...

There have been groups started all over Canada called Canadian Forum and adult education groups. There are several in Owen Sound. On Tuesday nights, the groups meet separately and listen to the Canadian Forum broadcast from 8:30 to 9 over C.B.C. Last week, for example, the subject was "The right to be healthy"...After their discussion broadcast, the groups all over Canada discuss it themselves. Each week before the broadcast, each member in a group gets a printed pamphlet presenting the topic in a concise form and on the back page there are questions for the group to ask themselves and answer. By rights, each group should have a secretary and report the decisions to the Canadian Forum office. It is something like a Gallup poll...

So help me, I'm never going to write another letter after the war. It is only my love for you that keeps me writing. Tell me the truth now dear, aren't you sick of writing them too? Gosh, we really are noble, aren't we?

Love and kisses galore, as ever,

Norah

~

Jan. 18

My dearest Norah:

We have been to sea now since Saturday...I wrote you before we pulled out and you will have had that letter now. I feel sure you will pardon the petty subterfuge of my saying I would not be writing because I was going out on a scheme. I did not want you to worry, and I did not want to evade the security regulations, so please excuse.

I have a very nice cabin, the only difference between it and a peacetime first-class being that there are two of us in it instead of one. That is no hardship, it being quite sizeable enough to hold us both. I sleep in the upper of the two bunks which, since I had the choice, was a poor choice as the mattress is not as soft as might be. I reflect, though, that I have been wise since my roommate, a dentist, is disposed to be in fear and trembling of sickness and has lain on his bed since we hit the first rollers. I should not enjoy a lower if he should be racked by suppressed retching…

It is amazing that we make so little of the trip. To be on a ship like this and on a voyage like this, we would pay much in hard cash if it were peacetime. Times and purposes being what they are, we sail along indoors most of the time as though we were packed into a blacked-out train. There is no deck sport, not yet at least and not likely to be, for the decks used for games in peace are now stacked with rafts, boats and gear…

We must wear our lifejackets wherever we go, carry a water bottle and an emergency ration. Besides, we have a little red light attached to our shoulder and powered by a battery in our pocket. Quite a sight to see us all so loaded up. We have had boat drill every day. First there is "action stations", when all troops get under cover except those manning the ack-ack guns which dot the top decks. Then "emergency station", when everyone goes to the position from which they would take to boats or rafts…

Our convoy is relatively small I would judge, though at least double in numbers the one I came to England in. The ships seem smaller and I judge the warships to be of smaller classes than those that protected us before…Tuesday:…We fooled about in circles some few hours in the Atlantic and then as it came night, passed through the Straits of Gibraltar…We all stayed up quite late that night watching the lights of Tangiers…A sight indeed, when you remember that for most on board, it's been two to four years since they've seen the lights of a town. It's a thing to think about - just try.

Since then we have been paralleling the North Africa shore, which we see in the distance. My God, what a rugged coastline it is! You must see it to have any notion of what faced the North Africa landing of the First Army…

I send you all my love, Norah darling, and my best to the family. Love and kisses to Waide and Cynthia.

Fred

~

Jan. 28

My dearest Fred:

…You would have laughed today. When we were coming along the street downtown, a very uncouth, dirty little boy came up and slapped Cynthia. Before I could even speak, the youngster was flat on his back on the sidewalk. Waide just gave him one blow and knocked him for a loop, as they say, and he very savagely told him to leave his sister alone.

Fred, I couldn't possibly describe how affectionate they are, one with the other. You will be so happy when you see them. Of course they scrap and tease, but most times they are so loving. You would laugh if you could see them coming down the stairs head-first on their tummies, and such a racket. Tonight at supper…Cynthia was tired and was crying and Waide said, "Mom, I simply can't stand the noise, I guess I'll have to go away". He has heard me say that, of course…

Could you not ask for a leave in June?…I heard a Col. Baker speak on the radio today, and he was addressing the Rotary Club on "Rehabilitation". He said they were considering bringing back men from the armed services overseas who were equipped to work at this work. He mentioned lawyers. It offers a great chance to serve, Fred. It is very necessary to have the right sort of men in that type of work because as you know, thousands will come back unable to work at their former work and will need vocational guidance and education. They need someone to see that they get that opportunity…

It is too bad when one isn't one hundred per cent enthusiastic over one's work. But you know, Fred, I do believe enthusiasm can be encouraged in one, or developed to quite a high degree if one tries a little harder…I feel no matter what, you could and would earn and provide for me and Waide and Cynthia, or you'd die in the attempt. But to someone like yourself, a living isn't enough, a good living isn't enough; you need, as you say, an outlet for your creativeness and if I were you I would do everything possible to find out what that is…

You see, I'm terribly ambitious for you, maybe you don't quite realize just how much. You are honestly the only one I've ever felt I would be glad to remain in the background for. That is because I love you so. Absolute love is absolute unselfishness. But remember Fred, as long as we live I expect your best, the same as I aim to give you my best.

Did I tell you I put an ad in the paper and phoned the selective service for a maid? I got two answers to my ad and the selective service sent me a girl, whom I engaged…Truly I believe she is heaven-sent…This afternoon I have two hours off to rest and write to you while Emma is out with Waide and Cynthia. She can cook and bake anything.

So darling, things are going to be okay. I'm horribly thin and tired, but I'm going to make an effort now, if ever I did, to rest. I refused invitations for Friday, Saturday and Sunday nights, just so I could rest and relax. And I feel sure when you arrive home, I'll be just dandy and plumper.

I've aged too, you know. You'll laugh, I know, but I've lost some of my youth, like you have, but I've got something better in its place...

My darling, I've not written as often of late for only one reason, I was too bushed, but things are going to be rosy again and the mail will flow again.

Good-bye, dear.

Norah

~

Feb. 7

Dearest Norah:

...Life is quite okay and in the last day or so, we've been having quite a bit of fun. Not the least is the fun of fixing up quarters. We have built a stove up against the wall with a pipe out the window, which is quite serviceable when the wind is in the right direction. When the wind is not right, it puffs back vigorously, temporarily disrupting our poker game...

It is true that we have cursed more at the damage done to the plumbing than any other thing. It has necessitated open-air latrines. Believe me, that is literal. They are uncovered from weather or sight, and in these cold days, one seeks them out only when pressed...

It's pretty apparent that I'll be doing little else than court martial work here in the reinforcement and hospital area. There are a lot of cases and few experienced men. Kitz has a murder case to defend, Norm Bergman one of the same to prosecute, and there seems to be little end to the variety. I've had nothing of real interest as yet, but odds and ends are coming along....

We get no first-hand news of fronts as they are too far off. Occasionally someone lands in back from the north who has interesting items, but little of an important import.

It's grand to have oranges, lemons etc. in abundance, and we do gorge on them...

Dearest I do hope you will take care of yourself and see that you get better speedily. You should have no worries on my behalf, and it's not going to be long now. Do be a dear and keep quiet and unexcited. I'm well and I love you and I want you to keep the same...

Fred

~

Feb. 15

My dearest Fred:

...Your letter which arrived yesterday was posted I don't know when because it was censored. The only thing cut out was the date at the top of the first page.

Of one thing I'm certain - you are terribly lonely. You don't say so in so many words, but you can't conceal it, dear. It naturally makes me unhappy. I can help little except write cheery letters and write often.

I was terribly down last evening after I got your letter. I even worry, silly and all as it is, and wonder if maybe you've met someone else whom you love and you don't want to tell me, and yet of one thing I feel sure though, dear, you would tell me, wouldn't you? It would only be fair to me.

But I can imagine you feeling when you read this that you would like to spank me for even thinking such nonsense. It is funny what strange things one's mind will do to one...

In spite of having Emma and in spite of having plenty of work and lots of outside activities, I feel so often lately that I just can't stick it out much longer. I've got now that I can hardly speak of you to anyone without getting an awful lump in my throat...

Last week on Wednesday and Thursday and Friday nights I tried to go to bed early, did in fact, but couldn't sleep, so read or as usually happens, was disturbed often because either one of the children seems to want something. Sometimes Fred, as much and all as I love them, I wish I could get away from them for even a day. They seem to be on top of me almost twenty-four hours a day...

Waide is, I think, old enough to dress himself, so in the mornings now I get him to dress himself while I dress Cynthia. You would just die at him. He whines and grouches and fumes and sighs, and this morning he said, "I'm just too lazy". But I keep sweet but firm, and he finally gets dressed, and then of course he is very pleased with his accomplishment...

Believe it or not, I've been reading my Bible every night for some time now. In fact, on my bedside table at present I have Jane Eyre by Charlotte Bronte, Personal Religion and the Life of Fellowship, by Temple, the Archbishop of York, and my Bible, and The Tudor Wench, by Thane, a biography of Queen Elizabeth...

Please don't feel I've gone off the deep end over religion. I haven't...I feel the children's religious education is very important and I can't be a hypocrite, and besides, I believe in God and in Jesus Christ, so why not live or try to live according to my beliefs? You'll find when you get home again and get to know the bairns, it makes one fully conscious of one's responsibility to one's self, one's family and one's community...

If you feel like grousing, dear, and writing me a really blue letter, well write it and get it off your chest. Also if you have something in particular bothering you perchance, get it off your chest too, darling. You really say so little, dear - you keep it all pent up like you always did when home, and as usual I'm never quite sure just what is the matter...

Darling, if you have any worries that I won't want to give up my active participation in the church groups, Hospital Aid, etc. etc. when you come home, please stop worrying from this moment. I will drop out of the run, shall I say, so fast it will make my or their or your head swim. In the meantime I do enjoy it simply because it gives me an interest...

Thought anything more of asking for a leave? I'll take a month's happiness anytime...
Norah

~

Feb. 21
My dearest Fred:
What a surprise to learn upon receiving your blue sheet air mail of Jan. 30 this afternoon that you are in Italy. It does take the feet from under one, you know.

Mary Wilkinson and I and Edna Johnston were sitting having tea, having returned from skating at the arena. I took Waide and Cynthia, too. It is quite some work holding Waide up, but he doesn't do badly. However, when we returned, we came back here for tea and I certainly was surprised when I opened your letter.

You sound so happy that that, at least, made me happy. Naturally until I receive further news I'm wondering how you came to go, whether your work will be similar to that in England, or have you gone and kicked over the traces again and got yourself into something new and bloody.

I'm really so surprised and worried and excited etc. that I'm cross inside. I had foolishly let myself believe that you would be coming home by summer if even on leave, and I've even gone so far as to order a particularly revealing and seductive nightie and a smart new suit so that I would look nice when you came - but I might as well throw them in the ashcan now for they will be moth-eaten by the time you get home now.

I know I'm being a poor sport and I don't care. It's horribly unfair, the whole bloody business. However, give me a day or two to pull myself together and I will go "nobly on", like a good and sensible wife in my position - but so help me, I'm going to stop looking for you home for another five years and then maybe I won't be disappointed…

Don't worry, I'll be all okay and peppy and optimistic in no time. Love and kisses galore,
Norah

~

Feb. 22
My dearest Norah:
…Firstly I must tell you of the trip Len Kitz and I had to Naples. We had a spot of work to do there…That was a real piece of luck, as Naples is "out of bounds", allegedly because of typhus - most believe that the real vermin wear skirts. Be that as it may, there we were with Saturday to put in and a town to see.

There are two items you must add into anything I may say…They are, dust and beggars. Besides the ordinary dust that ladens any city, Naples has a particular grime that I believe is crumbled mortar and brick resultant from bombing. The Italian buildings are largely built of tile, soft sandstone and a soft powdery mortar. When demolished, as so many are, they are a heap of stone and tile in chips floating in a greyish powder…and the large volume of traffic just stirs it up and sends it swirling through the streets.

Then the beggars. Near every alley or doorway, along every sidewalk, you will find women, usually old, usually visibly frail, always filthy, wearing black clothes…generally carrying a small child wrapped in a shawl. These are so filthy, so ragged and unkempt, so whining, that they do not evoke your sympathy but only your disgust. Do not mistake me, the people are not in need of food. These beggars are racketeering and the first to run them off the lot are the rest of the Italian people…

We were looking for the offices of the Maple Leaf (Canadian Army newspaper) and asked a man who was a member of a religious order directions. He was wearing brown robes and wore a queer brown flat derby. He took us around the corner and next thing we knew he was trying to sell us a string of beads! Holy orders!

Well, the padre, after two days in Italy, told us that there wasn't much comparison between our clergy and Italian, and I will believe him…

There is enormous war damage, some bombing, some

mines…One realizes what a magnificent opportunity we have in Canada after this war to destroy the unsocial and unhealthy buildings and still be in an advantageous position in regard to the rebuilding program that most certainly will sweep the world…

While Europe builds for bare necessities, we can build for superior living conditions and working conditions. There is no excuse for us failing to discard that which is not best…

Naples is in a lovely setting, with Vesuvius smoking away and visible from almost any street corner, the land sweeping away from the sea into high hills behind the city, a colourful shore with enticing islands lying off within easy sight, buildings that once were probably beautiful and imposing but are now rubble or dusty fragments or shabby. Peopled by dirty, ragged beings who slouch about gleaning a living off the army. That is the appearance; better there must be…

I must close this now, Norah darling, as it's 10:30 and this writing with a carbide lamp is no cinch. I have not heard from you yet and I admit it is depressing…
Fred

~

Feb. 27
My dearest Fred:
…I wrote you a short note on Tuesday last, after having received your letter which was written on the boat. I'm afraid it wasn't a very cheery letter, and I'm afraid this won't be much better unless I devote most of the pages to the children's doings and sayings and current interests and topics.

My mind has been like a maze all week. Maybe you will wonder why on earth you going to Italy (for I got my map out and traced your voyage and I feel you must certainly be in Italy) should upset me so, but it has. You seem so much farther away, and I'm in the dark so far as to what work you are doing…So it took the props right out from under me and I've had a sick feeling in the pit of my stomach all week…

So I don't feel happy, and why pretend I do. There is one thing I don't want you to do, unless because of regulations you can't, and that is to keep me in the dark so that I won't worry over you. I worry over you far more if I don't know. I've always felt I could face a thing if I knew what I had to face…

By the time you receive this, Waide will be five. I am going to give him a real nice party and use St. Patrick's Day decorations. He is looking forward to it so much...

Waide plays piggyback with Cynthia on his hands and knees, or they stand up facing one another with their arms around one another and then go around and around. Waide has music in him. He can't keep quiet when there is band music or dance music on the radio. You would die laughing if you heard the two of them singing Pistol-Packin' Mama...

Except for the fact I'm worried over and lonesome for you, I couldn't ask for things to run more smoothly. Emma is truly an answer to my prayers, and really things are running so smoothly. I have so much more time for Waide and Cynthia and they are so much happier of course when I have time for them...I do the upstairs work, all the planning of meals and shopping, the mending and the children, and Emma does all the cooking (I just go and sit down at the table) and the washing and ironing and together we keep the downstairs tidy...so I hope she stays for ten years...

Last week's citizens' forum group was well attended and quite interesting. The subject was "Canada and the Commonwealth" ...This Tuesday the subject is "Anglo-American relations". Since I know nothing about the subject whatsoever, I asked the librarian if she would hunt me up some material to skim through...

Due to all the talk over the Russo-Polish border, and due to the fact last week three different evenings the people assembled were arguing pro and con, I decided to read the history of Poland and Russia and find out for myself who aggressed or whether both did and when and why etc. No sense arguing without facts.

Gosh, I guess I should have been a man and gone into politics, for I'd almost rather argue than eat...

I so hope and pray this finds you well and happy...My fondest love and kisses as always, dearest.
Norah

~

March 24
Dearest Norah:
I'm sitting here eating olives, nice big green ones. It's a very sweet life. I have had little to do today, having just finished a court martial yesterday. I got the lad off two charges, one of assaulting an Italian woman and one of breaking up her furniture, but failed to get him out of "being concerned in a disturbance". Well, you cannot expect everything, I suppose.

I have at last received a letter directed here...disappointed that my coming to Italy seemed to somewhat depress you. It ought not to have. The letters I wrote you for nearly a month before should have assured you I was not getting into something. I had and have and do tell you all I can of my doings, and had thought you would be no longer concerned.

The only thing I said that was not the whole truth was when I said I was going on a scheme and therefore would not be able to write for a while. You must know I could not have said a word more.

As for Italy being farther away than England, well, that I don't comprehend - once out of Canada, anyplace seems just about the same distance to me. Physical miles, perhaps, but what do they, of themselves, signify?

I like Italy immensely. The weather is variable, but when we have sunny days, I feel like a king. I got so in England that I believed the sun only shone some unpredictable quarter of an hour a day. It is true that the people of England were grand to us all, and that to chat in a home or pub was a joy, but then you can't have everything...

I trust, darling, that when you get this, you will be feeling better...All my love, sweetheart,
Fred

~

April 6
My darling Fred:
...It's terribly silly, but when I go without mail for as long as we have, I feel somewhat desperate - mail, I mean, that hasn't crossed and where we don't reply to each other or chat. I have wondered all day if everything is all right with you. Most important of all, do you still love me and as much? What are you thinking about these days, do Waide and Cynthia and I still mean as much, are you as happy as it is possible for you to be, are you depressed and maybe a little cynical - oh, a thousand questions...

I've been writing regularly and as often and I so hope you get my mail, written since I knew you were in Italy, soon. Darling, will you write me a nice chatty love letter soon? It is really a long while since I've had one and I would love you to just chat to me since you're too far away to cuddle me.

This devilish separation. The lump in my throat seems always to be there. There is a tight, forlorn knot that has become almost part of me...I long for you so much. Good night, and a happy Easter...
Norah

~

April 14

My dearest Fred:

…I received your blue sheet of March 24…and here I just wrote you last Thursday asking you to write me a love letter so that I would be reassured of your love. I never doubt it, dear, but it is necessary since we are separated to make a point every so often to take time out and write a love letter - to make up for the kisses and loving we don't have.

I'm sorry I sounded so downhearted about you going to Italy. The zombie goof who made me believe you would come home on a leave was just myself letting myself believe that fate just couldn't keep us apart any longer, and then in a letter last summer, you said you felt sure you would be home this summer coming, to play with us on the sand. So I just let myself believe you were coming and then when I learned you were in Italy, it seemed to me to be so disappointing.

But I'm glad you're there now, dear. You do seem to like it and your letters are so interesting. And I'm certainly not going to let myself look for you at any fixed time from now on.

I wish I had some of those nice olives of yours. They are fifty cents a small bottle here.…

I meant to write last night, but was tired, so I read some material for a paper or speech I'm giving on Wednesday and Thursday nights next week. I was asked to speak to the Junior IODE on something in connection with the British empire for their empire study meeting. So I chose "Britain's Changing Foreign Policy". Then the president of the Y Women and Y Men's club called and asked if I would give the same speech on Thursday night to them…

So my dear, it may be a case of fools rush in - but I'm taking a crack at it anyway and my audiences are not critical since nine out of ten of them probably don't read half as much as I do…

On Thursday morning, I helped at the blood donor clinic from 8:30 to 12:30…Not being a graduate, I couldn't have a bed to supervise, but I and another nurse did all the haemoglobins - you know, stick a needle in their finger and then put some blood on a blotter and compare it with the colour card. There were a hundred and forty donors. It is one busy place…

On Friday noon, Waide was sitting eating his lunch with us and was obviously in a brown study. So we said, "A penny for your thoughts". He said, "What do you mean?" So when we told him, he was very amused and could hardly keep from laughing. So he told us and of course we each came through with a penny, and wasn't he tickled - never had he earned money so easily. Well, at night he was sitting eating again and he said, "I'm thinking of -" and looked to see if it was going to work again. The monkey...

Good night, my darling. Love and kisses galore,

Norah

~

April 18

My dearest Norah:

I'm up earlier than my usual this morning, dear, and have already had breakfast, washed, shaved etc. Since it's only 7:45, I should probably have stayed in bed. Well, I would have, too, had I been home with you. Tush, a nooner - and sometimes sooner.

A few days ago Len and I climbed partway up the mountain, stripped to a pair of shorts and basked in the sun. In a day or two, I was as itchy as sin. Thinking I was unquestionably lousy, I bathed and did all manner of things to relieve me of my unwelcome friends, to no avail. Then I discovered it was because I was getting a new skin. I've peeled my whole back, my legs and arms. Think! That's my first sunburn since the summer of 1940! Boy, it feels grand...

Sunday, Len and I climbed to a small village, through it to its highest point where the ruins of an ancient fortress dominate the whole of the mountain spur the town is on. We wore shorts and shirts only, and the freedom from heavy clothes was a real boon. Within the old fortress walls the ground is now completely green. The locals have grown there an olive orchard. We lay down for a quick game of chess...

All my love, darling. I get so damn impatient to see you. I'm fed up being away and look forward to nothing but being with you again...

Fred

~

April 25

My dearest Fred:

...I've had a busy week. Last Tuesday night I put the finishing touches on my speech. And Wednesday night, I spoke to the IODE (Junior). I was positively thrilled with the response, and most of them entered into a discussion at the end...

Last Thursday, two different people brought us maple syrup and my washing-machine man brought back the wringer, which was on the hummer, the radio man came for the radio which was also on the hummer, and to top everything, at noon that day Waide "beat up" David Cheer, a four-year-old around the corner, and nearly kicked his eye out.

So his dad came to me, was very, very nice but it did upset me. According to him and the neighbours, Waide, who usually plays nicely, just all of a sudden threw him down and beat him up. Well, what to do? In a case like that I always wonder what you would do or say to Waide. I would hate him to be a bully, and I feel sure he isn't. I really feel he is so belligerent because when I first moved here, he was so big for his age, and yet young, that he had one devil of a time with the older boys who were continually getting the best of him. However, he has learned to stand up for his rights, and still has to fight, but this time he picked on someone smaller.

So I had a long talk with him and I offered to pay the doctor's bill if David needed attention, and Waide went up and apologized to Mrs. Cheer. I didn't spank him. Should I have? And I know he realizes he mustn't do anything like that again. He really doesn't know his own strength, and often hurts Cynthia when he is playing with her.

Well, after such a busy day I was rather pooed out. However, I dressed in my new blue suit and hat etc. and went over to the Y for supper...I did enjoy the meeting. There must have been around fifty members present, all kids around eighteen to twenty, needless to say about three girls for every boy...The kids are so cute and so carefree and romantic in one way, and yet very serious in another. In other words, the kids of eighteen of today are essentially okay - made me feel rather old and settled and much too serious.

However, when the dancing commenced I had lots of dancing, so I guess I didn't seem too ancient. Made me think of us at eighteen, and also made me wonder what Waide and Cynthia will be like at eighteen. One thing I noticed, they were all free and frank and made me feel they knew a lot more about love and sex than I did at eighteen...

Silly to be nervous, but I was a bit, until I got on my feet. I know you're not fussy about me speaking in public, so I hadn't your enthusiasm as an incentive...

I do wish I had a really nice snap of you. I don't like the one of you you sent me at Christmas. You're much nicer looking than that. So please if you can, have one taken or get someone to snap you for me, dear. I want you to grow your moustache again, darling. I liked it so much. Any requests from you?...

All my love, dearest,
Norah

~

May 2
My dearest Fred:
…Waide has been sick for four or five days…Yesterday his temperature went to 104.6 and I was mighty worried…His tonsils may have
to come out after this, which is not pleasant but I do want him in
good condition for school in September…

I plan to houseclean this month, wash quilts and blankets etc.
and be all ready to move. It will probably be delightful at Leith in
June and perfect for sleeping. I feel very sad at times when I realize
it is my third, no, it will be my fourth summer without you. Really it
is a long time, isn't it, dear?…

You do seem happier in Italy. I suppose it is a combination of
things - plenty of work to do, nicer weather, a change of scenery, etc.
etc…

On May 21, the anniversary services are being held at the church.
Mr. Watson, from our old church in London, is the guest speaker. So
I thought Mom and Dad would enjoy entertaining some people after the Sunday night service, at coffee and a grate fire. So I phoned
our minister, Rev. Adams, and told him and he was delighted. He is
really a good scout - a little too timid perhaps, but in earnest and
ambitious.

We have no junior congregation in the morning, so I told him if
he would start one, I would take Waide and Cynthia and help or-
ganize it and conduct it. He was so pleased, Fred. He said he had
been anxious to start one but didn't know who to turn to. So I'm
hoping he will get the session to give the go-ahead.

Apparently some of the older men in the session feel when they
were young they had to go and sit and listen to the sermon and
were good, so, so can the children of our day. To that I say, "Yes, and
they'll know as little of the sermons as I did, and demand a more
tangible, workable religion, as I do and hundreds of others…

I, too, am getting so impatient to have you home. However, I'm
not looking for you until the war in Europe is over. Maybe you will
be kept on in the army of occupation, and maybe I could come over
- wouldn't that be a grand chance, for me to see something for a
change. Good night, my sweet. Pleasant dreams. Worlds of kisses.
Norah

~

May 6

Dearest Norah:

…Darling, a letter of yours to England arrived recently. I didn't reply directly to it. I felt sure it had been answered over and over again. You need never think I may have found another girl. No husband, I feel sure, ever loved his wife more completely than I you.

Perhaps at times I've been reserved, perhaps a word more would have settled you, I don't know, but I do know that I have never loved anyone but you and never felt the least inclination to review my feelings toward you. I always loved you from our first days together. That love has grown, is growing. It has added many new sides. Like the facets of a diamond the new have added to the brilliance, but never changed the stone.

You have outdone yourself in loyalty to me during the last three years. I expected it of you, I know, but your splendid showing with the children, the home, the family, have been more than one could expect. I expected much, in all honesty I say I demanded of you more than I probably had any right to do. I left with complete confidence, without really understanding what it would mean in work and bearing on your part. I understand now, and admire the strength you have put into your job…

I should tell you so daily, but of course I'm not one for saying much on any occasion. I only know, Norah dear, that I expected much of you and that I received that and more from you, which is just what I did expect.

All my love, darling,

Fred

~

May 15

My dearest Fred:

I meant to write you a long letter tonight and just chat, but I'm not particularly in the mood now, the reason being Emma, the maid, up and left today - just like that…no two weeks' notice or anything…Her tale of woe was things had gone wrong at home…

She was the best maid anyone could wish for and everything was running so smoothly here. I'm not quite through the house-cleaning and have the quilts and blankets yet to do since the washing-machine wringer has been and still is on the hummer. I had to cancel helping at the blood donor clinic Thursday morning, also I was in charge of a baking sale for the hospital aid this week.

Without help, I'm tied hand and foot and slug from morning un-

til night. It means I'm virtually a prisoner at the cottage, too, because I can't get anyone to mind Waide and Cynthia even a night at
the cottage, so I'll be putting in many a night just sitting by my own
little lonesome...

Am I not feeling sorry for myself? Well, there it all is in a nutshell.
I wouldn't mind working twelve hours a day if you were home,
because we would have our evenings together. Ain't it hell?

Waide and Cynthia are just dandy. Waide is all better and the
weather has been perfect, so they are out playing. I have to watch
Cynthia very closely because she does run away sometimes and
crosses the road of course, and we are so near the river...

I've been reading two interesting books. The Mastery of Sex, by
Weatherhead, an excellent book and a propos since there is so much
talk about sex education and I found and find there is a lot to learn
- he emphasizes we all have more sex energy than we need for bio-
logical purposes and should divert the energy into some other chan-
nel. I'll discuss it at length later. The other book is A Tree Grows in
Brooklyn, a novel. Darling, I love you so. What is there to say?...
Norah

~

May 16
Dearest Norah:
...It was Friday that we learned that the Italian offensive was going
again. Everyone's mighty happy that the beginning is made and
puzzling to know how it has been fitted in with the Western front.
No use to give my or our guesses...

I'm forever surprised at Italian scenery. It is not mountains as I
imagined them, that is, my concept was all wrong. One sees much
flat land with great towering peaks rising abruptly out of them.
Makes me think of a field of huge icebergs floating on a placid sea.
Vegetation is luxuriant. Fields bearing trees in regular rows with
grape vines strung from tree to tree so as to divide the whole in
squares, and floored by a full sowing of grain, are the common type.
Probably the most plentiful of all things at the present time is dust.
How a soil so dry can give birth to so much vegetation is a real
surprise to me...

One other matter is pending. I have applied for transfer back to
the Lorne Scots. If it goes through, I will also revert to lieutenant.
The reason is not communicable at the moment. Don't think I'm a
fool, or "kicking over traces". True, you'd have some supporters
among my friends here, but you must rely on my good judgement

relative to matters here - as I rely on yours relative to things at home. Well, extra dough was welcome while it lasted.

While I'm at it, this is my doing and not in any remote way to my discredit...

Night, m'love,

Fred

~

May 20

My dearest Fred:

...Wednesday evening I went to a C.C.F. meeting with Lorna Elliott. Her father was speaking on trade unions in Russia and how they operate, and compared them with the trade unions in Canada and the U.S.A. I'm almost convinced I believe in socialism, but I don't think the C.C.F. is the medium by which we will get it.

Nor do I feel we are ready for it yet. I do feel the germ is there and maybe we will live in the transition period only, but our children may live to see true socialism....

Thursday I baked three pumpkin pies and took two over to the Junior Hospital Aid baking sale. We made $15, which really didn't make up for all the work entailed. We would be farther ahead to each contribute fifty cents...

I managed to get my old stand-by, Dorothy, whom I had all last summer at the cottage, from four to eight weekdays and all day Saturday...

When you said in a letter not so long ago that you had a feeling you would never know complete satisfaction in your work, I naturally thought maybe you would have, had you finished in your honour course. So I will always feel I've got to work extra hard to make it up to you.

I suppose you could say the same thing, in that if I hadn't met you, I would have finished my course. I can say honestly, dear, I have no regrets. I would rather have you than a hundred B.A.s or R.N.s. But I do think maybe we both could have had both our education and each other. What say you?...

Please my dearest, don't feel I regret you one tiny bit. I feel it is not even necessary to say that. You know, darling, how much you mean to me, don't you? It is as much for the sake of an argument and have you answer it and thus have something to discuss in letters that I write the above.

I took Waide over to Al on Friday and the report is not good. He has very bad tonsils and adenoids and his glands are full...So if his ears are cleared up in two weeks, Al advises taking his tonsils out, and adenoids...

I feel Waide will have the summer ahead of him to pick up and be in good condition for school. Maybe you will feel I should wait for your opinion, but I felt you've been away so long, you wouldn't feel you could give an opinion and would be willing to leave it up to me and the judgement of Al as his doctor for nearly three years now...

I so wish you were home, dear. But it won't be too long now, my darling, will it?...

Norah

~

May 28

My dearest Norah:

...We are now camping out...Our camp is a fine one located in a natural amphitheatre. Surrounding the floor are small hills, while back of them three or four miles off are mountains. One trouble is that the wind scoops through the camp and raises quite a dust, and as the dust indicates, there is little if any surface or running water. Again I am amazed at the fertility of this place in spite of lack of rain. Every day is clear and sunny from morning to nightfall. Grand!

We hear less of the progress of hostilities than we would like to, though doubtless much more than do you, particularly as to individual units and their achievements. Suffice it to say that we are very proud of our own corps' accomplishments, and confident that Jerry has been and is being administered a sound thrashing and defeat in the Italian theatre...

I was pondering over in my mind my thoughts on reconstruction etc., and thought I might do worse than take you into my confidence. I mean I have never consulted you to any extent on this matter. Indeed I have never spoken much to anyone on it, though of course we have had arguments...

Briefly I think that all the planning boards and all the policies formulated will never scratch the surface of the problem unless each and every individual does his own little individual plan...You see, essentially I'm democratic and capitalistic, and I have no faith in the doings of "the theys" except as to matters whose character is such that individuals need not bother to do them, or that need to be done in a lump. That is poorly expressed. But I insist we should be thinking what "we" will do towards our rehabilitation, not what "they" must do...

Well, after this harangue perhaps I can give an example. It's an example only, but it will show what I mean. I intend to either set up a private practice, either by opening an independent office or joining a firm or partnership, or take a salaried job...In addition I hope to add to my income by possession of a farm or a summer camp or some other business that can be profitable and serviceable by management and control. Now here, too, plans can now be made. I have made some tentatively, to view the difficulties, of which there are many: location, equipment (kind, source) employment, revenue and expenses.

All these matters must be examined and carefully estimated, and it is a full-time job and certainly more profitable individually and more conducive to assisting reconstruction and rehabilitation than toying verbally with some minister's problem and crooning, "Why don't we do like the Russians (or others)?"...I shall close this letter, dear, by sending you all my love. Should those words ever grow dull or monotonous to your ear, let me assure you they carry with them such a wealth of feeling and so vast a collection of thoughts, that these things could be summed up no other way...
Fred

~

June 3
My dearest Fred:
...I have Dorothy of last summer engaged for July and August, and so I'm so tickled. She is so good with Waide and Cynthia, and they love her...

I've decided to have Cynthia christened a week from tomorrow, that will be June 11. I had always felt I would rather wait until you come home, but that may not be for some time yet and she is at the cutest stage right now...

Eleanor is being married two weeks from today, that is June 17. She is home this weekend, so you can imagine how busy we all are planning for the wedding, reception etc...

Waide is to be operated on on Monday at 10 a.m. I will be taking him in tomorrow, Sunday, at 5 p.m. I will stay with him until he goes to sleep...It is so nice to have the doctors and nurses as friends, because I know they will take a special interest. I haven't disillusioned Waide in any way, and as he says, he is going to be a good brave soldier. When it is your own child, it seems so much more important, doesn't it?...
Sunday: I have just come from the hospital. I took Waide up at 5 p.m....I stayed until ten, when they gave him his sedative. He said,

"Come here, Mom, while I put my arms around you," and then he said after he kissed me that he would be all right and to go home now. So I, having a hard time with the lump in my throat, said good night and walked home with our full moon shining on me.

Seems funny, leaving the tyke up there alone. Gosh, I love him...

I will close for tonight, darling, and finish this tomorrow noon when I can give you a report after the operation. Good news of the fighting in Italy today. My heart fairly sings when I think maybe in a few more months you will be home...

Monday, 10:30 a.m....Al just phoned and the operation is all over with and Waide is fine...He won't be out of the anaesthetic for a while, of course, but I'm sure he will be fine and dandy...

All my love and kisses and hugs, sweet.

Norah

~

June 4

Dearest Norah:

...Yesterday I and two others set out for Naples after the morning's work. That's on the q.t. of course, for we weren't quite within our rights in going. Right after dinner we set off and lo and behold, had not tramped more than one-half sweaty mile when we picked a lift going right through.

Arrived in Neopolita, we stepped smartly to a "hairdresser" shop and were shaved, haircut, shoeshined and generally tidied up. One of the other sissies even had a manicure. Then we boldly set off down the Via Roma. Armed with about forty-five lira, the better half of profits from the galloping dominoes and the pasteboards, I felt I could face even the world's most overcharging shops, which all know the said Via Roma to have. Ah, happy thought! Ah, sweet courage of the innocent and guileless! I have returned shorn of my wealth and possessed of a few baubles foisted upon me by wily merchants...

It really was quite some fun and in due course you will receive mother-of-pearl necklaces, also one of the same only different, and a coral ring guaranteed gold-plated...

It is now Tuesday. Much has happened since I wrote the beginning of this letter. Rome has fallen, the second front has been opened. Quite exciting days. It is wisest to save breath, for doubtless you have hugged the radio and heard far more than I...

I am sorry Waide has not been in better health. I agree he ought to have the operation on his tonsils and adenoids. The sooner the better...You are right in making decisions regarding operations and such-like for Waide and Cynthia. I would be and am willing and glad to give any advice I can, but as you realize, I can't give sensible decisions from here...

Your letter contained some two or three pages of the pros and cons of marriage and when to marry and how to marry...With the single exception of being somewhat sorry our parents weren't in on or present at our marriage, ours has my vote. I regret not a single item and I see no way it could have been different...

You appear to think you can read up on sex education. I don't. Nor do I think reading "the art of love" etc. is either a beneficial or good practice. Two human beings with a reasonable imagination and no preconceived notions are quite capable of stumbling along well enough. True, in nearly everything we do we lean on the wealth of knowledge of the ages, but in love, it is the discovery that is sweet.

Just think, at last the die is cast and the end of the war begun. Soon, dear, I hope it brings me home. All my love, many many kisses and hugs.

Fred

~

June 6

My dearest Fred:

Well, D-Day is here, dear. The radios were broadcasting since 1:30 a.m. The town curfew rang for fifteen minutes at 6 a.m...For most, I imagine it will be a relief. Everyone has been on edge for weeks. We have been told that it is no time for rejoicing, but I personally can't help feeling hopeful because of the fact it may not be many months before you come home to us. Just think, dearest - when I think of it, dear, I feel like crying with happiness.

I am up at the hospital now. It is Waide's second day and he is fine. He was very dopey yesterday naturally, and restless, but really, by now you wouldn't know he had been operated on...

With the fall of Rome to the Allies, I was wondering if you would see Rome soon. I'm sure you hope you do...

Waide says to tell you that jolly round red Mr. Sun is shining every day. And he sends his love and kisses and hugs, as do I dear, by the bushel.

Norah

~

June 8

My dearest Fred:

Your letter of May 28 arrived today, dear. A letter is always a joy and a pleasant surprise. I enjoyed it as usual, especially your comments on rehabilitation…

I personally decided I would be wise to do my job from day to day with a will and a smile, and that keeps me so busy when I do it well, I haven't much time for arguing. Not that I don't like to argue, but arguing won't make my children healthy or teach them good morals or make them good Canadians or give them companionship…

Waide is pretty well. It is Thursday. I wrote you on Tuesday and brought him home on Tuesday at 4:30 p.m. He can now eat pablum and milk and ice cream and mashed banana and soup and ginger ale.

I felt so sorry for him tonight. He started to cry and he just couldn't seem to stop. He said in fact, "Mummy, I can't stop crying." It was reaction, of course…He had it in his mind he wanted to be a brave soldier and I was to tell you he didn't cry. But it is a shock and he has been tired and listless the last two days…

I had Cynthia over town today for a fitting for her christening dress and she looks a dream - but she cut up capers. She runs away on me and hides and generally gets me tied up in knots. Where does she get it?…

Everyone is listening to war news of course, as are you, I suppose. The paper is scattered throughout with casualties - mostly from the Italian theatre, all in fact, so far. I thank God every night you're not in it. I could neither sleep nor eat if you were. I've got the jitters just worrying over others' loved ones…

It may not be long before I'll be able to cuddle up close for keeps. Doesn't that make your heart sing? It does mine.
Norah

~

June 13
My dearest Fred:
Well, here we are at Leith again for another summer. Do you realize it is three years yesterday since we saw one another? And this will be my fourth summer without you. However, it won't be long now, dear.

I do wish you could pop in right tonight. We have the darlingest cottage you can imagine. It is really a little house, and quaint as can be and everything in it. It has lots of lawn and a fence running all around with a gate. Waide and Cynthia are delighted with it, and I'm sure we will have a nice summer. We will be here until the end of July...

On Sunday Cynthia was christened and looked adorable and was very good...Waide was sitting in the front seat as we came in to the front of the church, so he was all smiles and got up and marched along beside me and stood with me while Cynthia was christened...

Last Friday Art Moore got word his younger son Donald, age 20, was killed in Italy. I went up to see him Friday night. There is nothing one can say or do. Art is very brave and very sensible...As he said though, he is only one of many who will be receiving bad news, for the casualties are coming in every day now...

As for your probable transfer - I don't know what to say. I was immediately worried and upset, then very angry. By dinner tonight I'd cooled down and decided to leave it up to your good judgement. You'll do as you see fit anyway, and after all, why not, I suppose. Maybe if you do get transferred you'll get home on a course, eh? However, I'm not going to bank on that and raise my hopes, only to have them shattered...

Love and kisses and hugs by the bushel,

Norah

~

June 15

Norah darling:

I am back into barracks again. We broke camp Sunday and came in under roof. Not sure just why, but I may say that it was not until I got upon a floor again that I realized how impregnated with dust was all my equipment, and myself too for that matter...

Am in a somewhat dull mind. Can't feel today that optimism in the future that is my more general mood. Oppressed by the waste these three years have been to me, how there seems never to be a thought in my mind, how much I've forgotten, what a paucity I've learned, how few friends I've made.

When I realize these things and know I'm becoming less attractive - weightier, heavier-featured - it makes me count up the little that war has given us personally and the huge cost it has been to us...

Enough. I do love you, darling, and today that is the one big bright star. It has not been said in vain that love finds a way.

Fred

~

June 20

Dearest Norah:

173

Little has happened since my last letter to you, i.e. of a personal nature. God knows there's been plenty of news of the invasion of Normandy and of the action on the other fronts. There is no need of me trying to add to the comments, just and only to say, dear, that every day brings us two together more closely, and one of these fine days it will be true...

I've received your letters telling of Waide's operation and of the next day. I'm very happy all has gone so well and I'm sure he'll be all the better for it...Your letters were cute. You were so full of love for the little fellow, you could hardly see the page. Waide and Cynthia are lucky to have such a loving mother...

Cynthia's christening and Eleanor's wedding are two things I'm very sorry to miss. I'm sure they'll both look grand at their respective does. I will write Eleanor and send you the letter for delivery. I hope she has great happiness, like ourselves, dear...

Your letters show you to be a busy, busy girl. I don't quite see how you manage to keep the whole works going. But I'm glad you are active and having some good times. I don't suppose I'll ever keep up with my whirlwind, I'm so sauntering about everything. Guess we'll keep each other from extremes.

It is amazing for me to think Waide is starting off to school this year, since my strongest mental image of him is him throwing sticks into the basement at Oakville...Gosh, when I look at the blue sky or the full moon or even at nothing at all, how I want to be home to all of you...

All my love and many kisses and hugs,
Fred

~

June 23
My dearest Fred:
...I must confess dear, I don't understand you entirely and I don't suppose I ever will. You are so very reserved that I couldn't always get through to you. So if I couldn't, I'm sure lots of people who are mere acquaintances couldn't.

I do know how you feel when you say the last three years have been wasted and you've forgotten so much. It's true, and there is no use fooling ourselves. Actually though, it isn't all wasted. I feel it is worth it in several ways.

The most important is the degree to which our love has grown and matured. I love you so much more than three years ago, and I know when our time comes to be reunited, we'll be happier, more considerate, more sensible, have so much more of a sense of values. Oh, in so many ways we will be happier.

We're still young, dear, and when you come home you'll be so thrilled with the children. They are so sweet (and bad at times)...They require a lot of guidance and teaching. I'm convinced to a large degree they'll be fine grown-ups only if we teach them how to live the right way, and we can best teach it by example. So if we want them to be honest, kind, energetic, enthusiastic, loyal etc., we must live that way ourselves, and it's a full-time job, Fred.

As for your work, I do often feel you would be happier in engineering or some such field. If you want to go back to school, why not? We can cut down drastically on expenses, and to be happy in one's work is a great thing. As you know, I'm with you and for you wherever you go or whatever you do.

I do feel, dear, you should try to be a little more interested in other people. I know everyone talks too much and a lot of it is wasted effort, but if you're interested in others, they'll be interested in you, and we all like people to be friendly. You can't have friends and not go sometimes more than halfway.

I don't very often have a new idea, and certainly jabber away about nothing most of the time, and yet you chose me as your wife knowing I was like that. Most people are pretty nice underneath...

I feel I'm finally and for all time self-sufficient, and I'm going to drum that into Waide and Cynthia...Most of the time I feel towards life like one feels on a cold morning when one would rather stay in bed where it's warm, but what one should do is get mad and jump out and put on a fire and beat the cold...

I've decided there is no escape from this hellish loneliness - I sometimes wonder if I'll ever have fun and happiness again, or have these three hectic years spoiled us? I think not, most of the time. We've kept as close as possible through our letters. I know several girls whose husbands only write once every month or so, any more. They've been separated so long, they've lost touch...

I do hope you don't get into action, but if you do I'll understand. I feel though that if you didn't come back, I would feel so very much sadder always feeling you walked into trouble.

I must close, sweetheart. This isn't a very good letter, but it is the best I can do. If you were here, I could say so much more, or would I need to say anything? I think not...

Norah

~

July 28

Dearest Norah:

...First about me, the regiment and all. You appear to be worried on that score...I have transferred to the Perth Regiment, home Stratford. The transfer is through and I am now a Perth...I figured if I didn't choose to move, it would not be long before I was moved.

Now as a result I will in all probability lose my captaincy. That just will be as it will, and I've got little or no control over it, okay? Now sweet, I do trust you have the picture and will cease forthwith to be worried...

The war news is very good this weekend. The whole affair seems so removed that one expects it to be all over before you could possibly catch up with it. The troops are all in good spirits and believe the end very much in sight.

I was censoring letters the other night and could not but remark the extremely high morale that pervaded the soldiers' written thought. Another thing gave me joy to see, was the enduring love they one and all expressed for their wives and sweethearts...

I was thinking only the other day that while I've always had a blind faith in the sanctity of marriage and of the home, and have believed in the necessity of these for the enjoyment of life, the development of personality and the orderliness of a state, I would not be able to express why these things were to my mind essentials...

I came to this conclusion: that in life we face many problems of the very greatest difficulty, the torture of this war being an example but an example only; for homes in war or peace, there will always be problems to face. I need not elaborate.

Well, I thought that it is to me almost impossible for a man or woman to face these entirely alone, indeed not in nature, and when a couple come up against these problems, there can be no half measures, they must be prepared to go to the end of the trail with full trust and confidence in the other, with a "no right or wrong" attitude.

The amount I've leaned on your support in difficulty is immeasureable. I feel certain I have helped you. I believe two persons who start life with a reservation, a "perhaps" attitude, will never go the whole course. There isn't a place in marriage for "perhaps" people, only for those who say, "We will"...

Fred

~

Aug. 2

My dearest Fred:

Just a short note, for I am very tired tonight. The children and Marg came up from the cottage on Sunday night and Dorothy and I cleaned the cottage all day Monday, and I must say we left it clean. On Tuesday morning I did a huge washing, Marg helping me of course. The wringer is on the hummer again so I had to wring by hand.

Mary Wilkinson called me at noon and suggested driving down to the club for afternoon tea, which we did. It was nice, but I have long since decided I'm not the clubby type...

Today I made jam and got about ten large jars....This afternoon I ironed and ironed and then prepared dinner. Mom helped me with the ironing. I just now finished bathing Waide and Cynthia, and really, I'm exhausted...

On Monday last, Waide had the misfortune to be riding his tricycle too fast, came to the corner and couldn't make the turn and ran out on the road and crashed into a moving car. Luckily he didn't hurt himself, but was badly frightened. He could so easily have broken his neck, for he crashed into the running board and had a red mark where his Adam's apple is.

I saw the whole thing, but was helpless to prevent it and was just trembling. I made a rule he can't cross the street under any circumstances and took his wagon and tricycle away for a few days, not as a punishment but as a reminder...

Waide said the other night, "I know you, when Daddy comes home you'll be loving and kissing him, and you'll like him better than us". So I'll have to be careful and not arouse any jealousy.

We're so excited over the war news these days, and over the hopeful words of Mr. Churchill and Mr. Eden. Maybe, or should we be so hopeful, you will be home for Christmas...

Our full moon is up, and if you were home I could be very romantic...

Norah

~

Aug. 23

Dearest Norah:

...Since I wrote last, I've been on an extensive trip about and saw many new and old places and scenes. Have had everything but an actual leave, and it certainly cost just as much. I sent off a number of parcels - a pipe to Don and one to Dad, a hat to you and a pipe to your father. I sent Waide a German rifle. I rather think you'd better not tell him so as to surprise him, and also there is many a chance it might not get there, though I boxed it well and had it disassembled…so as to disguise its shape as much as possible.

I was swimming at Salerno the other day and had the pleasure of rescuing an exhausted soldier from the water. It was easy, since I was enjoying a sail under the skippership of an Italian boatman and I just hauled him over to the side and then boosted him in and crawled in too. First bona fide rescue I've ever managed. Sure, pat yourself on the back, Freddie!

I'm back again with the Perth Regiment and am now a lieutenant again in accordance with the situation I outlined to you. I reverted, of course, at my own request, and I feel sure that in the long run it will be to my advantage…

Since I've started all the moving about from unit to unit, my mail has been nil. I expect in a week and a bit that much back mail will be in…All my love, sweetie,
Fred

~

Aug. 26
My dearest Fred:
…With the war news so good, I spend almost every hour of every day thinking about when you come home. Home - doesn't that sound wonderful? I could cry with happiness. They say some of the scenes at the Union Station are so exciting. Men and women shouting and yelling with joy at being reunited…

Tell me, when you were a little boy, did you get black as mud on Sunday when you had your best suit on? Six days a week, Waide wears overalls or pants and jersey shirts and I never say boo. But today by 3 p.m. his white pants, socks, white shirt, even his good navy suit coat were filthy - dirty legs, hands and face. What would you do? Should I just put old things on him after Sunday school, or should I insist he keep clean?

Cynthia is almost as bad. Her little powder-blue skirt was a sight. And when I scold, they just stand there and blink at me and do the same thing over again. It's no fun washing and ironing!…

Good night, dearest, and sweet dreams and write soon and tons and tons of love and kisses, darling,
Norah

~

Aug. 26
Dearest Norah:
…Today, as usual, has been gloriously hot. I like this so much as at

times to furtively hope the day is far off th...
Things go so well in all fronts, though, that ever...
geously good spirits, and predictions of the end vary o...
ters of days or weeks, or months to the most pessimistic.

Even at this stage, when it is not possible not to be exhilarated by the great successes we have had, one prays that no underestimation of the enemy or undue optimism among men or generals lead to a lamentable awakening…

Melons, grapes and tomatoes are the field order of the day, and a welcome addition to the army fare they are. All is well, darling, and I send you all my love, with stacks of hugs and kisses to the bairns. Fred

~

Sept. 3
My darling Fred:

I didn't have mail this last week, but I did receive my present of money and my hat and etchings and the pipes…The hat was so nice, but it was too small and I was very disappointed. It was such a pretty colour and style. I gave it to Eleanor…

Waide starts to school on Tuesday and I'm as excited as he is. He goes to kindergarten this year and Grade 1 a year from now. He just goes in the mornings…

The war news is good, is it not? I felt very sentimental about you all day today - felt like crying at the least provocation, I was so lonesome. Darling, I can't believe that you may be home before many months. I will be so happy to see you - I can't even describe or express my happiness.

Good night, my darling. I love you worlds and worlds.
Norah

~

Sept. 10
My dearest Fred:

Another week gone, dear. I received your blue-sheet letter dated I think it was Aug. 22. You were with the Perths and had reverted.

What your reasons are for wanting to change is all very perplexing, and so since I can't figure it out, or you either at times, I'll let it be. It makes me cross, as you can see, and of course the only reason I'm cross is because I'm worried over you.

Honestly dear, I sometimes feel when you get home, I'll love you first and then I'll give you the devil…

Tuesday morning, Waide started to school - a red-letter day in-

...ked very nice…I went with him
...d as punch. You'll be home to start
...I thought our Waide was the nicest-

...of death etc., and I explained to him about
..., and then about the good voice inside telling
...and the bad voice telling him wrong things to
..., "Waide, you have a lovely face and body, but it is
w... ...r heart that I love, that is really Waide."

H... ...stened very intently, and then he said, "Say, how'd we get on to this subject, anyway?" The next morning he came and got in with me when the alarm went off and he said, "You know, Mom, you've got a lovely face, but it is what is in your heart that I love". So you can see he had been thinking and understood.

Last night when I was bathing him he said, "Mummy, when I was inside you before you born me, was I peeking out your eyes?" What the kids come out with is amusing, there is no doubt about it.

Cynthia is equally interesting but in a different way…She is a typical girl, feminine and motherly. She loved the doll you sent her, which arrived this week. It has hardly been out of her arms…

Darling, won't you please send me a good snap of yourself? Take care of yourself…and please write me a nice chatty letter. Love and kisses and hugs, my darling,
Norah

~

Sept. 16
My dearest, darling Norah:
I'm out having a rest, and that is most welcome. Yesterday I swam in the sea and today I did the same. Hope tomorrow to sail and swim. It really is grand after so much…
Sept. 17: I'm going to hospital now due to desert sores. It is nothing, but will merely keep me from marching. I should get out in ten to fifteen days. There is absolutely no reason to worry. In fact, since I'm out of action I really should consider myself lucky…

Darling don't worry, I'm okay and I love you all the world…
Sept. 18
Well, so here I am…Now, these sores are nothing to worry about. I can get around, but since they are on my legs, the latter have stiffened a bit and I'm content to spend most of my time at ease. I'm in no danger whatever, but it will be a bit of time before they heal up…

Hard about being taken out, but now that I know I must come

out, I feel better about it and, I suppose, relieved, for that fighting, Norah, was the toughest show you could possibly imagine.

I did well, a man knows whether he has or not, and so I rest content…No worry, sweetheart. All my love and hugs and kisses to my sweet bairns.

Fred

~

Sept. 18

Dearest Fred:

…It is so long since I've received a long chatty letter from you, or one answering mine, that I feel very depressed about it. It is bad enough to have you away, but terrible to seemingly lose touch entirely…

I feel certain you are in action - I feel maybe you were trying to either hint it or conceal the fact. However, I think I'm right in guessing you are. As you know, it doesn't make me feel like a million dollars. Frankly, I've got the worst feeling in the pit of my stomach I've ever had…

Take care of your dear, dear self and Waide's and Cynthia's and my prayers are ever with you.

Good-bye for now, dearest,

Norah

~

Sept. 19

From the Gothic Line to Rimini

Dearest Norah:

…This narrative will be dotted with "I's" from start to finish. That is because it is not intended to be the story of the battle nor a part of the history of a unit, but simply all that I can recall of what I personally saw and heard…

The unit had begun its move up from Spoletti after an early breakfast Aug. 24…This movement was a slow one, the unit moving up behind the units of another division that was pushing the fighting line back to the Foglia river and the main Gothic defences…

The area was at the bottom of the steepest hill I think I've ever had the pleasure of coming down. It was not a regular road, but a track enlarged by our use and the dust lay heavily upon it. I thought several times that we would slither down the pillar of powder…

Since no one knew where we were headed or what echelon we were to join, prudence led me to order the carrying of small packs and blanket. It was prudent all right, but what a bugger of a job.

When we reached the end of our trail, we were exhausted and that completely. I believe I have never been so dead beat...

It was here that the matter of the packs really began to tell. The road seemed intent upon going straight up to heaven, and though we quickly peered around each bend as we came to it, believing the summit must be revealed, we were not rewarded until we were nearly too tuckered to be appreciative...

When we saw the position we were in on the morning of the thirtieth, we were pleased for we surrounded a sturdy farm building that was set quite picturesquely on the gentle slope of a spur that ran off onto the top of a lesser hill...

Just about 10 o'clock I found everyone retired to bed. Norm Root told me Lt. Cook had had to go to hospital sick and that I was to go up to the company. I moved fast; roused Wawro, put on my essential kit and the two of us started out for the next town...

When I arrived there were numerous vehicles crowded about and five or six prisoners could be made out standing under guard by the house wall...

Shell fire came down...intermittently during the night, but it was aimed at harassing the road more than demolishing the house so that, except for the odd bit of shrapnel striking the forward part of the house, the fire did not come dangerously close to us.

Just as the darkness was beginning to thin out, the colonel decided to go forward to recce for a headquarters on the north of the river. He took Wawro and I with him...We set off quickly to get benefit of what darkness was left, for it was lightening rapidly and we knew we had open ground to cover that was under enemy observation...

As we came along the road, the height of Montocchio lay before us on the left. It gave the enemy complete observation of the road and was within easy range. But although it was now light, no fire came at us from the feature and we reached the road junction quite easily and there used the deep ditch for cover till the company showed signs of activity.

Sgt. Reid showed me the platoon's positions and then shared his slit trench while he told me in detail what had happened the day and night before.

By now the Jerries on Montocchio had become active and were sniping particularly at the tanks...The snipers were accurate. I saw one tank lumber down the hill to a safer point where its crew were able to get out the tank commander, who apparently had been shot through the head while observing from his open turret.

More tank units began to move up the road...At the same time the Irish came up the road, cut through our position and proceeded up the slope to line the ridge. It was the right moment for Jerry, and he quickly brought down shell fire on the road junction. Baker company got its full share of this. One shell that landed right on top of company headquarters instantly killed a wireless operator, wounded CSM Sheardown and wounded another man.

Crouching in Reid's slit trench, I got the odd piece of spent shrapnel that fell into the trench, but no more...

Major Snellgrove led off company H.Q. and I came next, leading 12 Platoon. We were in the tank harbour area proceeding north from the main road and commencing to climb up a shallow draw leading to the top of the ridge when shells landed right in amongst us. I had been going along trying to see some of everything that was going on, at the same time searching the ground for hollows, furrows, folds or ditches that might give some cover...

I had just sighted one narrow, shallow ditch when I was in it and the shelling was on. I shall never know whether I dove into that ditch or was blown in, for I didn't consciously hear the shell that landed on top of the platoon, catching nearly eleven in a standing position, killing Cpl. Dube and wounding L/Cpl. Droshner...

The effect of the morning's trials on the men was all too apparent. They were nervous, hesitant, reluctant to go on. Nothing was said, but the major paused here and the platoons moved in closer and individuals found better spots of ground.

It is amazing what can be found to get one below the ordinary ground level: the ground turf where a tank had turned in its tracks, a grass-grown furrow where once a plow had ditched the ground, the gouges spring water had taken from the land, and the innumerable folds not normally visible to the eye, besides the more obvious ditches, banks and stream bottoms, give more hiding spots than one might expect...

Fifteen or twenty minutes after the shelling, we moved off up to the ridge...We had proceeded to a point from which we could see north and east, and there we halted...The men spread out on the track, which here was sunken, and removed their equipment. It was a welcome rest.

Peters pointed out a trench cutting off at right angles from the road, the entrance barred by the limb of a tree that had been drawn into it. He wanted to go into the trench but thought the limb might be booby-trapped. I got well to one side and jerked out the limb and then went on up the track on some errand or other.

When I came back, it was to be passed by platoon members proudly escorting back seven Jerry paratroopers Peters had found when he investigated the trench...It was just the same when we later investigated a similarly concealed trench system on the other side of the track and took out another nine paratroopers, including an officer. They were well-equipped and armed...If these troopers had sallied out when we were taking it easy in the road, they might well have taken the whole company for a mighty serious loss...

So long-winded...I tired of the task of setting down the detail. Writing what I did gave me a chance to blow off some of the excitement and desire to talk of what had happened. As you see, the narrative covers to Sept. 1...

~

Sept. 20

My dearest Fred:

...Yesterday afternoon Marg and I took the bairns down and had their photographs taken. They may look sweet and angelic and neat and clean, but if you could only have been an onlooker when I was bathing them and trying to keep them clean in their best bib and tucker etc., and the difficulties we had getting them to walk down and not run and fall, and the time Mr. Johnston had to get them to pose etc., you would or will appreciate the pictures twice as much.

He took four shots of me alone, but unless they are good, I won't have mine developed - I might scare you off from coming home...

By the by, if when the German show is over and if they ask for volunteers for the Japanese scrap, you had better not volunteer if you want to keep your sweetie. I'm feeling pretty depressed again, all because that awful lonely feeling is coming on me again...

You know, I know now why old maids get crabby and cynical and humourless - I really do. I feel that way a lot, but I know it will disappear when you come home. I never realized until you've been away how much easier and happier one's work and daily problems and annoyances are when one has one's sweetheart to look forward to at night - even if you only sit in two chairs at opposite ends of a room and read. You're there, and there is something awfully comforting and safe about it...

You hardly ever say how you feel, if you're lonely etc. Of course I know you are, and you've been so busy, and I'm glad you were in one way because when you're busy, you haven't as much time to think. That is one thing against housework, it gives one too much time sometimes to think…

Love and kisses and hugs galore,
Norah

~

Sept. 21
My dearest Norah:

…There was so much news and chatter-chatter streaming through my mind when I wrote my last two letters that I missed telling you many little things. Of major importance is the fact I received your lovely birthday parcel on Sept. 15 and two packages of 300 Buckinghams each…

I opened the lovely fruit cake and cut it so it just went round the room. Those lads - and me too, my sweet - enjoyed it to the full. They send their compliments through me, and let me assure you that for some, it was a spot of brightness in a rather grim day…

Have bad news for Waide re the rifle I sent. For some reason of length of parcel or something, the post is trying now to not send it. Infuriating. I wrote the chief postal authority but hold little hope. As a consequence, picked up another Jerry rifle, a bayonet, belt, buckle, badge and a revolver, all of which except the latter came from a fallen Jerry that got too close to my platoon, and I'm praying they remain with my kit till I get back to the unit and can make some arrangement for sending them. Tell Waide to keep his hopes up.

All my love, darling, and many hugs and kisses to your sweet self and the wee 'uns.
Fred

~

Sept. 23
My dearest Norah:

Today I'm feeling grand. Grand in several ways. Not only am I physically well, but I'm in high spirits and seldom in my life has the future looked so bright. So let me just ramble off to you what my imagining sees.

First, I think I'll practise in Goderich…I have a vivid scene before me of yourself gracefully coming down the long front staircase to greet a throng of happy guests pouring into the front hall and the lovely front room with its majestic French windows. I imagine grand parties on the lawn with magic lanterns strung from the trees and our healthy, happy children boisterously playing in the orchard…

But I'm nothing if not practical, and my dreamings do not displace hard thinking of how it's all going to be done. Where the clients, where the businesses. And I see that too, for coldly and calculatingly I can count up a good beginning for a practice...

Then too, I intend to see the Ontario government about their promise of a job. Well, a provincial government has lots of odd bits of business, and it's my intention to see that any in the Goderich area go to me...

You will be surprised at some of the changes in me that have taken place in the past six months. I have said nothing to you before, for I haven't been on this topic, but it is quite some time back that I decided that I will run for parliament after coming home. Precisely when I have not decided, and perhaps not till one or more elections have passed, for first I must have a stable business. But my dear, eventually you will have an MP in the family - or MPP, all depending.

All these things have been mulling and stewing within me, and now at last all seem desperately simple. Frankly and honestly, I think this last action had much to do with it, for I've come out with a new confidence in myself and a new knowledge of my own power. Strange, is it not?

Norah, I just dream of the days when we are together again. The long nights, the glorious days. Walking hand in hand in the moonlight and watching it dance on the lake's ripples. Fun on the lawn, tennis and swimming and gay scrambles into the car with all the rods and reels and hampers and paraphernalia for a day's picnic and fishing.

The future is bright and shining and now, oh how near. How very soon we will be stepping out into those days and nights that will go on forever. It is grand, sweet...

Fred

~

Oct. 6

My dearest Fred:

I'm an extremely happy girl tonight what with all the mail...It is just as well I didn't know where you were and what you were doing at that time, or I would have been almost worried sick. As it was, from the time I suspected you were in action, I went around most of the time in a sort of daze. I still can't believe that you were in all that and came out of it...

To hear you say that you have a new confidence in yourself was wonderful, dear. You seem so enthusiastic, and that makes me happy…Also I was pleased to hear you have decided to run for member of parliament. Really Fred, I can't believe it is you. It does make me feel all these years of separation and loneliness have been worth it…

Today was Cynthia's birthday and she was a very happy girl. I gave her a nice party with twelve guests…Waide went over and bought his presents for her himself, and he got three bows for her hair and a string of beads and a bracelet. He wrapped them up himself, too…

Pray take good care of yourself. I am praying you will not be sent back to your unit, but I suppose you hope you will be. I have a new confidence though, since receiving your letter - I feel you must come back to me. We have a job to do, and we must have each other…
Norah

~

Oct. 13
Dearest Norah:
…I am still doing well and my legs now are in pretty good shape, though still my chief worry. Otherwise I'm well except that I've got a slight case of jaundice…I'm not sick, just a bit disgusted…
All my love, dear,
Fred

~

Oct. 19
Dearest Norah:
I have at long last received letters from you, and feel very nearly human again…

Waide will by now be all over his first bit of excitement about starting to school. Somehow I can't quite feature him going to kindergarten…I hope they will manage to satisfy his serious mind…I'm inclined to think that if the work is too much like play, he may think the build-up was a bit on the extravagant side…

I enjoyed your howl in one letter re the condition of their Sunday clothes by mid-afternoon. I think you might relent and get them into second-bests after the morning show. Enough is enough for kids, and I don't want them to be too surprised at their dad chopping wood in his bare hide after the family is safely home from Sunday parade.

The fact is, I'm a bit puzzled about how my conduct will look to my Christian children, who may be somewhat scandalized by their dad's squirmings in church. I'm a believer in God, as you well know, but for the Christianity of the churches I have little use, nor for that matter have I much use for the large majority of Christian creed...

I was disappointed that the hat I sent was no fit for you. I want to send you presents, but refuse to just take something because I want to get a parcel together. It is so seldom that you see anything that is pleasing. Nearly everything is just high-priced junk...

The fact Waide's rifle didn't go is another thing that is irritating. Recently I sent him a revolver and hope that makes up to him to some degree, but I should have been much happier for him to have a rifle and I do think he would have been more pleased. Still, he ought to be the best armed in the cops and robbers gang...

You can tell Waide that little personal innovation of his in his prayers to keep those German bullets away from daddy came just in time, for about that time, Sept. 14 to be exact, a burst of fire from a Jerry machine gun only seventy-five yards off cut the air between I and another man standing together. I never did believe a burst could get through such a small space. Whew, it was close!

The same morning before light I and some Jerry had one of the nicest little revolver duels you would like to see. Just like a wild west barroom fight. If I hit him, he got away anyhow. As for me, nothing came closer than smelling range. After that I only needed my haircut, for I'd had my close shave...

It'll be at least another week before I can get up, although I'm feeling fit as can be...Then at least two weeks in convalescent camp...After that I start the tedious business of passing from camp to camp until being sent forward as a reinforcement. This is the process which I've not been able to give you much dope on, but it's hellishly boring and plays havoc with your mail...

When the war ends, I and many others will soon be on the way back to Canada, to be discharged from the army just about as soon as we get there. That will mean looking for a new income, and looking for one in a quick rush, for we do not want to spend our gratuity etc. for just the ordinary monthly expenses...

Besides our own problem of getting back into the groove, we have a responsibility in regard to...the problem that will present itself if we break up the Owen Sound house. It is not only the question of where will your parents live then, but also that bigger problem of whether it is fair to the children and to your dad and mom to suddenly sever the companionship that has meant so much to them all...

We must be pretty happy that we have stuck through it all with loyalty. It isn't the easiest path that's the best, is it?
Fred

~

Oct. 29
My dearest Fred:
It is a week Friday since I wrote to you - it is positively heartless of me, I know, when you are in hospital and so miserable with your latest development of jaundice. I have only one reason, dear, and that is that I've felt so rotten and have been so discouraged and depressed I just couldn't bring myself to write. I wouldn't tonight if it weren't that I don't want you to be too long without mail.

There is no point with you so far away going into all my troubles - it is absolutely hellish, though, and beyond me. The whole thing in a nutshell is simply this, Fred: I can't, any longer, cope with everyone's problems and do all the work and look after the children properly and keep my health and my sanity. I've stuck it out for three and a half years now, and I can't do it any longer. I know you would appreciate how I feel if you were here - it is no one person's fault, it is just the sum total of circumstances...

I'm definite something has got to be done or I'm going to go stark staring raving mad. You were frustrated for three and a half years until you got into action, so you won't need me to tell you how it feels. I've got to get alone with just Waide and Cynthia before you come home, or I won't be fit to live with.

The only thing that would deter me from acting is if the war were to end suddenly and I felt you would be home within a few months, or if by chance you were lucky enough to be posted home due to your illness...But I suppose that is a small hope. Couldn't you ask to be posted home? I'm serious...

Believe me, I think of you every hour and pray silently you will get home soon. Good night my darling...
Norah

~

Nov. 2
Dearest Norah:
...Regarding the question of what I should write you of what I am doing while with the regiment, you will of course realize that it is impossible to relate anything which indicates the unit's activity within the previous week or two, and at some times for a much greater period...

I was surprised, though, that you were never sure what I was doing, for once it was announced that the corps...was in action, I did not conceal the fact that I was tagging along...

I was and am very happy that you were happy about my plans for the future, and I await anxiously more of your comments along those lines.

I very nearly wrote you a still more prideful and boastful letter in relation to the future, then shamed myself into considering rationally what a high tone I was assuming. But I've lost none of my confidence...

You wrote on Cynthia's birthday and told of the good time she had and of the attentions paid her by Waide. It was a pleasant account. I have high expectations of being home before she has another...

You have really stuck to living as we would have lived, and done the job of a daddy and mother...I rejoice constantly in having the very grandest wife in all the world. I always did love you dear, but in the past years you have proven yourself in full and gained all my admiration and respect...

I know many here whose homes have broken up and I would hazard the guess that the percentage is greater than in civil life. I do believe that we both have felt the other was doing the job that we should when we were at war...

I dream of our days and nights together and think of you tight in my arms. All my love, dearest.
Fred

~

Nov. 2
My dearest Fred:
...I was amused at you wondering what your Christian children will think of their dad. Don't worry about them, dear. They aren't sissies or goody-goodies. I haven't preached creed to them yet, nor I don't intend to. I agree with you that there is not much to interest or inspire one in the average Christian church of today...

Meanwhile, you do agree with me sending them to Sunday school, don't you?...

Don't worry about presents for me, dear. It is ridiculous paying the Italians exorbitant prices...Waide's pistol arrived and of course he's thrilled to death...

Dad showed Waide how one would load it if one had bullets and how to fire it etc. So of course he in turn showed the kids I understand I'll have to register it.

Speaking of pistols, you must have a charmed life, my dear, or a very special guardian angel or, and I believe the latter is likely the answer, namely your son's prayers...when you had two such narrow escapes in the space of a few hours. I somehow can't realize you were in such danger. You must have lived a year in a few hours or minutes in a situation like that...

By the sound of Mr. Churchill, you don't need to worry about the war being over before you get back to the unit. He says, as you probably know, that it will probably be early summer...Waide will be having dates with girls, if it soon isn't over, before you get home... Love and kisses and hugs,
Norah

~

Nov. 5
My dearest Fred:
...Last week I went over to Al for a check-up...To make a long story short, I'm not in good condition...I have iron pills to take and thyroid pills, sedative and vitamin pills. I have to rest two hours every day in the afternoon and be in bed at 10 p.m. all but one night a week. I have three weeks to show him what progress I can make, and if it isn't considerable or sufficient, he's going to put me in the hospital for a week.

So believe me I've been doing as I'm told, for I got a real scare and with no one to look after Waide and Cynthia if I go under, I'm really going to get down to business...Rest assured, darling, I'll be all right - I intend to be in good condition soon and when you come home.

I do hope you're feeling better. I keep wondering if you've been more ill than you've let on to me.

Gen. McNaughton, the new minister of defence, said at a press conference that the men who have been away for a long while would have an opportunity to come home - I hope it means you. Mr. King spoke tonight on the reinforcement problem. He admitted they had to have more infantry reinforcements.

The government is still going to adopt the voluntary system, and he gave plenty of reasons, facts and figures why it was better than conscription...

Didn't you say, when you went active, something to the effect I was not to go around with my hatchet after people who weren't in the army or navy or air force, it was their own business etc? Well,

I've tried to do what you told me ever since you went away. There are lots of people I could get mad at and feel bitter about and don't. I feel you went because you felt it was your duty and I agreed, so I'll stick by that...

I'm certain we'll be happy though, dear. How could we be any other way?...

Norah

~

Nov. 12

My dearest Norah:

Well, I've been down town and about Rome. Truly it is quite a town...I saw the "ancient" part, the Colosseum, the Forum, the temples and ancient places. Of course except for the Colosseum, most is left to your imagination - only the outlines of buildings, a few columns and walls, now exist...

I have good news. You mustn't say to Waide at least, but his Jerry rifle is on its way...and perhaps he'll have it by Christmas. Your dad can see about getting it assembled...

I'm well cured now. Would have been discharged perhaps a week ago, but there has been no room at convalescent camp, so I've kicked my heels around here. Tomorrow I'll be discharged to the unit...

I am sorry you've been feeling discouraged of late. I am not surprised. I think it's fairly general and that it comes largely from expectations raised a bit too high, hopes of a quick and easy fall campaign to win a European victory.

I am very sure this is the cause of you and so many feeling let down, fed up, frustrated or what have you. That it seems for the moment that the causes lie closer to home is natural, but I fully believe is in error.

I sympathize with your disappointment. Indeed many of us have believed that a month more would see us home bound, and to realize it is not to be so easy is a blow. Each month away seems so very long to us...

I believe that we can spare no effort now, that we can ask for no personal pleasure, that we must press on to the finish. We have not yet won. Unless we put on every effort at this very moment to prevent him from recovering from the summer and fall defeats, we may not win! I'm serious...

I promise to get back home just as soon as it is possible. That is when the German war is finished. To hope for sooner is ridiculous. I am certain that the numbers of men in this theatre entitled to home leave as soon as or sooner than I, would amount to far more than present policy in Canada could ever hope to release. Further, if the punch is taken out of the Canadian army by the application of the home leave policy announced by McNaughton, I think it would be a disgrace to Canada and a betrayal of our allies…

I'd like to be hugging you tight right now, and soon will.
Fred

~

Nov. 13
My dearest Fred:
…I am feeling much better. I find it very hard to get my two hours of rest in the afternoon, though. There seem to be endless jobs to do…

Friday morning the mothers were invited to come and be guests at the kindergarten to observe our children. I dressed Cynthia all up and away we went…

Waide and Bill Prudham had gotten into a scuffle before I got there, before class in fact, and Waide had grabbed Bill's mother's umbrella and ripped the cover and bent five supports - so what could I do?

It wasn't all Waide's fault, one of those scuffles, you know, but I had to offer to fix it and so I took it in and it will cost about $4.50. I was provoked. I took $1 out of Waide's bank to help pay for it and gave Waide a good scolding.

Cynthia of course did not want to sit up and watch. No spectator is she! She wanted to be a participant. So it ended up I had to take her out. She ran away on me and when I found her, she was walking up with the Grade Four class. I almost missed her, for she had a devilish look on her face and wasn't batting an eyelash.

I came home wondering if our children were smarter and more energetic than most, or whether I was a failure as a disciplinarian…I miss you so much over such problems…

Mr. King made a radio address and said if conscription were put into force, there would be grave results…Mr. St. Laurent, the minister of justice, made a speech threatening what would happen if Mr. King put in conscription. Everyone, and I mean everyone, says the whole thing may end in civil war.

You've no idea how "hot" everything is - a nice kettle of fish with most of our good men away - who's going to protect us if we have a civil war? You may not think it is serious, or that serious, but Fred, things are bad…

I'm on the mend now, I really am. I do wish of course that you could come home. I'm so very lonesome for you. I think of you every day - I'm just never going to leave you for a minute when you do get here....

Norah

~

Nov. 19

My dearest Fred:

...I was delighted to hear you are recovering nicely. I keep wondering if you were not more ill than you revealed to me. Six weeks was a long time in bed dear, wasn't it? I do hope you will not find yourself back in action before you are in A-1 condition again. I wish you were not going to be back in action at all, of course. But I suppose that will not be....

Waide is just bursting with energy - he is a scream. He all of a sudden just shouts or yells or jumps or turns somersaults etc. Just bursting with energy...

The other evening after dinner, I was cross at both of them - in fact I sent them to their rooms. As they were going upstairs I heard Cynthia say, "Let's get rid of Mummy, she's worn out anyway, so let's throw her in the furnace."

Then as they got upstairs, Waide said, "Oh, I don't think we should, she's nice most of the time." Imagine the monkeys, and the age of them.

Cynthia is at the age where she is very disobedient. She is so determined, Fred, and just pays no attention and goes right on. When I ask her why she doesn't obey me, she says, "Well Mummy, I don't want to and I don't have to."

So I'm on the warpath and I've spanked her every day for a week now, and then of course she sobs and wants to kiss and make up and says she is sorry etc...

Parliament meets on the twenty-second. Everyone seems to be in a fog as to what Mr. King intends to do - ask for a vote of confidence, or what...Mr. King is being besieged or flooded with letters demanding conscription...

I went up to the high school on Tuesday and Thursday nights to a conversational French class...We read aloud in French, Ian Ferguson, the teacher, reading it first a few words at a time and then we read and then he asks each one to read a few sentences alone aloud. Then he gives us new vocabulary and reviews verbs, then we have conversation and then we sing. I enjoy it...

All my love, my dearest Fred,

Norah

~

Nov. 26
Dearest Norah:
I expect soon to be returned to the regiment. I am very happy about that. It means so very much to my everyday living that I be among people who have regard for me and in whom I have faith. Do not mistake me, I find much pleasure wherever I go, but it is difficult to be happy in a reinforcement unit where the personnel changes so often...

It will seem strange to you that a front line unit may mean peace and home, but it is so, for so very little time of a unit is spent in a war-like atmosphere, and I will, if I return to the unit, be no further forward than now, and indeed the unit itself will be in much the same status as the day I left them...

Norah, I do not know how I can keep going. I am so much dependent on you. I so much want to come home. I am nearly done, yet I feel I must keep on...
Love,
Fred

~

Dec. 5
My dearest Fred:
I received your letter of Nov. 11 today, the first in two weeks. I liked the snaps very much. You really haven't changed much, nor do you look much older...

You will no doubt be glad to hear I'm feeling better. I got a maid at $35 a month...Fred, just now it is necessary that I have help, so I want your opinion and your approval. As I explained, I have not only been discouraged and feeling generally lonesome, but my general health has not been good. I'm sure you realize I try my best to do my part and hope you'll understand the situation...

I regret the gloomy letters I have written of late, but Fred, I honestly felt so poorly I just couldn't write any more optimistic ones. However, when you receive this one you'll know I'm on the upgrade again.

By your letter today, I realize I've got to keep going alone for some months yet. I dread you going into action again - I can't help it, Fred, I worry over you and keep steeling myself all the time...

To say merry Christmas seems ridiculous, but I'll say it anyway. You know I'll try and make it merry for the kids becaue they are so

excited already. I will be thinking of you every minute of every hour...
Norah

~

Dec. 15

My dearest Norah:

...I will send you a Maple Leaf which recounts that the Canadians have bridged the Lamone River and given Jerry a solid walloping. I think things have been going really well and we here are pleased. The advances made may seem small to you at home, for they are but small gains on a large map, but a sight of the terrain would put an end to any criticisms or doubts as to the advances made being significant...

I'm somewhat worried about you, but your full explanation has been reassuring. I do trust you will look to yourself and do what you should for a recovery. I know it's tough to sit and take things quietly, but that's what you must do.

It is going to be so much easier for both of us when we get together that we will find things just coasting along by comparison to now...

This morning after breakfast I went with others on a trip to Ravenna...Boy, is it knocked down! It is supposed to contain historic monuments and I searched some for such but found nothing surprising. A search in the rubble is pretty hopeless at best...
I would so much be with you. Soon dear, I hope...
Fred

~

Dec. 17

My dearest Fred:

...Really I've had the best week I've had in months. Waide is better and although I have a bad cough and my ribs ached...I've really been feeling tip-top in spirits. The bairns are so good these days and obedient and polite and we've really had fun...

The bairns are greatly excited over Santa. We are going to put up our decorations tomorrow and our tree if we can get it...I have all my shopping done...Friday afternoon I made twelve dozen cookies and Cynthia and I decorated them with red and silver balls and they looked so nice.

Friday evening Mary and Bill Telford came in, and Don and Douglas (his wife) Adamson came in also and we sat around in front of a grate fire and drank Australian port (I was able to get one bottle) and ate Christmas cake and cookies…

Bill Telford of course is out of the army and has resumed his law practice. Bill…had spent the day with General McNaughton, who was up here to speak at the Liberal convention on Saturday last. Bill's dad recently resigned to allow General McNaughton to run in the byelection in February…

Our mayor is running on the Conservative ticket and is backed by the Legion, so it is quite exciting and all eyes are on North Grey. Everyone is betting two-to-one McNaughton will be beaten. I don't think the C.C.F. is putting a candidate into the field…

Darling, as you can see I am much better and it is mainly, all in fact, due to the fact I have Hazel and thus have time with the bairns instead of working all day and never getting through. Everything runs so smoothly and we're all much happier. And if you were here, you'd see how it works and I'd have time for you and we'd romp with Waide and Cynthia and read to them in the evening…

I love you worlds and worlds,
Norah

~

Dec. 25
My dearest Norah:

…Early today we got busy and found enough Italian plates, knives and spoons to go around and got them all washed up and trim. Then we got the room where we serve meals spicker and spanner than usual. By arranging small writing tables and abandoned doors, we had a good large U-shaped table capable of seating the whole platoon…

Clean sheets made grand tablecloths, and to add to the lustre we found some runners for the centers of the tables. Added frills and smartness, as you know. All was in place before quarters brought up our dinner, which was a special one. Roast chicken with stuffing, carrots and mashed potatoes, a grand pudding with a fine sauce all hot and steaming. Before dinner actually got to the table, each had a good tumbler of rum which we'd saved from issue…During dinner we had red wine, which I had forgotten to say had been placed on each table in three glass decanters - looked real bright and gay…

We just sat around afterward - around the table that is - joking, some singing, most reading books and papers…You would have thought there was a truce, the day was been so quiet…Jerry did a bit of boisterous singing that probably meant he had found the vino barrels too, and was enjoying himself…

Occupied as I was, dear, there was little time that I was not thinking of you and loving you and wishing you the best. I love you so very much that it is a sin I cannot be with you all the time, and particularly on days such as today. I hope your Christmas has been a good one...

I think too of Waide and Cynthia tonight and wish I was kissing them good night. Do that for me, my love, and tell them I love them dearly....

Fred

~

1945

Wounds and relief

"All I can say is, 'That was close'."

Waide and Cynthia, Goderich, 1945

Jan. 2

My dearest Fred:

…Waide is not quite so much my boy of late - not so loving, I mean. But I'm not surprised and I was prepared for that. They say a boy is more clinging than a girl until he's six or seven and then he's gone forever. I hope I'll never be stupid and be too possessive…

Another New Years has passed. I must say, the whole week went by with me practically in a daze…Really Fred, in the third-last letter I received from you, you said you felt you couldn't go on, you were so lonely for me. I hope you felt that way only for a day or so, because I've been feeling that way for weeks now, every day, with little exception, and it is really a very bad state to be in…

I must tell you about Waide and Cynthia and the rifle and pistol. The other afternoon when I was working at something in the living room, I was in a good position to observe them. Waide had the rifle and Cynthia the pistol. They were crawling on their bellies from the dining room to the living room. Waide was in the lead and was speaking in a low voice to Cynthia.

When I looked the second time, Cynthia was whimpering behind one of the big chairs - Waide was evidently making it too realistic and Cynthia was frightened, thinking the Germans were really here. However, she regained her courage and the two of them proceeded and finally sat up and fired. Waide can operate that rifle like a veteran, and he's pleased as punch with it…

I haven't had a letter yet acknowledging my letters of October or November, so it seems ages since we've had a talk together…As I've said before, I do wish you could get a leave home…

Love,

Norah

~

Jan. 5

My dearest Norah:

…I am in good form and fettle. I have been busy and have found it difficult to get a letter off to you, so please forgive my slackness in writing…

We've been having a great game this past while, and firmly believe we'll show a real bloody nose to old Bosch. Reports from other fronts are much better now too, so the picture brightens…

Kiss and hugs, dearest,

Fred

~

Jan. 8

My dearest Norah:

...Perhaps you will be surprised at this story. I've not told it before, since it would not have been right to indicate just when it happened.

We were teeing up for an attack, and for several days before it took place I was out doing recces and making arrangements. This is the usual procedure and it was by no means my first time to be doing it and I'd never thought about it before except as an irksome duty, and the same for the actual attack.

Well, for the two days I was engaged in preparations, I became increasingly nervous and fearful, until the last night I was properly scared. I could not sleep and I feared my legs just wouldn't carry me in the morning.

I was put out, and just got worse lying through the darkness wide awake. So I prayed to God and I asked for courage to carry out my duties. Shortly I fell asleep, and I dreamt I was home, with you and Don and Mother predominant in the family scene. We had fun, laughter, games, talking, general hilarity, everyone showing each other favourite and new possessions. We had a grand time and you were at my side the whole time as I enjoyed the assemblage.

I woke fully refreshed, all my shakes and qualms and fears were gone, and I was ready.

I could not have slept long. I had been terribly tired. I had been afraid. I seldom if ever dream, and when I do so, generally not of pleasure. I woke fully fresh and not at all as I had gone to bed.

What can a man think? I do believe, I am sure, that my prayers had been answered...

Fred

~

Jan. 18

My dearest Fred:

...The whole town and county here is buzzing with the election on Feb. 5. As I've told you, General McNaughton is seeking the Liberal seat, our former mayor, Mr. Case, the Conservative seat, and Air Vice-Marshal Godfrey, an outsider, the C.C.F. The C.C.F. are putting on a real campaign, and will probably poll a big vote.

I have been asked to speak over the radio in support of Mr. Case. So since I had decided to vote Conservative, I intend to speak. It is just for fifteen minutes and my speech is all typed ready for me to read, so unless I get "mike fright", I should be okay...

If one gives McNaughton a vote, one signifies one is in accordance with what Mr. King has done in Ottawa re the conscription question. At least that is how I see it...

Sweet, have you a wee bit of an idea how much I love you?

Norah

~

Jan. 19

My dearest Norah:

...I feel guilty. My last letter to you, written days ago, I carried for a couple of days, then tore up for it was so depressed. In fact I have been so down in the dumps I have not dared to write...

The task of being in the line, combined with horrible weather, combined I believe to depress my spirits. Truly I'm a summer-time man. I just succeed in existing during the cold and rain and slush of other seasons...

I am glad Waide got his rifle, but I had no intention that he should start marching with it. Instead, I had hoped he'd regard it as a hunting rifle or, if not that, as merely a curiosity to decorate a wall. I don't want the wee fellow getting too war-minded...

I feel myself that it is high time for me to be home, for your health and for mine. I am completely out of vigour these days, and at times wonder how much further I can push myself. I am afraid that it is not much further...

I am thoroughly tired of this life and admit that at the present time, I would take any means available to get home. I do not know of any means open to me. If you have any bright ideas, just let me know. I have no faith in the leave scheme until the numbers sent are substantially greater than at present.

Frankly, it seems a dead end, with the only route open through the heart of Germany. Well, the news being as good as it has been the last few days, perhaps that route will be clear soon...

All my love, Norah darling,

Fred

~

Jan. 24

Dearest Norah:

...I personally, and from my observations I am convinced it applies to the other men, am thoroughly tired of attempting to make fun and to arouse my interests in sights. It's a general lethargy of mind and body, and it irritates me to just think about it...

At times I believe I shall never play again, never have fun, never laugh from pure joy. That has been my mood this past month. I'd like to kick myself out of it, but I do not succeed. I know it dulls my letters, as it dulls the actual happenings that I write about...

I must try not to write so dully, but darling, it boils down to this: that I am miserably unhappy here so far from your love and from those places and things that are my only true interest. I have tried to develop my interest in matters European and in the world and world to be. That interest has flagged greatly...

My chief aim has been to build up and around our home those relationships and those things which make it a happy one. That endeavour has been seriously hampered by my absence, though I believe that both of us working toward that have done all that people could do to foster it.

I think we have made great progress. But for me it has been a long road and one that has had no pleasures except for your lovely letters...But for your unfailing encouragement, I know I'd be totally mad...

You wrote your Jan. 2 letter in bed with a cold. I do hope, dear, you will be well soon...If, dear, you worry about finances, I assure you you ought not. You need not write me explaining where money goes...It's true I sometimes wonder how we'll meet all expenses in our new home and life, but soon dismiss the subject from my mind. As always, I put off that worry until faced with it. Right now it seems we've got enough problems of the moment to look to...

I like Waide's independance. You must not imagine, dear, that less demonstration of love by him means less love. Not so, but likely the reverse. But Cynthia must be growing into a real child. God, I do wish I could see her now, before she becomes a child. I suppose even now she has lost most baby traits...

If I could only talk straight to you, I would have so much to tell you. In all likelihood, I suppose I'd be spellbound and be as slow to speak as I always have been, but I like to think of me rambling on hours just to you. Soon darling, I pray...
Fred

~

Feb. 2
Dearest Fred:
...You mentioned your dream and your prayer. I'm sure many a man has had a similar experience, especially the men in the air force. I don't suppose since you've been grown up you've ever before prayed for strength or guidance. I do feel it is a great pity that we don't pray more often, regularly in fact...

I pray almost every hour of every day and I do believe you will come home to us unharmed. I do worry, but I do think I would be much more distressed had I not that faith and confidence about you...

I gather, darling...that you have been in action since you wrote me the Dec. 15 letter...

I received today a letter from a Mrs. Kirk...She had heard me on the radio and wondered if I was the wife of a Lt. F.T. Egener who had written such a nice letter to her when her son, her only son, was killed.

Then she expressed their frustration re reinforcements, because they received word, a letter from him, on a certain date that he was wounded and in hospital, and nine days later received word he was killed. That letter which I received from her was read over the radio tonight by the Conservatives...She said after listening to me speak, she certainly was going to vote Conservative...

They gave me an introduction to the effect no doubt the listening audience had heard my two very fine radio speeches in which I pulled no punches etc. etc., and that my husband was in the thick of the fighting...

For every enemy I made, I made ten admirers. This all sounds very conceited, but I've either got to tell you or not mention the whole thing at all. This phone has hardly stopped ringing since I gave the speech Wednesday - I was amazed at the people who called or sent messages. Older, respected, intelligent people, a lot prominent in public life, every one complimenting me on my delivery, my voice and my courage to speak as I did...

For tonight, my dearest Fred, I send you all my love...
Norah

~

Feb. 18
Dearest Fred:
I haven't had mail from you for nearly three weeks now, and quite naturally I'm getting anxious...

Dad had pleurisy and bronchitis, since Thursday he has had pneumonia and is really very sick...Al had hoped to get him in at the hospital, but there wasn't a room and anyway since they are so busy, I feel certain he'll get better care at home...

I do wish you could apply to get home on compassionate leave. If Dad does pull through, he has failed so, he will be a long time recovering and with Mom's heart the way it is and the house to manage and the bairns and no one to fall back on, it is a frightening feeling at times to know you've simply got to keep going, no matter what...

I hate to complain, but I do need you so badly - however, don't feel if you can't ask for leave or don't get home soon that I'm going to go under. I'm not, it is just that I feel with you having been away going on four years now and me with so much responsibility, I could expect you might get leave.

Mom and Dad spoke for an apartment two weeks ago, and it is very comfy and warm and modern. It is available May 1, so if everything goes well they will be moving...They felt since you'll surely be home this year, it would be nice for you and I and Waide and Cynthia to have our home just to ourselves when you do come, and the children would adjust to Grandma and Grampa being away and it wouldn't be so hard a break as it would be if we suddenly moved away after the war and pulled up stakes suddenly.

However, all these plans hinge on how Dad gets along...

Both the children are well and are really pretty good. Waide can tell the time now and count away over a hundred. He seems to be happy at school and loves playing hockey. He is getting more like you every day, not only in his looks but in his ways - if things go even half well, he is good-natured and sweet...

Miss Cynthia is growing up, too. She has a mania for wearing my high heels and carrying a purse...She has been picking up the odd swear word from the kids and it is comical to hear her - however, we are ignoring it and hope she will forget the bad words...

Darling, don't worry over me - I'm really fine, and everything is running very well...

Norah

~

Feb. 20

My dearest Fred:

...Dad is a little better tonight, although it will be a day or so before we will be assured he is okay...

Last night I had to punish Waide severely since he arrived in for dinner at 6:45 and has been doing that of late, so I warned him etc...When I was kissing him good night he said, "Mom, will you and Daddy give me a watch for my birthday and then I won't be late for meals?" So I made some enquiries and I think I can get a pocket watch for a couple of dollars, which will be a start for him and won't be a terrible loss if he breaks it. He can tell the time, which is real good for a kid his age...

Cynthia's latest is, "You damn bugger" - it sounds awful, I know, but I'll have to be patient...

Did I tell you since my two radio speeches, I have had three invitations to speak - one to take part in a discussion at the Home and School Club on the subject of the child-parent relationship. Then the National Council of Women asked me to give the speech I gave to the IODE and the Y's Men last May, "The Changing Model of Britannia". The Lyceum Club asked me if I would prepare a little paper on my views on art...They want to get a novice's view on art, as a change from an artist's views...

It is hard to attempt to make fun. I've almost ceased to try. I'm never gay any more, and yet I do try to keep smiling and be generally pleasant - the children make it impossible for me to be too sad.

Darling, you certainly will laugh again, and we will be so very happy. As I said once before, what you and I need to see us through is endurance...

Why can't you apply for a course, or to get out entirely?...Darling, do you realize you'll be thirty-three this August? You're old to fellows twenty and twenty-four in the army...

I know how much you miss Waide and Cynthia. It is true Cynthia is no longer a baby, but Fred, she is cuter and more interesting every day. Actually, you've missed a lot of headaches, and when you get home they will both have some common sense...Children are sweet, but to me much more interesting from four years on...

Please for my sake, sweet, keep your old chin up...

Norah

~

March 7

My dearest Norah:

I have a whale of a lot of news, dear, and yet but a little. That that statement shall not long puzzle you, I'll step right into the news-telling.

I am now in the Western European theatre of operations... Censorship regulations are queer...I cannot for example put in a letter where I came from. Certainly you know, but it cuts down much of the news I'd stored up to tell you...

The company is billeted in a pleasant little village of less than a thousand inhabitants. It is the first time we have had a "company town". It is ours so completely that we hardly know what to do. The town officials do just whatever we wish. We can close or open the pubs, take over halls, run pictures or dances...

The town has had no war damage, the streets are not torn up, the windows are all in, there is electric light, running water and all the conveniences of modern life…

We have been most surprised at the amount of damage we have seen in this theatre. True, we may have bypassed the worst areas, I have no way of knowing, but comparatively, there just is no damage. My good God, the damage I have seen!…It is an agreeable sight, dear, to see whole buildings, fields and orchards. Damaged property depresses a person beyond expectation.

I'm sitting tonight in the company mess listening to the radio. It is perhaps a year and a half since I've just sat and listened to a radio. In that time I've listened only under strain to hear the news filtered through static and dilapidated machines. Tonight it's orchestras!

It is surprising, too, to find that there is nothing to indicate that we should ever return to action. Of course we shall, but the present immediate prospect is simply that of reorganizing…

We, as you will understand, cannot quite credit all this and most certainly do not know what to make of it. We will make the most of our good fortune…

One hopes, and wishful thinking leads us to speak of the end in one or two or three months. It does not seem that this could happen, that finally the end might be so near; at the same time it seems impossible that Germany shall be able to continue much longer…

Well darling, that's the news, and you will agree there is a lot and yet not much. Were I able to give a day-to-day recount of my recent travels, this letter would have been more interesting.

Do not get the idea the tour has been conducted by Cooks, nor that it ought not to have been missed, for in the end it has been boring and tedious. Men and officers the whole time have been interested in only three things: When will we get supper? Will it rain? When will we ever get a bath? And believe me, that last became a prayer. Yes, even me!…All my love, my darling,
Fred

~

March 20
My dearest Fred:
…Nearly everyone who has someone in Italy has received word in the last day or so that their husband or son is now in Belgium or England. So I'm all of a dither wondering where you are. It is a horrible feeling. I've even heard some of the Canadians from Italy are being sent to Burma. Maybe I'll hear in a day or so.

I haven't been able to sleep well for a week now. It is silly, but I've been so nervous about you; not since you went away have I been so upset. The other night I got into bed and my heart just pounded, so I got up and walked the floor...

I can't explain the reason for my feelings. I'm feeling fairly well and see no reason to be all a-jitter. Maybe it is the weather, which is generally dull, or maybe the war news, which is good and yet causes one to be anxious and excited. Oh well, I suppose no news is good news...

Dad is improving and is up for a short while each day now. He will never be as strong as before but should be fairly kipper in a month or so.

Waide had a nice day on his birthday...He had two guests for dinner and then I played them records and they went home at eight o'clock. He went in the day before, all by himself, to the radio station and asked them if they would announce his name over the air on their "happy birthday" program...He seems to be a very aggressive child, and more reliable every day...

You know I'm thinking of and praying for you in my heart constantly...
Norah

~

April 3
Mrs. Norah Elizabeth Egener:
Sincerely regret inform you Lieutenant Frederic Tristram Egener has been officially reported wounded in action thirty-first March 1945 nature and extent of wounds not yet available stop When further information becomes available it will be forwarded as soon as received stop When addressing mail add words in hospital in bold letters over name of addressee for quick delivery stop To prevent possible aid to our enemies do not divulge date of casualty or name of unit.

~

April 4
My dearest Fred:
It was yesterday morning that I received word from Ottawa that you had been wounded. I do not need to tell you it has upset me. I have been so jittery and nervous the last while that in a way the news came as a relief, if you can understand what I mean - but of course until I hear how badly you are wounded, I cannot rest easy...

We are all trying to be hopeful that you are not seriously wounded, and yet I hope it is serious enough to send you home so that you won't have to go into action again. I'm sure the fighting was grim. I have heard the Perths were used as the spearhead...

I can't help feeling bitter when I heard on the radio today that four thousand men are at large in Canada, evading army service. It would seem to me you boys who have been fighting so long are being called upon to do the fighting some of these "yellow slackers" should be doing.

Waide and Cynthia are not conscious of your plight, and I thank God for it...

I don't feel like writing much, dear. I hardly know what to say to you, darling. I do pray you are all right and not in pain. I realize the medical service is the best...

I will say good night now, darling. My love as always, sweetheart, and I will write often. The family, one and all, send their love and are thinking of you, dear, and hope you are all right...
Norah

~

April 10
Dearest Fred:
Just a note to let you know I received another wire from Ottawa this morning...I was very much relieved to say the least. I can tell you now that I was worried it might be your eyes or a head injury.

It has been a long and trying week waiting for news. I am now anxiously waiting for news from you - even though you will not be able to write, I feel sure you will get someone to write me a letter which you can dictate.

Don't think I am minimizing your wounds, dearest, but I am thankful they are not worse. I'm hopeful it will mean you are permanently out of action...

I do hope you improve quickly and are not too uncomfortable. The end should come soon now. My fondest love as always and forever.
Norah

~

April 24
Dearest Norah:
...My hand is progressing rapidly. I now attend daily the physiotherapy ward to do finger exercises and have the ladies there massage the fingers with oil. Quite pleasant!

I still am somewhat happily amazed at the relatively trivial wounds I received in the blaze of fire that was turned on me. As near as I could judge, the Jerry fired a whole magazine at me from a Spandau (equivalent of a Tommy gun) at point blank range (not more than ten yards).

The bullets were around me like a swarm of wasps. Only the two went home, but one ticked off a chunk of skin from my right thumb, one grazed my right thigh (front), one grazed the skin of my left cheekbone, on examining my tunic yesterday I found another had gone through my right sleeve and two or three had cut the threads in front of my right chest! Besides, several struck the Sten gun I carried, damaging it.

All I can say is, "That was close!"...I was out on night patrol about a mile and a half forward of our extreme forward positions. We wanted to know just where Jerry was. After searching several homes and positions suspected, I found him, or rather he found me.

I was ahead of the rest of the patrol and I think they thought I was done, for they hit out for home as the whole area opened up with enemy fire. But I'd chased the guy back by firing at him and then got up traction and left like a hundred-yard finalist. It seemed a long way back, but it didn't take long, hobble-legged and all.

All my love, Norah. I do hope my mail will soon begin coming through.

Fred

~

April 24

My dearest Fred:

...First thing, I want you to apply for your leave...I swear darling, if you don't answer this letter telling me you honestly will try to get your leave, I'm going to try somehow to get it for you...

I've been willing in my heart up to now for you to be away, because I felt we had decided to play our part, but now I'm not willing. I want you home, and I swear I'll go to no end of trouble to see if I can get you home if you don't try yourself to get leave. You don't want me to have a nervous breakdown, do you?...

On Monday and Tuesday all day I was enumerating for the provincial election...It was really quite fun. It is interesting meeting all kinds of people. One certainly sees life's other side.

Mr. Case wrote me asking me if I would work for him as before. I don't know what I'll do yet. I'm known by some Tories as Mrs. E. who got so many votes for Mr. Case, and by some Grits as Mrs. E. who lost so many for Mr. Case...

Last night I was dreaming all night about you. I was trying to find you and you were evading me. Imagine! I woke up exhausted this morning. Only once in four years when I've been dreaming about you have I been able to find you. One of these days I will, though, and it will be really you, my sweet...

Everyone is well, and I do hope you are improving every day...
Norah

~

May 15
My dearest Norah:
I woke up this morning to find two splendid letters from you awaiting me. Gee, that was grand!...

My chief impressions are two: first, that you're a busy, busy girl. How do you find time and energy to take part in the multitude of things that you are into? Church and Red Cross and politics and all. You are amazing.

Secondly, I feel sure you have been unduly worried about me. I wrote as soon as I could...hoping to forestall worry about me. After all, lots got wounded and as for me, my wounds were far from serious.

I still have a stiff hand...It looks like being stiff a couple of months. Hope I'll be home long before that!

You are anxious for me to get home, and I'm at least as anxious. As a matter of fact, I'd applied before I left the unit and had I not been hospitalized, might now have been en route...

Please don't worry, Norah, and remember, I'll get me home just as soon as I possibly can. Good night, darling...
Fred

~

May 20
My dearest Fred:
...As each day passes, I get more excited about you coming home because I've more or less decided in my mind you'll be home in June, or July at the latest. I still can't really believe it is true, Fred - really I can't.

After four years of separation, loneliness, fear for your safety, trying to prepare myself for the worst but all the time hoping, praying for your safety - at last it is over...

Believe it or not, Fred, I'm a little nervous. We've gotten along so well apart. We've been able to talk things over and come to an understanding. We've been frank and honest over every problem. Let's always do that, dear - I never really could get you to talk to me before like you have the last four years.

I feel if we both try every day, in every way, to make the other one happy, we will be happy...

My love and all of it for now. It won't be long now. I can hardly wait...

Norah

~

June 16
Halifax
Mrs. F.T. Egener
Arrived. Meet me Royal York Tuesday. Make a reservation.
Love.
Fred

~

EPILOGUE
Joan Barfoot

Two days before she received the telegram announcing Fred's arrival in Halifax, Norah, acting on a strong premonition, made a reservation at Toronto's Royal York Hotel.

Then, she says, "when we were reunited physically and spiritually, it was as if our time apart had never existed. It was as if I'd seen him yesterday."

They were together for another forty-three years. "Our marriage not only survived the four-year separation, it was eternally enriched."

They rarely spoke about the war again.

Fred Egener established his own law practice in Owen Sound in late 1945. Within two years he had been sworn in as sheriff of Grey County, local registrar of the Supreme Court of Ontario, registrar of the surrogate court and clerk of the county court of Grey County.

In 1967 he was appointed Grey County's first Legal Aid director, and in 1969 became the first family court judge for Grey, Bruce and Huron counties. He retired in 1987, a year before his death.

Both he and Norah were widely active in other local activities. Among other things, Fred was the first president of the Grey-Bruce branch of the Canadian Mental Health Association, chaired the board of the Grey County Children's Aid Society, served on the Senate of the University of Western Ontario and was on the board of governors of the Owen Sound hospital.

Norah was at various times president of the local Home and School Association, a trustee on the Owen Sound board of education, and chair of the Owen Sound library board, the Tom Thomson Art Gallery board and the Grey-Owen Sound Housing Authority. She helped found the Grey-Bruce Women's Centre and received the centre's woman of the year award as well as a volunteer workers' award from the Ontario government. She was also named an honorary citizen of Owen Sound.

Four decades after she interrupted her university education to marry Fred, she received her B.A. in geography in 1977 from the University of Western Ontario.

Norah and Fred did not, as they had intended, wait a year or two before starting to add to their family. Daughter Elizabeth was born in April, 1946. In 1949, their second son, Hugh, was born, and their third daughter, Kristen, arrived in 1954.

Waide, who has a master's degree in city planning, now works for the foreign buildings office of the U.S. state department in Washington. Cynthia is assistant head of mathematics at East York Collegiate Institute in Metro Toronto.

Elizabeth, a self-described "adventurer" who has degrees in music and nursing, and Kristen, who has an M.A. in English, live in Owen Sound with their families. Hugh has a bachelor's degree in psychology and is a captain in the Canadian armed forces.

There are twelve grandchildren.

When Fred died, Norah composed a death notice that summarized more than his professional and family lives. "Fred was a yachtsman, curler, wood-carver, chess and duplicate bridge player."

Also, she wrote, "he was an adventurous, wise, compassionate, non-judgmental, charitable human being."

Fred

Norah

The Egener Family